HARVARD THEOLOGICAL REVIEW

TOWARD A HERMENEUTIC OF THE IDEA OF REVELATION*

Paul Ricoeur

The University of Chicago
Chicago, Ill 60637

The question of revelation is a formidable question in the proper sense of the word, not only because it may be seen as the first and last question for faith, but also because it has been obscured by so many false debates that the recovery of a real question in itself constitutes an enormous task. My lecture today will be devoted to just this enterprise.

The way of posing the question which, more than any other, I will seek to overcome is the one that sets in opposition an authoritarian and opaque concept of revelation and a concept of reason which claims to be its own master and transparent to itself. This is why my presentation will be a battle on two fronts: it seeks to recover a concept of revelation *and* a concept of reason that, without ever coinciding, can at least enter into a living dialectic and together engender something like an understanding of faith.

I. The Originary Expressions of Revelation

I will begin on the side of revelation and my first remarks will be devoted to rectifying the concept of revelation so that we may get beyond what I have spoken of as the accepted opaque and authoritarian understanding of this concept.

By an opaque concept of revelation, I mean that familiar amalgamation of three levels of language in one form of traditional teaching about revelation: first, the level of the confession of faith where the *lex credendi* is not separated from the *lex orandi;* second, the level of ecclesial dogma where a historic community interprets for itself and for others the understanding of faith specific to its tradition; and third, the body of doctrines imposed by the magisterium as the rule of orthodoxy.

---

*The material in this lecture was first presented to the "Symposium sur l'idée de la révélation" at the Faculté Universitaire St. Louis in Brussells, on February 17, 1976, then in a somewhat condensed form as the Dudleian Lecture at the Harvard University Divinity School on November 11, 1976. The translation is by David Pellauer.

The particular amalgamation that I deplore and that I am seeking to combat is always made in terms of the third level, which is why it is not just opaque, but also authoritarian. For it is on this level that the ecclesiastical magisterium is exercised and this is where it puts its stamp of authority in matters regarding faith. Hence the rule that we should consider the levels that we named in ascending order as contaminated in a descending order. The doctrine of a confessing community, e.g., loses the sense of the historical character of its interpretations when it places itself under the tutelage of the fixed assertions of the magisterium. In turn, the confession of faith loses the suppleness of living preaching and is identified with the dogmatic assertions of a tradition and with the theological discourse of one school whose ruling categories are imposed by the magisterium. It is from this amalgamation and this contamination that the massive and impenetrable concept of "revealed truth" arises. Moreover, it is often expressed in the plural, "revealed truths," to emphasize the discursive character of the dogmatic propositions that are taken to be identical to the founding faith.

I do not intend to deny the specificity of the work of formulating dogma, whether at the ecclesial level or the level of theological investigation. But I do affirm its derived and subordinate character. This is why I am going to endeavor to carry the notion of revelation back to its most originary level, the one, which for the sake of brevity, I call the discourse of faith or the confession of faith.

In what manner is the category of revelation included in this discourse? This question seems all the more legitimate to me in that, on the one hand, the philosopher can hardly discover or learn much from a level of discourse organized in terms of philosophy's own speculative categories, for he then discovers fragments borrowed from his own discourse and the travesty of this discourse that results from its authoritarian and opaque use. On the other hand, he may discover and learn much from nonspeculative discourse—what Whitehead called barbaric discourse because it had not yet been illuminated by the philosophical *logos*. What is more, it is an old conviction of mine that the philosopher's opposite in this type of debate is not the theologian, but the believer who is informed by the exegete; I mean, the believer who seeks to understand himself through a better understanding of the texts of his faith.

The principal benefit of such a return to the origin of theological discourse is that from the outset it places reflection before a variety of expressions of faith, all modulated by the variety of discourses within which the faith of Israel and then of the early church is inscribed. So instead of having to confront a monolithic concept of revelation, which is only obtained by transforming these different forms of discourse into propositions, we encounter a concept of revelation that is pluralistic, polysemic, and at most analogical in form—the very term revelation, as we shall see, being borrowed from one of these forms of discourse.

1. Prophetic Discourse

Which of the biblical forms of discourse should be taken as the basic referent for a meditation on the idea of revelation? It seems legitimate to begin by taking prophetic discourse as our basic axis of inquiry. Indeed, this is the discourse which declares itself to be pronounced in the name of . . . , and exegetes have rightly pointed out the importance of its introductory formula: "The word of Yahweh came to me, saying, 'Go and proclaim in the hearing of Jerusalem, . . .'" (Jer 2:1). Here is the original nucleus of the traditional idea of revelation. The prophet presents himself as not speaking in his own name, but in the name of another, in the name of Yahweh. So here the idea of revelation appears as identified with the idea of a double author of speech and writing. Revelation is the speech of another behind the speech of the prophet. The prophetic genre's central position is so decisive that the third article of the Nicene creed, devoted to the Holy Spirit, declares: "We believe in the Holy Spirit . . . who spoke through the prophets."

Yet if we separate the prophetic mode of discourse from its context, and especially if we separate it from that narrative discourse that is so important for the constituting of Israel's faith, as well as for the faith of the early church, we risk imprisoning the idea of revelation in too narrow a concept, the concept of the speech of another. Now this narrowness is marked by several features. One is that prophecy remains bound to the literary genre of the oracle, which itself is one tributary of those archaic techniques that sought to tap the secrets of the divine, such as divination, omens, dreams, casting dice, astrology, etc. It is true that for the great prophets of Israel symbolic visions are subordinated to the eruption of the Word, which may appear without any accompanying vision. But it also remains true that the explicit form of double speaking tends to link the notion of revelation to that of inspiration conceived as one voice behind another.

When extended to all the other forms of biblical discourse we are going to consider, this concept of revelation, taken as a synonym for revelation in general, leads to the idea of scripture as dictated, as something whispered in someone's ear. The idea of revelation is then confused with the idea of a double author of sacred texts, and any access to a less subjective manner of understanding revelation is prematurely cut off. In turn, the very idea of inspiration, as arising from meditation on the Holy Spirit, is deprived of the enrichment it might receive from those forms of discourse which are less easily interpreted in terms of a voice behind a voice or of a double author of scripture.

Finally, the ancient bond between an oracle and techniques of divination establishes an almost invincible association between the idea of prophecy and that of an unveiling of the future. This association tends to impose the idea, in turn, that the content of revelation is to be assimilated to a design in the sense of a plan that would give a goal to the unfolding of history. This concentration on the idea of revelation as God's plan is all the more insistent in that apocalyptic literature which was subsequently grafted on to the prophetic trunk, calls "apocalypse"—i.e., revelation in the strict sense of the word—the unveiling of God's plans concerning the "last days." The idea of revelation thereby tends to be identified with the idea of a premonition of the end of history. The "last days" are the divine secret that apocalyptic proclaims by means of dreams, visions, symbolic transpositions of earlier writings, etc. In this way, the notion of the divine promise tends to be reduced to the dimensions of a divination applied to the "end of time."

2. Narrative Discourse

For these reasons, we must not limit ourselves to simply identifying revelation with prophecy. And the other modes of discourse bear this out. To see this, we need surely to begin by considering the narrative genre of discourse that dominates the Pentateuch, as well as the synoptic Gospels and the Book of Acts.

What does revelation mean as regards these texts? Should we say that as with the prophetic texts, these texts have a double author, the writer and the spirit that guides him? Should we really attend above all else to the question of the narrator? Theoreticians of narrative discourse have noted that in narration the author often disappears and it is as though the events recounted themselves. According to Emile Benveniste, for example, historical assertions, that is the telling of past events, exclude the speaker's intervening in the story.[1] Every linguistic form of autobiography is banished. There is no longer even a narrator: "events are posited as though they were produced to the extent that they appeared on the horizon of history. No one speaks here. The events tell themselves."[2]

Can we annul this specific feature of narration by advancing the trivial argument that someone nevertheless wrote it and that he stands in relation to his text analogous to that of the prophet and the double author of prophecy? I am not unaware that when the Nicene Creed proclaims "who spoke through the prophets," the creed engulfs narration into prophecy, following the tradition that Moses was the unique narrator of the Pentateuch and that he was the prophet *par excellence*. But in following this route, has not the classical theory of inspiration missed the instruction proper to the narrative genre? What I am hereby suggesting is that we should pay more attention to the things recounted than to the narrator and his prompter. We then see that it is within the story itself that Yahweh is designated in the third person as the ultimate *actant*—to use the category of A. J. Greimas[3]—i.e., he is one of the personages signified by the narration itself and intervenes among the other actants of the goings on. It is not a double narrator, a double subject of the word that we need to think about, but a double actant and consequently a double object of the story.

Let us follow this trail. Where does it lead? Essentially to meditation on the character of the events recounted, such as the election of Abraham, the Exodus, the anointing of David, etc. in the Old Testament, and the resurrection of Christ for the early church. The idea of revelation then appears as connected to the very character of these events. What is noteworthy about them is that they do not simply occur and then pass away. They mark an epoch and engender history. In this vein, the Jewish scholar Emil Fackenheim is correct when he speaks of "history-making events." These events found an epoch because they have the twofold characteristic of both founding a community and of delivering it from a great danger, which, moreover, may take diverse forms. In such instances, to speak of revelation is to qualify the events in question as transcendent in relation to the ordinary course of history. The whole faith of Israel and of the

---

[1] See his "Les relations de temps dans le verb français," in *Problèmes de linguistique générale* (Paris: Gallimard, 1966) 237-50.
[2] Ibid., 241.
[3] *Sémantique structurale* (Paris: Larousse, 1966).

early church is tied up here in the confession of the transcendent character of such nuclear founding and instituting events.

As Gerhard von Rad has established in his great work, *The Theology of the Old Testament,* and principally in volume one, "The Theology of Traditions," Israel essentially confessed God through the ordering of its sagas, traditions, and stories around a few kernel events from which meaning spread out through the whole structure.[4] Von Rad believes he has discovered the most ancient kernel of the Hebraic *Credo* in a text such as Deut 26:5b-10b which says:

> My Father was a wandering Aramaean. He went down to Egypt to find refuge there, few in numbers; but there he became a nation, great, mighty, and strong. The Egyptians ill-treated us, they gave us no peace and inflicted harsh slavery on us. But we called on Yahweh the God of our fathers. Yahweh heard our voice and saw our misery, our toil and our oppression; and Yahweh brought us out of Egypt with a mighty hand and outstretched arm, with great terror, and with signs and wonders. He brought us here and gave us this land, a land where milk and honey flow. Here then I bring the first-fruits of the produce of the soil that you, Yahweh, have given me. (*Jerusalem Bible*)

Notice how the recitation first designates Yahweh in the third person, as the supreme actant, then raises to an invocation that addresses God in the second person: "Here then I bring the first-fruits of the produce of the soil that you, Yahweh, have given me." We will return to this change from the use of the third to the second person when we discuss the hymnic literature. First, however, let us continue our examination of the narrative form.

What is essential in the case of narrative discourse is the emphasis on the founding event or events as the imprint, mark, or trace of God's act. Confession takes place through narration and the problematic of inspiration is in no way the primary consideration. God's mark is in history before being in speech. It is only secondarily in speech inasmuch as this history itself is brought to language in the speech-act of narration. Here a "subjective" moment comparable to prophetic inspiration comes to the fore, but only after the fact. This subjective moment is no longer the narration insofar as the events recount themselves, but the event of narration insofar as it is presented by a narrator to a community. The word event is thus emphasized at the expense of the first intentionality of the narrative confession, or rather the confessing narrative. The latter does not distinguish itself from

---

[4]Gerhard von Rad, *Old Testament Theology* (trans. D. M. G. Stalker; New York: Harper, 1962-65).

the things recounted and the events that present themselves in the story. It is for a second order reflection that the questions "who is speaking? who is telling the story?" are detached from *what* is narrated and said. For this reflection the author of the narration comes to the fore and appears to be related to his writing as the prophet is to his words. The narrator, in turn, may by analogy be said to speak in the name of . . . , and then he is a prophet and the Spirit speaks through him. But this absorption of narration into prophecy runs the risk of voiding the specific feature of the narrative confession—its aiming at God's trace in the event.

To recognize the specificity of this form of discourse, therefore, is to guard ourselves against a certain narrowness of any theology of the Word which only attends to word events. In the encounter with what we could call the idealism of the word event, we must reaffirm the realism of the event of history—as is indicated today by the work of a theologian such as Wolfhart Pannenberg in his attempts to rectify the one-sided emphasis of Ernst Fuchs and Gerhard Ebeling.

Then, too, narration includes prophecy in its province to the extent that prophecy is narrative in its fashion. Indeed, the meaning of prophecy is not exhausted by the subjectivity of the prophet. Prophecy is carried forward toward the "Day of Yahweh," which the prophet says will not be a day of joy, but of terror. This term, the Day of Yahweh, announces something like an event that will be to impending history what the founding events were to the history recounted in the great biblical narratives.

There is as well, however, a tension between narration and prophecy that first occurs at the level of the event in the dialectic of the prophetic event. The same history which narration founds as certain is suddenly undercut by the menace announced in the prophecy. The supporting pedestal totters. It is the structure of history which is at stake here, not just the quality of the word which pronounces it. And revelation is implicated in this now narrative, now prophetic understanding of history.

Did we say understanding? But this understanding cannot be articulated within any specific form of knowledge or within any system. Between the security confessed by the recitation of the founding events and the menace announced by the prophet there is no rational synthesis, no triumphant dialectic, but only a double confession, never completely appeased; a double confession that only hope can hold together. According to the excellent phrase of André Neher, from his fine book on the prophets, a gulf of nothingness separates the new creation from the old.[5] No *Aufhebung* can suppress this deadly fault. This is why this double relation to history is profoundly betrayed when we apply the Stoic idea of providence to it and when the tension between narration and prophecy is assuaged in some teleological representation of the course of history.

Such sliding over into teleology and the idea of providence would no doubt be unstoppable if we left the narrative discourse and the prophetic discourse of history face to face. Reduced to this polarity, the idea of revelation indeed tends to be identified with the idea of God's design, the idea of a decreed plan that God has unmasked to his servants and prophets. But the polysemy and polyphony of revelation are not yet exhausted by this coupling of narration and prophecy. There are at least three other modes of biblical religious discourse that cannot be inscribed within this polarity of narration and prophecy. The first of these is the *Torah*, or instruction, conveyed to Israel.

3. Prescriptive Discourse

Broadly speaking, we may call this aspect of revelation its practical dimension. It corresponds to the symbolic expression "the will of God." If we may still speak of a design here it is no longer in the sense of some plan about which thought may speculate, but in the sense of a prescription to be brought into practice. But this idea of a revelation in the form of instruction is, in turn, full of pitfalls for the traditional understanding of revelation. In this regard, the translation, beginning with the Septuagint, of the word *Torah* by *nomos* or "law" is completely misleading. It leads us, in effect, to enclose the idea of an imperative from above within the idea of a divine law. If, moreover, we transcribe the idea of an imperative in terms of Kant's moral philosophy, we are more and more constrained to lean the idea of revelation on that of heteronomy; that is, to express it in terms of submission to a higher, external command.

The idea of dependence is essential to the idea of revelation, but really to understand this originary dependence within the orders of speaking, willing, and being, we must first criticize the ideas of heteronomy and autonomy both as taken together and as symmetrical to each other.

Let us concentrate for the moment on the idea of heteronomy. Nothing is more inadequate than this idea for making sense of

---

[5] André Neher, *L'Essence du Prophétisme* (Paris: P.U.F., 1955).

what the term *Torah* has signified within Jewish experience. In order to do justice to the idea of a divine *Torah,* it does not even suffice to say that the Hebrew *Torah* has a greater extension than what we call a moral commandment and that it is applied to the whole legislative system that the Old Testament tradition connected with Moses. By thus extending the commandment to all the domains of life of the community and the individual, whether moral, juridic, or cultic, we only express the amplitude of this phenomenon without thereby really illuminating its specific nature.

Three points are worth emphasizing.

First, it is not unimportant that the legislative texts of the Old Testament are placed in the mouth of Moses and within the narrative framework of the sojourn at Sinai. This means that this instruction is organically connected to the founding events symbolized by the exodus from Egypt. And in this regard, the introductory formula of the Decalogue constitutes an essential link connecting the story of the Exodus and the proclamation of the Law: "I am Yahweh, your God, who brought you out of the land of Egypt, out of the house of slavery" (Exod 20:2). At the level of literary genres this signifies that the legislative genre is in a way included in the narrative genre. And this in turn signifies that the memory of deliverance qualifies the instruction in an intimate way. The Decalogue is the Law of a redeemed people. Such an idea is foreign to any simple concept of heteronomy.

This first comment leads to a second. The Law is one aspect of a much more concrete and encompassing relation than the relation between commanding and obeying that characterizes the imperative. This relation is what the term "Covenant" itself translates imperfectly. It encompasses the ideas of election and promise, as well as of menace and curse. The idea of the Covenant designates a whole complex of relations, running from the most fearful and meticulous obedience to the Law to casuistic interpretations, to intelligent mediation, to pondering in the heart, to the veneration of a joyous soul—as we shall see better with regard to the Psalms. The well-known Kantian respect for the law, in this regard, would only be one modality of what the Covenant signifies, and perhaps not the most significant one.

This space of variations opened by the Covenant for our ethical feelings suggests a third reflection. Despite the apparently invariable and apodictic character of the Decalogue, the *Torah* unfolds within a dynamism that we may characterize as historical. By this we do not mean just the temporal development that historical criticism discerns in the redaction of these codes, the evolution of moral ideas that may be traced out from the first Decalogue to the Law of the Covenant, on the one hand, and from the Decalogue itself through the restatements and amplifications of the book of Deuteronomy to the new synthesis of the "Holiness Code" in the book of Leviticus and the legislation subsequent to Ezra, on the other; more important than this development of the content of the Law is the transformation in the relationship between the faithful believer and the Law. Without falling into that old rut of opposing the legalistic and the prophetic, we may discover in the very teaching of the *Torah* an increasing pulsation that turn by turn sets out the Law in terms of endlessly multiplying prescriptions and then draws it together, in the strong sense of the word, by summing it up in one set of commandments which only retain its being directed towards holiness.

Thus the book of Deuteronomy, to cite one example, proclaims long before the New Testament gospel: "You shall love Yahweh your God with all your heart, with all your soul, with all your strength. Let these words which I urge on you today be written on your heart" (6:5-6). This inscription on human hearts gave rise to the proclamation of a new covenant by some of the prophets, not in the sense of the proclamation of new precepts, but in the sense of a new relational quality as expressed precisely by the phrase "engraved on your hearts." Ezekiel wrote, "I will give them a new heart and I will put a new spirit in them; I will remove the heart of stone from their bodies and give them a heart of flesh . . ." (Ezek 11:19).

Without this pulsation in the *Torah,* we would not understand how Jesus could have, on the one hand, opposed the "traditions of the elders," which is to say, the multiplication and excess load of commandments put forth by the scribes and Pharisees, and, on the other hand, have declared that in the Kingdom the Law would be fulfilled to its last iota. For Jesus, the Law and the Prophets were summed up in the Golden Rule from Deuteronomy: "So always treat others as you would like them to treat you; that is the meaning of the Law and the Prophets" (Matt 7:12). In this sense, the Sermon on the Mount proclaims the same intention of perfection and holiness that runs through the ancient Law.

It is this intention that constitutes the ethical dimension of revelation. If we consider this instituting function of revelation we see how inadequate the idea of heteronomy is for circumscribing the wealth of meaning included in the teaching of the *Torah.* We see also in what way the idea of revelation is enriched in turn. If we may still apply the idea of God's design for humans to it, it is no longer in the sense of a plan that we could read in past or future events, nor is it in terms of an immutable codification of every communal or individual practice. Rather it is the sense of a requirement for perfection that summons the will and makes a claim upon it. In the same way, if we continue to speak of revelation as historical, it is not only in the sense that the trace of God may be read in the founding events of the past or in a coming conclusion to history, but in the sense that it orients the history of our practical actions and engenders the dynamics of our institutions.

4. Wisdom Discourse

But would this deepening of the Law beyond its being scattered in precepts be perceived clearly if another dimension of revelation was not also recognized in its specificity? I mean, revelation as wisdom. Wisdom finds its literary expression in wisdom literature. But wisdom also surpasses every literary genre. At first glance, it appears as the art of living well, expert advice on the way to true happiness. It seems to turn the transcendent commandments of the Decalogue into minute details, practical advice, only adding a kind of lucidity without any illusions about human wickedness to the teaching of the Law. But behind this somewhat shabby facade, we need to discern the great thrust of a reflection on existence that aims at the individual behind the people of the Covenant, and through him, every human being. Wisdom overflows the framework of the Covenant, which is also the framework of the election of Israel and the promise made to Israel.

The counsels of wisdom ignore the frontiers where any legislation appropriate to a single people stops, even if it is the elect people. It is not by chance that more than one sage in the biblical tradition was not Jewish. Wisdom intends every person in and through the few. Its themes are those limit-situations spoken of by Karl Jaspers, those situations—including solitude, the fault, suffering, and death—where the misery and the grandeur of human beings confront each other. Hebraic wisdom interprets these situations as the annihilation of humans and the incomprehensibility of God—as the silence and absence of God. If the question of retribution is so acute here, it is so to the extent that the discordance between justice and happiness, so cruelly emphasized by the triumph of the wicked, brings to light the overwhelming question of the sense or nonsense of existence.

In this way, wisdom fulfills one of religion's fundamental functions which is to bind together *ethos* and *cosmos,* the sphere of human action and the sphere of the world. It does not do this by demonstrating that this conjunction is given in things, nor by demanding that it be produced through our action. Rather it joins *ethos* and *cosmos* at the very point of their discordance: in suffering and, more precisely, in unjust suffering. Wisdom does not teach us how to avoid suffering, or how magically to deny it, or how to dissimulate it under an illusion. It teaches us how to endure, how to suffer suffering. It places suffering into a meaningful context by producing the active quality of suffering.

This is perhaps the most profound meaning of the book of Job, the best example of wisdom. If we take the *dénouement* of this book as our guide, could we not say that revelation, following the line of wisdom, is the intending of that horizon of meaning where a conception of the world and a conception of action merge into a new and active quality of suffering? The Eternal does not tell Job what order of reality justifies his suffering, nor what type of courage might vanquish it. The system of symbols wherein the revelation is conveyed is articulated beyond the point where models for a vision of the world and models for changing the world diverge. Model of and model for are rather the inverse sides of one indivisible prescriptive and descriptive symbolic order. This symbolic order can conjoin *cosmos* and *ethos* because it produces the *pathos* of actively assumed suffering. It is this *pathos* that is expressed in Job's final response:

> Then Job answered Yahweh,
>
> I know that you are all-powerful:
>   what you conceive, you can perform.
> I am the man who obscured your designs
>   with my empty-headed words.
> I have been holding forth on matters I cannot understand,
>   on marvels beyond me and my knowledge.
> (Listen, I have more to say,
>   now it is my turn to ask questions and yours to inform me.)
> I knew you then only by hearsay;
>   but now having seen you with my own eyes,
> I retract all I have said,
>   in dust and ashes I repent. (Job 42:1-6)

What did Job "see"? Behemoth and Leviathan? The orders of creation? No. His questions about justice are undoubtedly left without an answer. But by repenting, though not of sin, for he is righteous, but by repenting for his supposition that existence does not make sense, Job presupposes an unsuspected meaning which cannot be transcribed by speech or *logos* a human being may have at his disposal. This meaning has no other expression than the new quality which penitence confers on suffering. Hence it is not unrelated to what Aristotle speaks of as the tragic *pathos* that purifies the spectator of fear and pity.

We should begin to see at what point the notion of God's design—as may be suggested in different ways in each instance, it is true, by narrative, prophetic, and prescriptive discourse—is removed from any transcription in terms of a plan or program; in short, of finality and teleology. What is revealed is the possibility of hope in spite of. . . . This possibility may still be expressed in the terms of a design, but of an unassignable design, a design which is God's secret.

It should also begin to be apparent how the notion of revelation differs from one mode of discourse to another; especially when we pass from prophecy to wisdom. The prophet claims divine inspiration as guaranteeing what he says. The sage does nothing of the sort. He does not declare that his speech is the speech of another. But he does know that wisdom precedes him and that in a way it is through participation in wisdom that someone may be said to be wise.

Nothing is further from the spirit of the sages than the idea of an autonomy of thinking, a humanism of the good life; in short, of a wisdom in the Stoic or Epicurean mode founded on the self-sufficiency of thought. This is why wisdom is held to be a gift of God in distinction to the "knowledge of good and evil" promised by the Serpent. What is more, for the scribes following the Exile, Wisdom was personified into a transcendent feminine figure. She is a divine reality that has always existed and that will always exist. She lives with God and she has accompanied creation from its very beginning. Intimacy with Wisdom is not to be distinguished from intimacy with God.

By this detour wisdom rejoins prophecy. The objectivity of wisdom signifies the same thing as does the subjectivity of prophetic inspiration. This is why for tradition the sage was held to be inspired by God just as the prophet was. For the same reason, we can understand how prophecy and wisdom could converge in apocalyptic literature where, as is well known, the notion of a revelation of the divine secrets is applied to "the last days." But intermingling in no way prohibits the modes of religious discourse—and the aspects of revelation which correspond to them—from remaining distinct or from being held together only by a tie of pure analogy.

5. Hymnic Discourse

I do not want to end this brief survey of modes of biblical discourse without saying something about the lyric genre best exemplified by the Psalms. Hymns of praise, supplication, and thanksgiving constitute its three major genres. Clearly they are not marginal forms of religious discourse. The praise addressed to God's prodigious accomplishments in nature and history is not a movement of the heart which is added to narrative genre without any effect on its nucleus. In fact, celebration elevates the story and turns it into an invocation. Earlier we spoke of the example of the ancient creed from Deuteronomy—"My father was a wandering Aramaean, etc." In this sense, to recount the story is one aspect of celebration. Without a heart that sings the glory of God, perhaps we would not have the creation story, and certainly not the story of deliverance. And without the supplications in the psalms concerning suffering, would the plaint of the righteous also find the path to invocation, even if it must lead to contestation and recrimination? Through supplication, the righteous man's protestations of innocence have as their opposite a Thou who may respond to his lamentation.

In its conclusion, the book of Job has shown us how, instructed by wisdom, the knowledge of how to suffer is surpassed by the lyricism of supplication in the same way that narration is surpassed by the lyricism of praise. This movement toward the second person finds its fulfillment in the psalms of thanksgiving where the uplifted soul thanks someone. The invocation reaches its highest purity, its most disinterested expression, when the supplication, unburdened of every demand, is converted into recognition. Thus under the three figures of praise, supplication, and thanksgiving human speech becomes invocation. It is addressed to God in the second person, without limiting itself to designating him in the third person as in narration, or to speaking in the first person in his name as in prophecy.

I freely admit that the I-Thou relation may have been hypostasized to an excessive degree by what we might call the religious personalism of a Martin Buber or a Gabriel Marcel. This relation is really only constituted in the psalm and above all in the psalm of supplication. We cannot say therefore that the idea of revelation is completely conveyed by this idea of a communication between two persons. Wisdom, we have seen, recognizes a hidden God who takes as his mask the anonymous and non-human course of events. We must therefore limit ourselves to noticing that in passing through the three positions of the system of first person personal pronouns—I, you, he—the origin of revelation is designated in different modalities that are never completely identical with one another.

If we were to say in what sense the Psalter may be said to be revealed, it would certainly not be so in the sense that its praise, supplication, and thanksgiving were placed in their disparate authors' mouths by God, but in the sense that the sentiments expressed there are formed by and conform to their object. Thanksgiving, supplication, and celebration are all engendered by what these movements of the heart allow to exist and, in that manner, to become manifest. The surpassing of *pathos,* that we have discerned in the movement of wisdom when it transforms suffering into knowing how to suffer, thus becomes in a way the theme of the Psalter. The word forms our feeling in the process of expressing it. And revelation is this very formation of our feelings that transcends their everyday, ordinary modalities.

If we now look back over the path we have covered, certain important conclusions are discernible.

First, I will reiterate my original affirmation that the analysis of religious discourse ought not to begin with the level of theological assertions such as "God exists," "God is immutable, omnipotent, etc." This propositional level constitutes a second degree discourse which is not conceivable without the incorporation of concepts borrowed from speculative philosophy. A hermeneutic of revelation must give priority to those modalities of discourse that are most originary within the language of a community of faith; consequently, those expressions by means of which the members of that community first interpret their experience for themselves and for others.

Second, these originary expressions are caught up in forms of discourse as diverse as narration, prophecy, legislative texts, wisdom saying, hymns, supplications, and thanksgiving. The mistaken assumption here would be to take these forms of discourse as simple literary genres which ought to be neutralized so that we can extract their theological content. This presupposition is already at work in the reduction of the originary language of faith to its propositional content. To uproot this prejudice we must convince ourselves that the literary genres of the Bible do not constitute a rhetorical facade which it would be possible to pull down in order to reveal some thought content that is indifferent to its literary vehicle.

But we will not get beyond this prejudice until we possess a generative poetics that would be for large works of literary composition what generative grammar is to the production of sentences following the characteristic work of a given language. I will not, in this context, consider the implication of this thesis for literary criticism. It concerns the type of discourse that is always a work of a certain genre, i.e., a work produced as narration, as prophecy, as legislation, etc. Instead, I will proceed directly to what concerns our inquiry about revelation. To be brief, I will say that the confession of faith expressed in the biblical documents is directly modulated by the forms of discourse wherein it is expressed. This is why the difference between story and prophecy, so characteristic of the Old Testament, is *per se* theologically significant. Not just any theology may be attached to the story form, only a theology that celebrates Yahweh as the great liberator. The theology of the Pentateuch, if the word theology itself is not premature here, is a theology homogeneous with the structure of the story; i.e., a theology in the form of the history of salvation. But this theology is not a system to the extent that at the same level of radicality or originariness prophetic discourse undoes the assurance founded on the recitation and the repetition of the founding events. The motif of the "Day of Yahweh"—a day of mourning, not of joy—is not a rhetorical motif that we can simply eliminate. It is a constitutive element of the prophetic theology. The same thing applies to the *Torah,* as well as to the spiritual tenor of the hymn. What announces itself there is in each instance qualified by the form of the announcement. The religious "saying" is only constituted in the interplay between story and prophecy, history and legislation, legislation and wisdom, and finally wisdom and lyricism.

Third, if the forms of religious discourse are so pregnant with meaning, the notion of revelation may no longer be formulated in a uniform and monotonous fashion which we presuppose when we speak of *the* biblical revelation. If we put in parentheses the properly theological work of synthesis and systematization that presupposes the neutralization of the primitive forms of discourse and the transference of every religious content onto the plane of the assertion or proposition, we then arrive at a polysemic and polyphonic concept of revelation.

Earlier I spoke of such a concept as analogical. Now I want to explain this analogy. It proceeds from a reference term: prophetic discourse. There revelation signifies inspiration from a first person to a first person. The word prophet implies the notion of a person who is driven by God to speak and who does speak to the people about God's name and in God's name. If we do not see the analogical bond between the other forms of religious discourse and prophetic discourse we generalize in univocal fashion the concept of inspiration derived from the prophetic genre and assume that God spoke to the redactors of the sacred books just as he spoke to the prophets. The Scriptures are then said to have been written by the Holy Spirit and we are inclined to construct a uniform theology of the double divine and human author where God is posited as the formal cause and the writer is posited as the instrumental cause of these texts.

However, by taking up this generalization, we do not render justice to those traits of revelation that are not reducible to being synonymous with the double voice of the prophet. The narrative genre invited us to displace onto the recounted events that revealing light that proceeds from their founding value and their instituting function. The narrator is a prophet, but only inasmuch as the generative meaningful events are brought to language. In this way, a less subjective concept than that of inspiration is roughed out. In a similar manner, the nuances of revelation that are derived from the prescriptive force of instruction, the illuminating capacity of the wisdom saying, and the quality of lyrical *pathos* in the hymn, are connected to these forms of discourse. Inspiration, then, designates the coming to language of the prescriptive force, this illuminating capacity, and this lyric *pathos,* but only as analogous to one another.

We over-psychologize revelation if we fall back on the notion of scripture as dictated in a literal fashion. Rather it is the force of what is said that moves the writer. That something requires to be said is what the Nicene Creed analogically signifies by the expression, "We believe in the Holy Spirit who spoke through the prophets." Yet we do not have, at least in the West, an appropriate theology that does not psychologize the Holy Spirit. To discover the objective dimension of revelation is to contribute indirectly to this non-psychologizing theology of the Holy Spirit that would be an authentic pneumatology.

Allow me now to draw one final conclusion. If one thing may be said unequivocally about all the analogical forms of revelation, it is that in none of its modalities may revelation be included in and dominated by knowledge. In this regard the idea of something secret is the limit-idea of revelation. The idea of revelation is a twofold idea. The God who reveals himself is a hidden God and hidden things belong to him.

The confession that God is infinitely above human thoughts and speech, that he guides us without our comprehending his ways, that the fact that human beings are an enigma to themselves even obscures the clarity that God communicates to them—this confession belongs to the idea of revelation. The one who reveals himself is also the one who conceals himself. And in this regard nothing is as significant as the episode of the burning bush in Exodus 3. Tradition has quite rightly named this episode the revelation of the divine name. For this name is precisely unnameable. To the extent that to know God's name is to have power over him through an invocation whereby the god invoked becomes a manipulatable thing, the name confided to Moses is that of a being whom human beings cannot really name; that is, hold within the discretion of their language.

> Moses asked, "If I come to the people of Israel and say to them, 'The God of your fathers has sent me to you,' and they ask me, 'What is his name?' what shall I say to them?" God answered, "I am who I am." And he added, "Say this to the children of Israel, 'I am has sent me to you.'" (Exod 3:13-14)

Thus the appellation Yahweh—he is—is not a name which defines God, but one that signifies, one that signifies the act of deliverance. Indeed, the text continues:

> And God also said to Moses, "You will say to the children of Israel, 'Yahweh, the God of your fathers, the God of Abraham, the God of Isaac, and the God of Jacob, has sent me to you.' This is my name forever by which future generations will invoke me." (Exod 3:15)

In this way the historical revelation—signified by the names of Abraham, Isaac, and Jacob—leans on the secret of the name, to the very extent that the hidden God proclaims himself the meaning of the founding events. The revelation takes place between the secret and the revealed.

I am well aware that tradition has interpreted the *Ehyeh asher ehyeh* in the sense of a positive, ontological assertion, following the Septuagint translation: "I am who I am." Far from protecting the secret, this translation opened up an affirmative noetics of God's absolute being that could subsequently be transcribed into Neoplatonic and Augustinian ontology and then into Aristotelian and Thomistic metaphysics. In this way, the theology of the name could pass over into an onto-theology capable of taking up and bracketing the theology of history, and in which the meaning of narration and of prophecy was sublimated and rationalized. The dialectic of the hidden God who reveals himself—the nuclear dialectic of revelation—was thereby dissipated into the knowledge of being and the comprehension of providence.

But to say that the God who reveals himself is a hidden God is to confess that revelation can never constitute a body of truths which an institution may boast of or take pride in possessing. So to dissipate the massive opacity of the concept of revelation is also at the same time to overthrow every totalitarian form of authority which might claim to withhold the revealed truth. In this way, my first reflections end by returning to the point where we began.

II. The Response of a Hermeneutic Philosophy

What is philosophy's task in response to the claim which proceeds from a concept of revelation as differentiated as the one I have just outlined? Claim—*Anspruch*—can signify two different things: undue and unacceptable pretension or an appeal which does not force one to accept its message. I want to understand claim in this second sense. But this reversal in listening to a claim can only be produced if, in symmetry with the critique of an opaque and authoritarian concept of revelation, philosophy proceeds in its own self-understanding to a critique of its own pretension which causes it to understand the appeal of revelation as an unacceptable claim opposed to it. If the unacceptable pretentious claim of the idea of revelation is in the final analysis that of a *sacrificium intellectus* and of a total heteronomy under the verdict of the magisterium, the opposed pretentious claim of philosophy is the claim to a complete transparency of truth and a total autonomy of the thinking subject. When these two pretensions simply confront each other, they constitute an unbridgeable canyon between what some call the "truths of faith" and others call the "truths of reason."

I want to direct my remarks to a critique of this double pretension of philosophy, with the idea that at the end of such undertaking the apparently unreasonable claim of revelation might be better understood as a nonviolent appeal.

But before undertaking this critique, allow me to say which ways I will not follow. First, I set apart from my own proposal the project of a rational theology which other philosophers whom I respect believe to be possible in practice. If I do not seek to restate the proofs for the existence of God, and if I do not inquire into the relation of concordance or of subordination that might exist between two orders of truth, it is as much for reasons based on the interpretation of biblical revelation given above as for the idea of philosophy that I make use of. My remarks in part one essentially tried to carry the idea of revelation back to a more originary level than that of theology, the level of its fundamental discourse. This discourse is established close to human experience and it is therefore in experiences more fundamental than any ontotheological articulation that I will seek the traits of a truth capable of being spoken of in terms of manifestation rather than verification, as well as the traits of a self-awareness wherein the subject would free himself of the arrogance of consciousness. These are those cardinal experiences, as language brings them to expression, which can enter into resonance or consonance with the modes of revelation brought to language by the most primitive expressions of the faith of Israel and of early Christianity.

This homology in no way requires that philosophy know God. The word God, it seems to me, just belongs to the pretheological expressions of faith. God is the one who is proclaimed, invoked, questioned, supplicated, and thanked. The meaning of the term God circulates among all these modes of discourse, but escapes each one of them. According to the vision of the Burning Bush, it is in a way their vanishing point.

The experiences of manifestation and of dependence therefore need not be referred to God, and still less serve to prove God's existence, in order to remain in resonance with those modes of experience and expression that alone signify God in the first place.

There is another way that I also will not follow—the way of an existentialism based on the wretchedness of the human condition, where philosophy provides the questions and religion the answers. No doubt, an apologetic based on the wretchedness of existence does satisfy the existential conditions imposed by the level of discourse we attained in our first section. Furthermore, it numbers among its practitioners such worthy names as Pascal and Tillich. But its apologetic character is suspect inasmuch as it is apologetic. If God speaks by the prophets, the philosopher does not have to justify His word, but rather to set off the horizon of significance where it may be heard. Such work has nothing to do with apologetics. Also, recourse to anxiety, to a sense of something lacking, is no less suspect. Bonhoeffer has said all that needs to be said against the God of the gaps, whether it be a question of explaining things or of understanding humanity. The philosophy of misery, even if one is not a Marxist, remains the misery of philosophy.

This is why I prefer to turn toward some structures of the interpretation of human experience to discern there those traits through which something has always been comprehensible under the idea of revelation understood in a religious sense of the term.

It is this comprehension that may enter into consonance with the nonviolent appeal of biblical revelation.

My analysis will consist of two parts, corresponding to the twofold claim of philosophical discourse to transparent objectivity and subjective autonomy. The first remarks will be directed toward the space of the manifestation of things, the second toward that understanding of themselves that humans gain when they allow themselves to be governed by what is manifested and said. These two dimensions of the problem correspond to the two major objections that are usually directed against the very principle of a revealed word. According to the first objection, any idea of revelation violates the idea of objective truth as measured by the criteria of empirical verification and falsification. According to the second objection, the idea of revelation denies the autonomy of the thinking subject inscribed within the idea of a consciousness completely in control of itself. The double meditation I propose will address in turn these claims to transparency founded on a concept of truth as adequation and verification, and to autonomy founded on the concept of a sovereign consciousness.

If I begin with the former point, it is for a fundamental reason, namely that the conquest of a new concept of truth as manifestation—and in this sense as revelation—demands the recognition of our real dependence which is in no way synonymous with heteronomy. The choice of this order of discussion also is in perfect agreement with the critique I offered in my first part of the subjectivism and psychologism engendered by a certain inflation of the idea of inspiration. I said, in effect, let us rather first look on the side of those events that make history or that are part of the impending future. Let us look on the side of the prescriptive force of the law of perfection, toward the objective quality of the feelings—the *pathos*—articulated by the hymn. In the same way, I now say, let us allow the space of the manifestation of things to be, before we turn toward the consciousness of the thinking and speaking subject.

1. The World of the Text and the New Being.

My first investigation, into what I will call the space of the manifestation of things, takes place within precise limits. I will not speak of our experience of being-in-the-world, beginning from a phenomenology of perception as may be found in the works of Husserl and Merleau-Ponty, nor in terms of a phenomenology of care or preoccupation as may be found in

Heidegger's *Being and Time*—although I believe that they may be connected by means of the detour I propose. Instead I will begin directly from the manifestation of the world by the text and by scripture.

This approach may seem overly limited due to the fact that it proceeds through the narrow defile of one cultural fact, the existence of written documents, and thus because it is limited to cultures which possess books, but it will seem less limited if we comprehend what enlargement of our experience of the world results from the existence of such documents. Moreover, by choosing this angle of attack, we immediately establish a correspondence with the fact that the claim of revealed speech reaches us today through writings to be interpreted. Those religions which refer back to Abraham—Judaism, Christianity, and Islam—are in their different ways, and they are often very different ways, religions of the book. So it is therefore appropriate, I believe, to inquire into the particular revelatory function attached to certain modalities of scripture which I will place under the title *Poetics,* in a sense I will explain in a moment. In effect, under the category of poetics, philosophical analysis encounters those traits of revelation which may correspond with or respond to the nonviolent appeal of biblical revelation.

To introduce this idea of a revelatory function of poetic discourse, I will draw upon three preparatory concepts that I have examined at greater length in my other writings on hermeneutics.[6]

The first one is the very concept of writing itself. We underestimate the phenomenon of writing if we reduce it to the simple material fixation of living speech. Writing stands in a specific relation to what is said. It produces a form of discourse that is immediately autonomous with regard to its author's intention. And in this autonomy is already contained everything that I will call in a moment, following Hans Georg Gadamer, the *issue* of the text which is removed from the finite intentional horizon of the author. In other words, thanks to writing, the world of the text can burst the world of the author. This emancipation with regard to the author has its parallel on the side of whoever receives the text. The autonomy of the text also removes this reader from the finite horizon of its original audience.

The second preparatory concept is that of the work. By this I mean the shaping of discourse through the operation of literary

[6] See, e.g., my recent book, *Interpretation Theory: Discourse and the Surplus of Meaning* (Fort Worth: Texas Christian University, 1976).

genres such as narration, fiction, the essay, etc. By producing discourse as such and such a work taking up such and such a genre, the composition codes assign to works of discourse that unique configuration we call a style. This shaping of the work concurs with the phenomenon of writing in externalizing and objectifying the text into what one literary critic has called a "verbal icon."

The third preparatory concept continues in the same direction and goes a bit further. It is what I call the world of the text. By this I mean that what is finally to be understood in a text is not the author or his presumed intention, nor is it the immanent structure or structures of the text, but rather the sort of world intended beyond the text as its reference. In this regard, the alternative "either the intention or the structure" is vain. For the reference of the text is what I call the issue of the text or the world of the text. The world of the text designates the reference of the work of discourse, not what is said, but about what it is said. Hence the issue of the text is the object of hermeneutics. And the issue of the text is the world the text unfolds before itself.

On this triple basis—autonomy through writing, externalization by means of the work, and the reference to a world—I will construct the analysis central to our discussion of the revelatory function of poetic discourse.

I have not introduced the category of poetics heretofore. It does not designate one of the literary genres discussed in the first part of my presentation, but rather the totality of these genres inasmuch as they exercise a referential function that differs from the descriptive referential function of ordinary language and above all of scientific discourse. Hence I will speak of the poetic function of discourse and not of a poetic genre or a mode of poetic discourse. This function, in turn, is defined precisely in terms of its referential function. What is this referential function?

As a first approximation, we may say that the poetic function points to the obliterating of the ordinary referential function, at least if we identify it with the capacity to describe familiar objects of perception or the objects which science alone determines by means of its standards of measurement. Poetic discourse suspends this descriptive function. It does not directly augment our knowledge of objects.

From here it is only a short step to saying that in poetry language turns back on itself to celebrate itself. But if we say this we accede too quickly to the positivist presupposition that empirical knowledge is objective knowledge because it is verifiable. Too often, we do not notice that we uncritically accept a certain concept of truth defined as adequation to real objects and as submitted to a criterion of empirical verification. That language in its poetic function abolishes the type of reference characteristic of such descriptive discourse, and along with it the reign of truth as adequation and the very definition of truth in terms of verification, is not to be doubted. The question is whether this suspension or abolition of a referential function of the first degree is not the negative condition for the liberating of a more primitive, more originary referential function, which may be called a second order reference only because discourse whose function is descriptive has usurped the first rank in daily life and has been supported in this regard by modern science.

My deepest conviction is that poetic language alone restores to us that participation-in or belonging-to an order of things which precedes our capacity to oppose ourselves to things taken as objects opposed to a subject. Hence the function of poetic discourse is to bring about this emergence of a depth-structure of belonging-to amid the ruins of descriptive discourse. Once again, this function is in no way to be identified with poetry understood as something opposed to prose and defined by a certain affinity of sense, rhythm, image, and sound. I am first defining the poetic function in a negative manner, following Roman Jakobson, as the inverse of the referential function understood in a narrow descriptive sense, then in a positive way as what in my volume on metaphor I call the metaphorical reference.[7] And in this regard, the most extreme paradox is that when language most enters into fiction—e.g., when a poet forges the plot of a tragedy—it most speaks truth because it redescribes reality so well known that it is taken for granted in terms of the new features of this plot. Fiction and redescription, then, go hand in hand. Or, to speak like Aristotle in his *Poetics,* the *mythos* is the way to true *mimesis,* which is not slavish imitation, or a copy, or mirror-image, but a transposition or metamorphosis—or, as I suggest, a redescription.

This conjunction of fiction and redescription, of *mythos* and *mimesis,* constitutes the referential function by means of which I would define the poetic dimension of language.

In turn, this poetic function conceals a dimension of revelation where revelation is to be understood in a nonreligious, nontheistic, and nonbiblical sense of the word—but one capable of entering into resonance with one or the other of the aspects of biblical revelation. How is this so?

[7] *La Métaphore vive* (Paris: Seuil, 1975) 273-321.

In the following manner. First the poetic function recapitulates in itself the three preparatory concepts of the autonomy of the text, the externality of the work, and the transcendence of the world of the text. Already by means of these three traits an order of things is revealed that does not belong to either the author or the original audience. But to these three traits the poetic function adds a split reference by means of which emerges the Atlantis submerged in the network of objects submitted to the domination of our preoccupations. It is this primordial ground of our existence, of the originary horizon of our being-there, that is the revelatory function which is coextensive with the poetic function.

But why call it revelatory? Because through all the traits that it recapitulates and by what it adds, the poetic function incarnates a concept of truth that escapes the definition by adequation as well as the criteria of falsification and verification. Here truth no longer means verification, but manifestation, i.e., letting what shows itself be. What shows itself is in each instance a proposed world, a world I may inhabit and wherein I can project my ownmost possibilities. It is in this sense of manifestation that language in its poetic function is a vehicle of revelation.

By using the word revelation in such a nonbiblical and even nonreligious way, do we abuse the word? I do not think so. Our analysis of the biblical concept of revelation has prepared us for a first degree analogical use of the term and here we are led to a second degree analogy. The first degree analogy was assured by the role of the first analogue, prophetic discourse, with its implication of another voice behind the prophet's voice. This meaning of the first analogue was communicated to all the other modes of discourse to the extent that they could be said to be inspired. But we also saw that this analogy with reference to the *princeps* discourse, that of prophecy, did not do justice to the specific character of each of the other modes of discourse, above all narrative discourse where what is said or recounted, the generative historical event, came to language through the narration. And the philosophical concept of revelation leads us back to this primacy of what is said over the inspiration of the narrator by means of a second analogy that is no longer that of inspiration, but that of manifestation.

This new analogy invites us to place the originary expressions of biblical faith under the sign of the poetic function of language; not to deprive them of any referent, but to put them under the law of split reference that characterizes the poetic function. Religious discourse is poetic in all the senses we have named. Being written down as scripture removes it from the finite horizon of its authors and its first audience. The style of its literary genres gives it the externality of a work. And the intended implicit reference of each text opens onto a world, the biblical world, or rather the multiple worlds unfolded before the book by its narration, prophecy, prescriptions, wisdom, and hymns. The proposed world that in biblical language is called a new creation, a new Covenant, the Kingdom of God, is the "issue" of the biblical text unfolded in front of this text.

Finally, and above all, this "issue" of the biblical text is indirectly intended beyond the suspension of descriptive, didactic, and informative discourse. This abolition of the reference to objects that we can manipulate allows the world of our originary rootedness to appear. Just as the world of poetic texts opens its way across the ruins of the intraworldly objects of everyday existence and of science, so too the new being projected by the biblical text opens its way across the world of ordinary experience and in spite of the closed nature of that experience. The power to project this new world is the power of breaking through and of an opening.

Thus this areligious sense of revelation helps us to restore the concept of biblical revelation to its full dignity. It delivers us from psychologizing interpretations of the inspiration of the scriptures in the sense of an insufflation of their words into the writers' ears. If the Bible may be said to be revealed this must refer to what it says, to the new being it unfolds before us. Revelation, in short, is a feature of the biblical world proposed by the text.

Yet if this areligious sense of revelation has such a corrective value, it does not for all that include the religious meaning of revelation. There is a homology between them, but nothing allows us to derive the specific feature of religious language—i.e., that its referent moves among prophecy, narration, prescription, wisdom, and psalms, coordinating these diverse and partial forms of discourse by giving them a vanishing point and an index of incompleteness—nothing, I say, allows us to derive this from the general characteristics of the poetic function. The biblical hermeneutic is in turn one regional hermeneutic within a general hermeneutic and a unique hermeneutic that is joined to the philosophical hermeneutic as its *organon*. It is one particular case insofar as the Bible is one of the great poems of existence. It is a unique case because all its partial forms of discourse are referred to that Name which is the point of intersection and the vanishing point of all our discourse about God, the name of the unnameable. This is the paradoxical homology that the category of the world of the text establishes between revelation in the broad sense of poetic discourse and in the specifically biblical sense.

2. Mediating Reflection and Testimony.

We may now turn to the second pretension that philosophy opposes to the claim of revealed truth. This is its claim to autonomy. It is founded on the concept of a subject who is master of his thoughts. This idea of a consciousness which posits itself in positing its contents undoubtedly constitutes the strongest resistance to any idea of revelation, not only in the specific sense of the religions of the book, but also in the larger, more global sense that we have just connected to the poetic function of discourse.

I will proceed here with regard to the second part of my analysis in the same manner as for the first. That is, instead of taking up the question of the autonomy of consciousness in its most general sense, I will attempt to focus the debate on a central concept of self-awareness which is capable of corresponding to one of the major traits of the idea of revelation brought to light by our analysis of biblical discourse. This central category will occupy a place comparable to that of poetic discourse in relation to the objective aspect of philosophical discourse. This category which to me best signifies the self-implication of the subject in his discourse is that of *testimony*. Besides having a corresponding term on the side of the idea of revelation, it is the most appropriate concept for making us understand what a thinking subject formed by and conforming to poetic discourse might be.

But before undertaking a properly philosophical reflection on the category of testimony, I will again call on some preparatory concepts which I have explicated at greater length in my other work on hermeneutics.

First, the concept of the *cogito* as mediated by a universe of signs. Without appealing to the mediation by means of the text, the written work, I would like to recall in general terms that general dependence that upholds a subject who, contrary to Descartes's assertion, does not have at his disposal an immediate intuition of his existence and his essence as a thinking being. From the *Symbolism of Evil*[8] on I have perceived this constitutional infirmity of Descartes's *cogito*. To pierce the secret of the evil will, we must take the detour of a semantics and an

---
[8] New York: Harper, 1967.

exegesis applied to those symbols and myths in which the millenary experience of the confession of evil is deposited.

But it is with *Freud and Philosophy*[9] that I decisively broke away from the illusions of consciousness as the blind spot of reflection. The case of the symbolism of evil is not an exception, one tributary of the gloomy experience of evil. All reflection is mediated, there is no immediate self-consciousness. The first truth, I said, that of the "I think, I am," "remains as abstract and empty as it is invincible; it has to be 'mediated' by the ideas, actions, works, institutions, and monuments that objectify it. It is in these objects, in the widest sense of the word, that the Ego must lose and find itself. We can say, in a somewhat paradoxical sense, that a philosophy of reflection is not a philosophy of consciousness, if by consciousness we mean immediate self-consciousness."[10]

Adopting the language of Jean Nabert—as I will do again in my analysis of testimony—I defined reflection by "the appropriation of our effort to exist and of our desire to be, through the works which bear witness to that effort and desire."[11] In this way, I included testimony within the structure of reflection without as yet having determined the importance of this implication. At least I saw that "the positing or emergence of this effort or desire is not only devoid of all intuition but is evidenced only by works whose meaning remains doubtful and revocable."[12] This is why reflection had to include interpretation; that is, "the results, methods, and presuppositions of all the sciences that try to decipher and interpret the signs of man."[13]

The second preparatory concept is that of participation or "belonging-to" (*appartenance*) which I borrow from Gadamer's *Truth and Method*.[14] For me, the conquest of this concept marked the end of a difficult struggle with Husserlian idealism which was not yet broached by the preceding avowal of the mediated character of reflection. It was still necessary to call into question Husserl's scientific ideal, especially in the sense of a final justification or a self-founding of the transcendental ego, to discover in the *finite* ontological condition of self-understanding the unsurpassable limit of this scientific ideal.

---

[9] New Haven: Yale University, 1970.
[10] Ibid., 43-44.
[11] Ibid., 46.
[12] Ibid.
[13] Ibid.
[14] New York: Seabury, 1975.

The ultimate condition of any enterprise of justification or of grounding is that it is always preceded by a relation that already carries it:

> Are we speaking of a relation to the object? Precisely not. What hermeneutics just questions in Husserlian idealism is that it has inscribed its immense and unsurpassable discovery of intentionality in a conceptuality which weakens its import, especially for the subject-object relation. . . . Hermeneutic's declaration is, so to speak, that the problematic of objectivity presupposes as prior to itself an inclusive relation which englobes the allegedly autonomous subject and the allegedly adverse object. It is this inclusive or englobing relation that I call participation or belonging-to.[15]

As you can see, my ongoing work undercut the primacy of reflection that at first was left out of the critique of the illusions of consciousness. Reflection does not disappear. That would make no sense at all. But its status is to be always a "second order reflection," to speak like Gabriel Marcel. It corresponds to that distanciation without which we would never become conscious of belonging to a world, a culture, a tradition. It is the critical moment, originally bound to the consciousness of belonging-to, that confers its properly historical character on this consciousness. For even a tradition only becomes such under the condition of a distance that distinguishes the belonging-to proper to a human being from the simple inclusion of a thing as a part of a whole. Reflection is never first, never constituting—it arrives unexpectedly like a "crisis" within an experience that bears us, and it constitutes us as the subject of the experience.

Our third preparatory concept is caught sight of in the prolongation of this dialectic of participation and distanciation. It makes more specific our mode of belonging to a culture where the signs are texts, i.e., writings and works arising out of distinct literary genres. This third concept corresponds in the "subjective" order to the concept of the world of the text in the "objective" order. You will recall my insistence on defining the hermeneutic task not in terms of the author's intention supposedly hidden behind the text, but in terms of the quality of being-in-the-world unfolded in front of the text as the reference of the text. The subjective concept that corresponds to that of the world of the

---

[15]"Phénoménologie et herméneutique," in Ernst W. Orth, ed., *Phänomenologische Forschungen 1: Phänomenologie heute: Grundlagen und Methodenprobleme* (Freiburg/Munich: Alber, 1975) 38. English trans.: "Phenomenology and Hermeneutics," *Nous* 9, 1 (April 1975) 88-89; trans. altered.

text is the concept of appropriation. By this I mean the very act of understanding oneself before the text. This act is the exact counterpart of the autonomy of writing and the externalization of the work. It in no way is intended to make the reader correspond with the genius of the author, for it does not respond to the author, but to the work's sense and reference. Its other is the issue of the text, the world of the work.

This third preparatory concept marks the final defeat of the pretension of consciousness to set itself up as the standard of meaning. To understand oneself before the text is not to impose one's own finite capacity of understanding on it, but to expose oneself to receive from it a larger self which would be the proposed way of existing that most appropriately responds to the proposed world of the text. Understanding then is the complete opposite of a constitution for which the subject would have the key. It would be better in this regard to say that the self is constituted by the issue of the text.

How, you might ask, are these three concepts of mediated reflection, belonging-to or second order reflection, and appropriation as self-understanding before the text preparatory concepts? They are preparatory insofar as they bring about on a purely epistemological, even a methodological, plane consciousness' abandoning of its pretension to constitute every signification in and beginning from itself. This abandonment (*dessaisissement*) takes place even on the terrain of the historical and hermeneutical sciences, at the very heart of the problematic of understanding, where the tradition of Romanticist hermeneutics had thought to establish the reign of subjectivity. It is the final consequence of a critique of Romanticist hermeneutics, at the end of which the concept of the world of the text has taken the place of the author's intention.

Perhaps you have begun to realize how the pretension of consciousness to constitute itself is the most formidable obstacle to the idea of revelation. In this regard, the transcendental idealism of a Husserl contains implicitly the same atheistic consequences as does the idealism of consciousness of a Feuerbach. If consciousness posits itself, it must be the "subject" and the divine must be the "predicate," and it can only be through an alienation subsequent to this power of self-production that God is projected as the "subject" for whom the human being becomes the "predicate." The hermeneutical movement I have just traced brings about a conversion diametrically opposed to that of Feuerbach. Where consciousness posits itself as the origin of meaning, hermeneutics brings about the abandonment of this pretension. This abandonment is the reverse of Feuerbach's critique of alienation.

But such a consequence can only be anticipated and glimpsed on the unique basis of a hermeneutic where self-understanding is the reply to notions as narrowly "literary" as those of the text, the work, and the world of the text. It is precisely the function of the category of *tes-ti-mony*—the central category of this second phase of our philosophical inquiry—to dismantle a little further the fortress of consciousness. It introduces the dimension of historical contingency which is lacking in the concept of the world of the text, which is deliberately nonhistorical or transhistorical. It throws itself therefore against one fundamental characteristic of the idea of autonomy; namely, not making the internal itinerary of consciousness depend on external events.

As Jean Nabert puts it in his *Essai sur le mal*, "Do we have the right to invest one moment of history with an absolute characteristic?"[16] You may recall that this is what in the phenomenon of religion also scandalized Karl Jaspers. According to him, "philosophical faith" ought to eliminate the arbitrary privileging of this or that moment of humanity's spiritual history. This refusal of historical contingency therefore constitutes one of the most dug-in defenses of the claim to autonomy and a meditation on the category of testimony is meant to confront this refusal.

Few philosophers, to my knowledge, have attempted to integrate the category of testimony into philosophical reflection. Most have either ignored it or abandoned it to the realm of faith. One exception is Jean Nabert in his volume entitled *Désir de Dieu*.[17] I want to draw on this work to show how this category governs the abandonment of or letting go of the absolute claim to self-consciousness, and how it occupies on the subjective side of a hermeneutic of revelation a strategic position similar to that of the category of poetics on the objective side.

Recourse to testimony occurs in a philosophy of reflection at the moment when such a philosophy renounces the pretension of consciousness to constitute itself. Thus Jean Nabert, e.g., recognizes the place of testimony at that point of his itinerary where concrete reflection exerts itself to rejoin what he calls that originary affirmation which constitutes me more than I constitute it. This originary affirmation has all the characteristics of an

---

[16]Paris: P.U.F., 1955, p. 148.
[17]Paris: Aubier-Montaigne, 1966.

absolute affirmation of the absolute, but it is unable to go beyond a purely internal act that is incapable of outwardly expressing itself or of even inwardly maintaining itself. Originary affirmation has something about it that is indefinitely inaugural and that only concerns the idea which the ego makes of itself. For a philosophy of reflection, this originary affirmation is in no way one of our experiences. Although numerically identical to each person's real (*réelle*) consciousness, it is the act that accomplishes the negation of those limitations which affect an individual's destiny. It is the letting go (*dépouillement*) of self.

In one sense, this letting go of self is still part of the reflective order. It is both an ethical and a speculative act. And it means renouncing not only the empirical objects that are ordered by reason, but also those transcendental objects of metaphysics that might still provide support for thinking the unconditioned. Consequently, this letting go takes up from and continues the Kantian meditation on the transcendental illusion as presented in the section on "Dialectic" in the first *Critique*. It could also be expressed by the language of the *Enneads* where Plotinus writes *Aphele panta*—"abolish everything." It is precisely this movement of letting go which bears reflection to the encounter with contingent signs of the absolute which the absolute in its generosity allows to appear.

This avowal of the absolute can no longer be Kantian (nor no doubt Plotinian), for Kantian philosophy would incline us to look only for examples or symbols, not for testimonies, understood as accounts of an experience of the absolute. In an example, the case is effaced before the rule and the person is effaced before the law. An abstraction, the abstraction of the norm, takes the place of the originary affirmation. But the encounter with evil in the experience of what cannot be justified does not allow us the leisure to grant our veneration to the sublimity of the moral order. The unjustifiable constrains us to let go of this very veneration. Only those events, acts, and persons that attest that the unjustifiable is overcome here and now can reopen the path toward originary affirmation.

As for the symbol, it is no less feeble than the example with regard to the unjustifiable. Its inexhaustible richness of meaning no doubt gives it a consistency that the example lacks. But its historicity places it at the mercy of the work of interpretation that may dissipate it too quickly into too ideal forms of significations. Only testimony that is singular in each instance confers the sanction of reality on ideas, ideals, and ways of being that the symbol depicts to us and which we uncover as our ownmost possibilities.

Therefore testimony better than either an example or a symbol places reflection before the paradox which the pretension of consciousness makes a scandal of, I mean that a moment of history is invested with an absolute character. This paradox ceases to be a scandal as soon as the wholly internal movement of letting go, of abandoning the claim to found consciousness accepts being led by and ruled by the interpretation of external signs which the absolute gives of itself. And the hermeneutic of testimony consists wholly in the convergence of these two movements, these two exegeses: the exegesis of self and the exegesis of external signs.

Testimony, on the one hand, is able to be taken up internally in reflection thanks to several dialectical features that arouse and call for this reflective repetition in us. It first proposes the dialectic of its object, which is an event as well as a meaning at the same time, similar to what we spoke of in part one with regard to the narration of the founding events of the history of Israel. For the Hebraic confession of faith, the event and its meaning immediately coincide. It is the moment that Hegel called the moment of absolute or revealed religion.

But this moment of fusion of event and meaning fades away. Its appearance is immediately its disappearance. We might recall at this point Hegel's admirable pages on the empty tomb and the vain quest of the crusades. In short, a scission appears here that engenders an unending mediation of immediacy. This is why testimony requires interpretation. Interpretation is also required by the critical activity that testimony gives rise to. It needs to be tested. This tight bond between testimony and a process of examination is not abolished when testimony is transferred from a tribunal to the plane of reflection. On the contrary, the judicatory dimension of testimony then takes on its full depth. We must always decide between the false witness and the truthful one for there is no manifestation of the absolute without the threat of a false testimony, and without the decision that separates the sign from the idol. This role for judgment will find its counterpart in a moment in the movement by means of which reflection replies to testimony's critique, what Nabert calls the criteriology of the divine.

Lastly, testimony calls for interpretation through a more fundamental dialectic, the dialectic of the witness and the things seen. To be a witness is to have participated in what one has seen and to be able to testify to it.

On the other hand, testimony may break away from the things seen to such a degree that it is concentrated on the quality of an act, a work, or a life, which is in itself a sign of the absolute. In this second sense, which is complementary to the first sense, to be a witness is no longer to testify that . . . , but to testify to. . . . This latter expression allows us to understand that a witness may so implicate himself in his testimony that it becomes the best proof of his conviction.

When this proof becomes the price of life itself, the witness changes names. He becomes a martyr. In Greek, though, μάρτυς means witness. I am well aware that any argument from martyrdom is suspect. A cause that has martyrs is not necessarily a just cause. But martyrdom precisely is not an argument and still less a proof. It is a test, a limit situation. A person becomes a martyr because first of all he is a witness.

This proximity between a witness and a martyr is not always without effect on the very meaning of testimony. Its purely juridical sense may rise and fall. In a trial, for example, a witness enjoys immunity. Only the accused risks his life. But a witness can become the accused and the righteous may die. Then a great historical archetype arises: the suffering servant, the persecuted righteous, Socrates, Jesus. . . . The commitment or risk assumed by the witness makes testimony more than and other than a simple narration of what was seen. Testimony is also the commitment of a pure heart and a commitment unto death. It thus belongs to the tragic destiny of truth.

This tragic destiny of truth outside of us in a wholly contingent history may accompany the letting go by means of which reflection abandons the illusions of a sovereign consciousness. Reflection does so by internalizing the dialectic of testimony from which it records the trace of the absolute in the contingency of history. The three dialectical moments of testimony—event and meaning, the trial of false testimony, and testimony about what is seen and of a life—find their echo, their reverberation, in the movement of consciousness that renounces its sovereignty.

The dialectic of event and meaning? A whole structure of self-understanding is declared here which enjoins us to renounce any idea of a self-constituting of consciousness within a purely immanent temporality. We exist because we are seized by those events that happen to us in the strong sense of this word—such and such entirely fortuitous encounters, dramas, happinesses or misfortunes that, as one says, have completely changed the course of our existence. The task of understanding ourselves through them is the task of transforming the accidental into our destiny.

The event is our master. Each of our separate existences here are like those communities we belong to—we are absolutely dependent on certain founding events. They are not events that pass away, but events that endure. In themselves, they are event-signs. To understand ourselves is to continue to attest and to testify to them.

The dialectic of true and false testimony? This process has its counterpart on the side of reflection in what Nabert calls the criteriology of the divine, and which he couples precisely to the examination of testimony. For a finite existence like ours, appropriation can only be a critical act. It is not a unitary intuition or a form of absolute knowledge in which consciousness would become aware of itself as well as of the absolute. It is in sorting among and sifting its predicates that we seem most worthy of signifying the divine, that we form a certain idea of it. This sorting takes the form of a trial. It is easy to see why. To discern the predicates of the divine is to follow what the medievals call the way of eminence. For how else are we to carry a certain idea of justice or goodness to extremes if not by conforming our judgment of eminence to the testimony given outside of us in history by the words, the deeds, and the lives of certain exceptional people who are not necessarily famous, but who testify by their excellence to that very way of eminence that reflection attempts to reproduce in itself and for itself? It appears therefore that the two trials or judgments criss-cross: in forming predicates of the divine we disqualify the false witness; in recognizing the true witnesses we identify the predicates of the divine. This fine hermeneutic circle is the law of self-understanding.

Yet the third dialectic, the dialectic of historical testimony, is the most significant for a self-understanding that would attempt to reproduce its movement in itself.

The witness to things seen, we said, at the limit becomes a martyr for truth. Here reflection must confess its inequality with the historical paradigm of its movement of letting go if it is not to abuse its words and become radically deceitful. The philosophy of reflection tends to use big words: *epoché,* reflective distance, letting go, etc. But in its use of them it indicates more that it can signify of the direction of a movement, that movement which we have simply wanted to point to with the expression "letting go" as the abandonment of the sovereign consciousness. Philosophy must internalize what is said in the Gospel: "Who would save his life must lose it." Transposed into the realm of reflection, this means, "Whoever would posit himself as a constituting consciousness will miss his destiny." But reflection cannot produce this renouncing of the sovereign consciousness out of itself. It may only do so by confessing its total dependence on the historical manifestations of the divine.

Once again, Nabert expresses this dependence in terms of a complementarity. "For the apprehension of the divine," he says, "the letting go essential to mystical experience and the liaison of the divine to a historical manifestation are complementary to each other. Thanks to the former, the grasping of the divine tends to be confused with the advance of reflection through the sole exercise (*ascèse*) of the philosophical consciousness; through the latter, the divine is inscribed in history through a testimony whose meaning consciousness has never exhausted."[18] And a few pages later he adds, "The essential idea is to demonstrate a well founded correspondence between the historical affirmation of the absolute and the degrees through which a consciousness is raised up and transformed by an originary affirmation. . . ."[19] For my part, I would emphasize the non-reciprocal nature of this complementarity inasmuch as the initiative belongs to historical testimony.

To account for this priority of historical testimony over self-consciousness, I would refer you to the description Kant gives of "aesthetic ideas" in the *Critique of Judgment*. You will recall the circumstances where he has recourse to this theme. At the moment of accounting for the aesthetic productions of genius, he invokes that power of the imagination "to present" (*Darstellung*) those ideas of reason for which we have no concept. By means of such representation, the imagination "occasions much thought (*viel zu denken*) without however any definite thought, i.e., any concept, being capable of being adequate to it; it consequently cannot be completely compassed and made intelligible by language."[20] Hence what the imagination thus confers on thought is the ability to think further:

> If we now place under a concept a representation of the imagination belonging to its presentation, but which occasions in itself more thought than can ever be comprehended in a definite concept and which consequently aesthetically enlarges the concept itself in an unbounded fashion, the imagination is here creative, and it brings the faculty of intellectual ideas (the reason) into movement; i.e., by a representation

---

[18] Ibid., 267.
[19] Ibid., 279.
[20] Immanuel Kant, *Critique of Judgment* (trans. by J. H. Bernard; New York: Hafner, 1966) 157.

more thought (which indeed belongs to the concept of the object) is occasioned than can in it be grasped or made clear.[21]

Historical testimony has the same structure and the same function. It, too, is a "presentation," of what for reflection remains an idea; namely, the idea of a letting go wherein we affirm an order exempt from that servitude from which finite existence cannot deliver itself. The Kantian relation between an idea and its aesthetic "presentation" well expresses the kind of relation we are seeking to formulate between originary affirmation (which would require an impossible total mediation between self-consciousness and its symbolic experience) and its historical presentation in testimonies whose meaning we have never exhausted.

Such is the non-heteronomous dependence of conscious reflection on external testimonies. And it is this dependence that gives philosophy a certain idea of revelation. As earlier with regard to poetic discourse on the objective side of the idea of revelation, so too on the subjective side, the experience of testimony can only provide the horizon for a specifically religious and biblical experience of revelation, without our ever being able to derive that experience from the purely philosophical categories of truth as manifestation and reflection as testimony.

Allow me to conclude with this expression of dependence without heteronomy. Why, I will ask at the end of this meditation, is it so difficult for us to conceive of a dependence without heteronomy? Is it not because we too often and too quickly think of a will that submits and not enough of an imagination that opens itself? Beginning from this question it is possible to catch sight of the dividing line between the two sides of our investigation. For what are the poem of the Exodus and the poem of the resurrection, called to mind in the first section, addressed to if not to our imagination rather than our obedience? And what is the historical testimony that our reflection would like to internalize addressed to if not to our imagination? If to understand oneself is to understand oneself in front of the text, must we not say that the reader's understanding is suspended, de-realized, made potential just as the world itself is metamorphosized by the poem? If this is true, we must say that the imagination is that part of ourselves that responds to the text as a Poem, and that alone can encounter revelation no longer as an unacceptable pretension, but a nonviolent appeal.

[21]Ibid., 158.

4QLXXNUM: A PRE-CHRISTIAN REWORKING OF THE SEPTUAGINT*

Patrick W. Skehan

The Catholic University of America
Washington, D.C. 20064

The MS published here in all its extant fragments[1] represents the remains of 3 successive columns, about 30 letters to the line, 34 lines to the column, from a scroll written at about the turn of the era.[2] Contrary to the writer's earlier published impression,[3] its text is not such as can be supposed to underlie the form presented in later Septuagint codices; it is instead a considerable reworking of the original LXX to make it conform both in quantity and in diction to a Hebrew consonantal text nearly indistinguishable, within the limited scope of our evidence, from that of MT. The

---

*Abbreviations used in this article are as follows. LXX =Alan E. Brooke and Norman McLean, *The Old Testament in Greek,* vol. 1: *The Octateuch* (Cambridge: Cambridge University, 1917). Individual LXX MSS and hexaplaric readings are cited from this source, using its sigla. G^B=B a Ethiopic;G^L=gndpt (G^{L^1}=gn; G^{L^2}=dpt); G^O=G ckx Syhex; G^A=AFM etc. These groupings are not proposed as definitive or exhaustive, but as pointing to identifiable currents of LXX evidence. $\alpha' \sigma' \theta'$=Aquila, Symmachus, Theodotion (medieval citations). MT=Rudolf Kittel, Paul Kahle, et al., *Biblia hebraica* (3d ed.; Stuttgart: Württ. Bibelanstalt, 1937 and later imprints). Sam. =August Freiherr von Gall, *Der hebräische Pentateuch der Samaritaner* (Giessen: Töpelmann, 1918). Syhex = Paul de Lagarde, *Bibliothecae syriacae . . . quae ad philologiam sacram pertinent* (Göttingen: Dieterich, 1892). PAM = Palestine Archaeological Museum (photographs).

[1]Preliminary notice in my article "The Qumran Manuscripts and Textual Criticism," *VTSup* 4: *Volume du Congrès: Strasbourg 1956* (Leiden: Brill, 1957) 155-57; see the discussion by Paul Kahle, "The Greek Bible and the Gospels: Fragments from the Judaean Desert," *SE* I (TU 73; Berlin: Akademie-Verlag, 1959) 615-18.

[2]See the opinion of C. H. Roberts, quoted by Kahle, "Greek Bible,"616: "[to] the end of the first century B.C. or [to] the opening years of the first century A.D."

[3]"That a somewhat awkward Greek rendering of Numbers has been reworked anciently to yield the recension contained in our later codices" ("Qumran Manuscripts," 157).

manner of this reworking is therefore that of the καίγε, or proto-Theodotionic, recension. Nevertheless there are indications (see with 3:40 below) that the reviser here at work cannot be identified with the καίγε reviser of LXX Samuel and Kings.[4] Agreement with distinctive readings of G^L does occur, but to a very limited degree.

4QLXXNum Col i (fragments): Num 3:40-43

]ἈΡΙΘΜΗϹΟ[υπανπρωτοτοκοναρσεν
τωννι]ῶΝΙϹΡΑΗΛΑΠ[ομηνιαιουκαιεπανω
καιλα]ΒΕΤΟΝΑΡΙΘΜΟ[ναυτωνεξονοματος
⁴¹καιλημ]ΨΕΙΤΟΥϹΛΕΥΙΤΑ[ϛεμοιεγωΚυριος
αντιπαντων]ΤῶΝΠΡ[ωτοτοκωντωνυιων   5
Ισραηλκαιτακτη]ΝΗΤ[ωνλευιτωναντι
παντωντωνπρ]ῶΤΟΤΟΚῶ[νεντοιϛκτηνεσιν
τωνυιωνΙσρα]ΗΛ ⁴²ΚΑΙΕΠεσκεψατοΜωυσης
οντροπονενετ]ΕΙΛΑΤ[οΚυριοσαυτωι
πανπρωτοτοκονεντο]ΙϹΥΙΟ[ι]ϹΙϹΡΑ   10
ηλ⁴³καιεγενετοπανπρωτο]ΤΟΚΟ[ναρσε]Ν
καταααριθμονεξονοματοσαπ]ΟΜΗ[νιαιου

Num 3:50-51 (?)

πεν]ΤΕϹΙ[κλους
αργ]ΥΡΙ[ον

Col. ii: Num 4:1, [2-4], 5-9, [10]

line

1 Μωυσηνκαι]ΑΑΡΩΝ[λεγων ²λαβετοκεφα

9 lines missing

---

[4]As discussed by James Donald Shenkel, *Chronology and Recensional Development in the Greek Text of Kings* (Cambridge: Harvard University, 1968), esp. 5-21, 113-20, 124-29, following on Dominique Barthélemy, O.P., *Les Devanciers d'Aquila* (*VTSup* 10; Leiden: Brill, 1963) and Henry StJohn Thackeray, *The Septuagint and Jewish Worship* (2d ed.; London: Oxford University, 1923). Nor does 4QLXXNum relate directly to the "Theodotionic" version of Exodus, which is also καίγε material. See Kevin O'Connell, *The Theodotionic Revision of the Book of Exodus* (Cambridge: Harvard University, 1972) 292-93.

11 υιοιαυτουοτανεξαιρηι]ἨΠΑΡΕΜΒΟΛ[η
12 καικαθ]ΕΛΟῚ[σι]ΝΤΟ̇[καταπετ]ΑΣΜΑῚ[ο
13 συσκιαζο]Ν ΚΑΙΚΑΤΑΚ[αλυψουσινεναυτ
14 ωιτηνκιβω]ῚΟΝΤ[ουμαρτυρι]ΟΥ⁶ΚΑ[ιεπι
15 θησουσινεπαυ]ΤΟ[κατακαλυμμαδ]ΕΡ[μα
16 υακινθινονκαιεπιβαλουσινεπαυτην
17 ιματιονολονυακινθινονανωθεν
18 καιδιεμβαλουσιντουσα]Ṗ̇ΤΗΡΑΣ[⁷και
19 επιτηντραπεζαντηνπρο]ΚΕΙΜΕΝΗΝ Ε
20 πιβαλουσινεπαυτηνιμ]ΑΤΙΟΝΥ[α]Κ̇ΙΝΘΙ
21 νονκαιδωσουσινεπαυ]ΤΗΝ̇ΤΑΤ[ρ]Ῡ̇ΒΛΙ
22 ακαιτασθυισκασκαιτ]ΟΥΣΚΥΑΘΟΥΣΚΑΙ
23 τασπονδειαενοιςσπε]Ν̇ΔΕΙΕΝΑΥΤΟΙΣ
24 καιοιαρτοιοιδιαπαντ]ΟΣΕΠΑΥΤΗΙΕΣΟ
25 νται⁸καιεπιβαλουσινεπαυτ]ΗΝΙΜΑῚ[ιον
26 κοκκινονκαικαλυψουσι]Ν̇ΑΥΤΗΝ ΚΑ[λυ
27 μματιδερματινωιακ]ΙΝΘΙΝ̇[ωικαιδι
28 εμβαλουσινδιαυτηστους]ΑῬΤΗΡΑΣ
29 ⁹καιλημψονταιιματιονυακιν]ΘΙΝΟΝΚΑΙ
30 καλυψουσιντηνλυχνιαντη]Σ̇ΦΑΥΣΕῶΣ
31 καιτουςλυχνουςκαιταςλαβιδασκ]ΑΙ

3 lines missing

Col. iii: Num 4:[10], 11–16

line

4 lines missing

5 ιματιαυακιν]ΘΙΝΑ ΚΑΙΚΑ[λυψουσιναυ
6 τοκαλυμματ]ΙΔ̇ΕΡΜΑΤΙΝῶΙῚ[ακινθινωι
7 ΚΑΙΕ̇[μβαλο]ΥΣΙΝΤΟΥΣΑΡΤ[ηρασαυτου
8 ¹²ΚΑΙΛ[ημ]Ψ̇ΟΝΤῚΑ̇Ι̇Π̇ΑΝΤΑΤΑΣ[κευηταλειτουρ
9 ΓΙ̇ΚΑΟ̇ΣΑΛΕ̇[ιτ]Ο̇[υ]ΡΓΟΥΣΙΝΕΝ[αυτοισεν
10 [το]Ι̇ΣΑ[γιοις]ΚΑΙΘΗ̇ΣΟΥΣΙΝΕΙ[σιματιον
11 υακινθινον]ΚΑΙΚ̇ΑΛΥΨΟΥΣΙΝ[αυτακαλυ
12 μματιδερμ]ΑΤΙΝῶΙῩΑΚΙΝ[θινωικαιεπι
13 θησουσινεπ]ΑῬῚΗΡΟΣ[¹³καιεκσποδιασ
14 ουσιντοθυσιαστ]Η̇ΡΙΟΝΚ̇[αιεπιθησουσιν
15 επαυτοιματιονολο]Π̇Ο̇ΡΦΥῬ[ον¹⁴καιεπιθ

3 lines missing

19 ΚΑΙΤΑΣΙ̇Ι[ονδειακαιπαντατασκευητουθυ

20 CIA[σ]ΤΗΡΙ[ουκαιεπιβαλουσινεπαυτοκα
21 ΛΥΜΜΑΔ[ερματινοννακινθινονκαιδιεμ
22 βαλουσιντουςαρτηραςαυτου¹⁵καισυντε
23 λεσουσινΑαρωνκαι]ΟΙΥΙΟΙΑ[υ]ΤΟΥ[καλυ
24 πτοντεςτααγιακαιπ]ΑΝΤ[ατασκευητα
25 αγιαεντωιεξαιρειντη]ΝΠΑΡΕΜ[βολην

        5 lines missing

31 ελαιο]ΝΤΟ[υφωτοςκαιτοθυμιαματης
32 συνθε]ϹΕΩ[ςκαιηθυσιαηκαθημερανκαι
33 τοελαιοντηςχρισεωςηεπισκοπηολης
34 τηςσκηνηςκαιοσαεστινεναυτηι]ΕΝΤ[ωι

Col. i. Though not enough margin survives to prove it, the fragment beginning with Num 3:40 should be from the top of the column. LXX, MT and Sam. show no variation in quantity of text toward the end of Num 3. In the format of the 4Q scroll the LXX text here would seem to call for up to 36 lines, rather than the 34 lines of cols. ii, iii. 4QLXXNum will therefore have had a slightly shorter text (see with ?3:50–51 below). The discrepancy would be the greater were the first fragment from lower than the column top.

3:40 ἀρίθμησον: no LXX codex is cited for this alternative to the generally attested ἐπίσκεψαι in this place. However, between Num 2:4 and 7:2 (though not in ch. 1, nor later in the book, e.g., chs. 26; 31) finite, participial and noun forms from the ἀριθμεῖν stem are often, though not everywhere, substituted for forms related to ἐπισκέπτειν: this by varying numbers of witnesses, with A, b, w and the Old Latin prominent among them. The practice is not that of the three later translators α′, σ′ and θ′: see the hexaplaric notes in Brooke-McLean for Num 1:19, 21, 45, 47; 2:9, 24, 31; 3:15, 22, which should suffice to establish that the three worked regularly with forms related to ἐπισκέπτειν. This means that ἀρίθμησον should not be καίγε/proto-Theodotion either. Nor is it: in Samuel-Kings both the Old Greek and the καίγε sections present us with ἐπισκέπτειν = פקד in a variety of forms and meanings, including those associated with a census.[5] We may

[5]Compare for the Old Greek 1 Sam 11:8; 13:15; 14:17 (twice); 15:4; 20:6, 18, 25, 27; 1 Kgs 21 (MT 20):15 (twice), 26. For the καίγε sections, 2 Sam 18:1; 24:2, 4; 2 Kgs 3:6; 9:34; 10:19; 11:15.

also compare Exod LXX 30:12-13; 39:2-3 (MT 38:25-26), where the text gives forms related to ἐπισκέπτειν, unchallenged in the Brooke-McLean apparatus,[6] and with α'σ'θ' attested at 30:13 for similar readings. Our scroll shows that the practice of introducing ἀριθμεῖν in Numbers has pre-Christian beginnings, parallel to, but distinct from, the καίγε revision.

λαβέ: with all LXX witnesses except BF, λάβετε. The lower right of the *beta* is present (most clearly in the early PAM photograph E[xcavation] 13); too close to the extant *epsilon* to permit of the plural reading, since the trace cannot be from *tau*— compare the *beta* in παρεμβολή, col ii, line 11, in the photograph.

αὐτῶν: was present,[7] with G^{L^2A} etc. as against G^{BL^1}, to judge from the letter count. There is no way of telling whether the pronoun preceded ἐξ ὀνόματος, or followed it as in G^O=MT.

3:41 λήμψει: sic for λήμψῃ. Λευίτας with B^bAF etc. against the Λευείτας orthography of B*.

Κύριος: unfortunately, our fragments of this scroll do not enable us to know how the divine name was written, here or in line 9 of this fragment. Either Κύριος or יהוה in square letter script (as in Fuad papyrus 266 of Deut) would seem to fit the space requirements. IAω as in pap4QLXXLev^a, and $\overline{KC}$, are certainly too short. Paleohebrew or ΠΙΠΙ forms in a Greek MS this early are improbable, in the present writer's opinion.

πάντων: was present twice in this verse, judging from the letter count, contrary to G^L which omits the second occurrence. For ἀντὶ πάντων τῶν πρωτοτόκων ἐν τοῖς κτήνεσιν as required in 4Q from space considerations, G^L (only) has ἀντὶ τῶν κτηνῶν τῶν πρωτοτόκων τῶν ἐν τοῖς κτήνεσιν.

---

[6]Except for a hexaplaric note to 30:12 in MS j, attached to ἐν τῇ ἐπισκοπῇ αὐτῶν, reading ἄλλος ἤτοι κατὰ τὸν ἀριθμὸν αὐτῶν. This ἄλλος is not α', σ' or θ': see above. Also, under 30:13 MS M has a hexaplaric note including ἀριθμόν, giving no source. Syhex, which in 30:12 has bĕmenyānāʾ dīlĕhōn 3 times, once with a σ'θ' attribution, and which gives bĕmenyānāʾ again in 30:13, must be rated a doubtful witness. In 38:25-26 it uses ʾestĕʿar for ἐπισκέπτεσθαι, as regularly in Numbers (see the discussion with 3:42 below) and elsewhere. If it does not do the same in Exod 30:12-13 the reason may easily have been the presence of ἀριθμόν in one or two places in its prototype, though surely not in all four.

[7]Contrary to what is supposed in "Qumran Manuscripts," 155.

Ισραηλ: there is an observable horizontal line above the traces of the *ēta*. Space considerations for this name, as for Κύριος (see above), preclude the understanding of this as an abbreviation stroke. Ισραηλ is spelled out fully at the end of the next verse, line 10 of this col. i fragment.

3:42 ἐπεσκέψατο: the universal reading of LXX witnesses in this place, compare 3:40 where 4Q's substitute ἀρίθμησον is unique. In the present verse Syhex's note, *waseʿar hānāw dên wamĕnāʾ*, means that the text seen by the authors of that version actually read ἐπεσκέψατο; there is a similar Syhex gloss on ἐπίσκεψις at Num 1:44, and Syhex saw no variant for these places.

Μωυσης: the orthography of 4Q, for this name also, remains unknown. Nor can we determine the word order as between Κύριος αὐτῷ with G^{AO} etc. and the αὐτῷ Κύριος of G^{L2} and N; but, judging from the letter count, the pronoun was present, contrary to G^{BL1}. Aaron was not present in 4Q of v 42, as he is in MSS b, w.

3:43 καὶ ἐγένετο πᾶν πρωτότοκον ἄρσεν. Little as is left of v 43 in this fragment, it is enough to guarantee the short rendering quoted, and to exclude καὶ ἐγένοντο/-ετο πάντα τὰ πρωτότοκα τὰ ἀρσενικά of the LXX witnesses generally. Only MS n gives (reconstructing from Brooke-McLean) καὶ ἐγένετο πᾶν πρωτότοκον ἐν τοῖς υἱοῖς Ισραηλ τὰ ἀρσενικά. The other Lucianic MSS (dgpt) have καὶ ἐγένοντο (g: -ετο) πάντα τὰ πρωτότοκα ἐν τοῖς υἱοῖς Ισραηλ τὰ ἀρσενικά. 4Q does not have the Lucianic expansion, which has been influenced by the preceding v 42; while the readings of n and 4Q represent a harmonizing of v 43 with vv 40, 42 on the basis of the close correspondence of the Hebrew phraseology in the 3 places.

?3:50–51 If this fragment is correctly placed, it supposes (1) the word order of G^{BL} as against G^{AO} (and MT) for the numerals in v 50; (2) the omission in 4Q of a quantity of text not quite equal to κατὰ τὸν σίκλον τὸν ἅγιον; and (3) a reading including τὸ ἀργύριον in v 51 (as in v 49). For this last, witnessed by FG and many minuscules (but not ndpt), if in fact κατὰ τὸν σίκλον τὸν ἅγιον was the omission, a word order τὰ λύτρα τὸ ἀργύριον (τῶν πλεοναζόντων) would best fit the letter count in the lines of this scroll. This word order is in fact attested by only two minuscules: g and Holmes-Parsons 130 (the latter without τά).

Col. ii

4:1 Ααρων: the fragment containing this word shows enough upper margin to establish that it comes from the top of the column. For the missing lines that follow, the text of G^{BL} in 4:2-5 corresponds rather precisely to the 9 lines required by the format of the scroll; and it cannot be supposed that the expansion ἐκ μέσου . . . πατριῶν αὐτῶν after Κααθ in 4:4 of G^{AO} etc. (repeated from the same position in 4:2) was represented in 4QNum.

4:6 ἀρτῆρας: lines 11-15, 18 of the column yield only small fragments of text; nothing remains of lines 16, 17. What little there is conforms to the text of G^B, which also fits the space requirements quite well, including in line 16, v 6, ἐπ' αὐτήν with Sam. but against MT. The term ἀρτῆρας, where LXX codices generally give ἀναφορεῖς for Hebrew בדיו, occurs in 4Q at the end of vv 6, 8, 11; all 3 occurrences are fragmentary,[8] but the reading is certain, the first 3 letters being clear in 4:11 and all but the first two in 4:6, 8. The plural of ἀρτήρ occurs nowhere else in LXX codices.

For בדים, the LXX offers a variety of terms. In Exod 25 we meet with ἀναφορεῖς 5 times, vv 12-14, 26, 27 (MT 13-15, 27, 28); there are no variants in the codices. In Exod 27:6, 7 (twice) this becomes φορεῖς, but is harmonized with ch. 25 (ἀναφορεῖς) again in B^ab and a number of MSS. Exod 30:4, 5 have σκυτάλαι without variants; a universally attested ἀναφορεῖς reappears in Exod 35:11 (MT 12). Then in Exod 38:4 (twice), 10, 11; 39:15; 40:18 (MT 37:4, 5, 14, 15; 39:35; 40:20) διωστῆρες appears consistently;[9] it survives in the last two places even in those hexaplaric

---

[8] In "Qumran Manuscripts," 156, the writer, influenced by LXX Exodus, tried to read διωστῆρας in vv 6 and 8; he cited ἀρτῆρας as the reading of v 11. At the end of v 12, the Hebrew and 4Q's Greek (ἀρτηρός, singular) are not the same as in vv 6, 8, 11; and it is from v 12 that the missing v 10 in 4Q must be reconstructed. In v 14a LXX ἀναφορεῖς again renders בדים and 4Q needs to be reconstructed with ἀρτῆρας. The extension of v 14, with ἀναφορεῖς in LXX, also found in Sam., was not present in 4QNum, see below. Kahle therefore states the case inaccurately when he affirms ("Greek Bible," 617): "In 5 places in these short fragments (4, 6, 8, 11, 12) Hebrew בדים is translated by αρτηρας (not διωστηρας, as Skehan supposes)."

[9] The μοχλοί for בדים in Exod 38:24 (MT 7) is sheer confusion; it normally renders בריחים.

witnesses which adopt the MT order for the later chapters of Exodus. The originality of ἀναφορεῖς in Num 4:6, 8, 11, 14a LXX seems guaranteed by the extension of the same term to those places (Num 4:10, 12, 14b LXX; 13:24 [MT 23]) where the Hebrew/Samaritan equivalent is מוט: see with Col. iii, Num 4:12, below. Two further indications that ἀρτῆρας is secondary are: (1) the distinction in number introduced with ἀρτηρός where the Hebrew is מוט (see with 4:12); and (2) the absence of αὐτῆς after ἀρτῆρας in vv 6, 8 where the ἀναφορεῖς reading is not qualified in this way,[10] whereas (see with col. iii) space considerations require that αὐτοῦ was present in 4Q after ἀρτῆρας in vv 11, 14a, where it occurs also with the ἀναφορεῖς reading of the codices. The Hebrew in all 4 cases is בדיו, with suffix; we are dealing, therefore, with a lexical substitution of the noun at a period too early to require the explicit insertion of a dependent pronoun (in addition to the Greek definite article) to reflect form as well as sense of the Hebrew phrase. The analogy of ἀρίθμησον (3:40), ὑακίνθινον (4:7), and φαύσεως (4:9) then suggest that here again the scroll reading is the substitute, and ἀναφορεῖς the original.

4:7 ἐπ'αὐτήν (1° loco, line 20): this LXX expansion as against MT and Sam. must have been present in the scroll, on the basis of the letter count for the line.

ὑακίνθινον: with MT and Sam. (תכלת) as against the LXX codices' ὁλοπόρφυρον, which would suppose a reading ארגמן, compare col. iii, Num 4:13. The form ὁλοπόρφυρον in LXX seems to have been induced by the ὅλον ὑακίνθινον of 4:6; a combination כליל ארגמן does not exist.

[καὶ δώσουσιν ἐπ' αὐ]τήν: the 3 extant letters and the required letter count for line 21 show that the scroll here agreed with MT, Sam. (and G^O, which reads αὐτῆς) in having this clause, which is lacking in G^BLA etc.

ἐν αὐτοῖς: here 4Q agrees with G^L against G^BAO etc. This fuller form is patterned on the language of Exod 25:28 (MT 29) and 38:12 (MT 37:16), to which the ἐν οἷς σπένδει of G^B, for MT and Sam. הנסך, already alludes.

ἐπ'αὐτῇ (line 24): the codices read ἐπ'αὐτῆς.

4:9 τῆς φαύσεως: nearly all other LXX witnesses read τὴν φωτίζουσαν. The exceptions are MSS b, w, which read τοῦ φωτός

---

[10]The δι'αὐτῆς of G^B in v 8 preceding τοὺς ἀρτῆρας serves the same function, and is required by the letter count in col. ii, line 28.

(as Exod 35:16 [MT 14]; 39:17 [MT 37]) and the Armenian, which reflects a nominal form. The φαῦσις reading for Hebrew מאור harks back to Gen 1:14-15 LXX, εἰς φαῦσιν, a first time where MT has no Hebrew to correspond (cf. Sam. להאיר and Gen 1:17), and the second time where MT and Sam. read מאור(ו)ת. Symmachus uses φαῦσις for מאור in Exod 35:8; and a hexaplaric variant to the same effect, without attribution, is quoted by MSS M and s at Lev 24:2. That τὴν φωτίζουσαν[11] is from the translator of Numbers, and τῆς φαύσεως secondary, is certain: compare (τὴν) προκειμένην, 4:7,[12] extant in 4Q, and τὸ συσκιάζον[13] in 4:5. Compare col. iii, line 31 below, φωτός for מאור in 4:16.

[κ]αι: this suggests a short reading in 4Q, with αὐτῆς twice omitted, against LXX codices and MT. Following this, the format of the scroll calls for 7 lines of text before our evidence begins again with col. ii line 5; 3 of these lines will have been lines 32-34 of col. iii. The text of G^B fits comfortably into this framework, and there are no variants in the codices for this part of the LXX text that suggest notable problems as to quantity.[14]

Col. iii

4:11 ἱμάτια ὑακίνθινα: of the cloth covering the golden altar. The plural ἱμάτια in Num LXX is restricted to human clothing, and is unexampled in the codices among the 8 instances of ἱμάτιον in 4:6-14, except in the Armenian rendering of 4:12.

καλύψουσιν: with G^BLO as against ἐπικαλύψουσιν G^A.
ἐμβαλοῦσιν: with G^L as against διεμβαλοῦσιν G^BAO etc.
ἀρτῆρας: see with 4:6 above.

4:12 θήσουσιν: the codices consistently read ἐμβαλοῦσιν here (compare 5:17), as they do for Hebrew ונתנו אל in vv 10 and (with Sam.) 14b. Simple τιθέναι for נתן does not appear in LXX Num.

καλύψουσιν with G^BAO etc. as against κατακαλύψουσιν G^L.
ἀρτηρός: in the singular, for MT המוט, which occurs again in MT v 10 (not extant in 4Q) and in Sam. v 14b (lacking in MT and

---

[11] This is also the reading of G^L in Exod 38:13 LXX (37:17 MT) as against ἡ φωτίζει of G^BAQ etc.
[12] This reading parallels Exod 38:9 LXX (37:10 MT) in both G^BLA etc. and G^O.
[13] This form is cited from θ' at Exod 39:34 in G^O.
[14] The αὐτῇ of G^O (=MT לה) near the end of v 9 was probably not present in 4Q.

4Q, see below). In these 3 places, and in Num 13:24(23); 1 Chr 15:15 (במטת, plural), the LXX codices use ἀναφορεῖς for this, as for בדים elsewhere (see with v 6 above). Chronicles LXX thinks this is κατὰ τὴν γραφήν (misreading Hebrew בכתפם to obtain this seeming allusion to Exod 25:13-14 LXX). A hexaplaric note at Num 13:24 in MS v attributes ἐν ἀναφορεῦσι to G^O; ἐν ἀναφορεῖ to α'θ'; and ἐν ἀρτηρί to σ' for the only other occurrence of such a reading. Neh 4:11 uses ἀρτήρ for MT סבל, making it the *guffa* of a Palestinian basket-boy.

4:13 The reading of G^B and, with minor variations, G^LOA etc. for the beginning of this verse (καὶ τὸν καλυπτῆρα ἐπιθήσει ἐπὶ τὸ θυσιαστήριον)[15] clearly cannot fit in lines 13-14 of this column in the scroll. On the other hand, the prefixed καὶ ἐκσποδιάσουσιν τὸ θυσιαστήριον of MS a (= MT) fills the space perfectly, and leaves no room for the alternative reading anywhere, since lines 14-15 were filled by v 13b (ὁλοπόρφυρον is partly extant). Since the scroll avoids τὸν καλυπτῆρα again in v 14, line 19 (see below), it evidently made some attempt to come to grips with the faulty treatment of the two places by the original LXX; this much only can be guaranteed.

ἐπιθήσουσιν: the reading of G^O; at this point the scroll must have had a short reading such as this for MT's ופרשו. The ἐπικαλύψουσιν of G^BA etc. and the κατακαλύψουσιν of G^L are too long. The ἐπιβαλοῦσιν of vv 6, 7, 8, 14b (LXX generally) where the Hebrew is the same, is perhaps even more likely as the missing reading of 4Q; α'σ'θ' also have distinctive readings alleged, which (ἐκπετάσουσιν, ἐκτενοῦσιν, περιβαλοῦσιν) hardly enter into consideration.

4:14 καὶ τὰ σπ[ονδεῖα]: the extant lettering is certain, as is (see lines 20, 21) the placement of these broken lines in the text of Numbers. The missing lines 16-18 are the required space for the beginning of v 14, with the names of 3 utensils mentioned in line 18 (which line the present writer reconstructs as πύρια καὶ τὰς κρεάγρας καὶ τὰς φιάλας). This presumes (see with v 13 above) that a reviser had difficulties with τὸν καλυπτῆρα, or, more basically, with Hebrew היעים.[16] For that reason he kept

---

[15]On this hopelessly wrong rendering and its parallel (and source) in Exod 27:3 LXX, see David W. Gooding, *The Account of the Tabernacle* (Cambridge: University Press, 1959) 60-61.

[16]Compare Gooding, *The Account of the Tabernacle*, 61.

φιάλας=מזרקת as the third of the 4 utensils, with LXX against MT, and then on the false analogy of v 7 read σπονδεῖα =קשות as the fourth class of instruments to be enumerated. For ἀρτῆρας, line 22, cf. with 4:6 above.

4:14b LXX, καὶ λήμψονται . . . , about the λουτῆρα=כיור and its stand, found also in Sam. but not in MT, would occupy 4 1/2 lines in the format of the scroll. It is not possible that this sentence or any part of it was present in lines 22ff. of col. iii, in the present writer's judgment. This depends on the correct placement of the tiny bits from 4:16 in lines 31-32, 34 of this column, and the postulate that we have extant remains of 3 columns only; these and (less critically) Ααρων in col. ii, line 1, are means to establishing the exact format of the columns. In that format, as here reconstructed, lines 22-34 of col. iii meet the space requirements for vv 15-16 (minus the last 5 words of G^B) very neatly, and there is no room for anything else. The inference is that the reviser represented in this scroll excised 14b of LXX upon comparing his Greek exemplar with a Hebrew MS that corresponded, in this respect at least, with MT.

4:15 The text of this verse, beginning in line 22 as indicated, when reconstructed in the scroll's column format on the basis of G^B, corresponds to lines 23-29 with no features that call for comment.

4:16 ἐπίσκοπος: with approximately the first 3 letters of this word ending line 29 of the column, the verse will have continued as in G^B (the codices show no notable variants) through the missing line 30 and on to the end of the column, as indicated.

το[ῦ φωτός]: with LXX generally; the extant *omicron* precludes a reading τῆς φαύσεως, as in v 9, for מאור.

ἐν τ[ῇ]: the wide bottom margin of this bit shows it is from the last line of a column. It fits here, and can by no means have come from the last line of a column in any part of the preceding materials: except that on the basis of v 15, ἐν τῇ σκηνῇ, it would be possible to end the column with what has here been taken to be line 29. If this were done, one would have to allege that the fragment assigned here to lines 31-32 of col. iii was in fact the sole surviving bit of an otherwise unrepresented column iv. Besides which, the horizontal correspondence (see the photograph) between lines 19-21 of cols. ii and iii as here given would become impossible to account for. It is that alignment which does most to establish the number of lines to a column in the format of the 4QNum scroll.

Notes on the plate. All fragments as they appear on PAM photograph 43.291 except four: the two at the lower left and right corners, from 42.039; the two with black background, from 41.933. Courtesy of the Palestine Archaeological Museum. In col. i, lines 9–10, the fragment with (το)ις υιο(ις) could—less likely—be from Num 3:51 and belong just under the piece here assigned to ?3:50–51. There are traces of ink for an upper line (here line 9); but abraded so that nothing can be read. The three bits at the bottom left of the plate are unplaced; they read ΑΥ[, ΔΥ[, and]ΚΙΝΘΙΝ̊[. The ink traces above and below]ΚΙΝΘΙΝ̊[are illegible. The height of the columns is not fully reflected in the plate, because the extant fragments have been drawn closer together in the vertical plane when gaps exist for which the adjoining columns furnish no direct control.

THE ENOCHIC PENTATEUCH AND THE DATE OF THE SIMILITUDES*

Jonas C. Greenfield and Michael E. Stone

The Hebrew University
Jerusalem, Israel

I

In a recent, extensive article in this Journal, J. T. Milik made public some of the conclusions which he had drawn from his studies of the Qumran Enoch fragments,[1] conclusions which have serious implications for the history of Jewish literature in the last centuries before the destruction of the Temple. Two of Milik's conclusions about the Enochic literature will be examined here: first, that there was at Qumran an Enochic Pentateuch, and second, that the *Similitudes of Enoch* (chaps. 37-71 of the Ethiopic *Enoch* book) are a late, Christian composition.

Milik's first step was his identification among the Qumran fragments of *The Book of the Giants*,[2] a work which had been in circulation among the Manicheans and was reconstructed from diverse fragments by W. B. Henning in 1943.[3] Only four of the five constituent parts of Ethiopic *Enoch* were uncovered at Qumran. Milik, however, considered this as a fifth Enochic work extant at Qumran. Second, he noted that *The Book of the Luminaries*, as it is found among the Qumran fragments, is almost twice as long as the form of the work preserved in the Ethiopic version.

---

*J. T. Milik's major study of the Qumran Enoch fragments appeared after the completion of this article; see J. T. Milik with M. Black, *The Books of Enoch* (Oxford: Clarendon, 1976). As well as publishing relevant Qumran texts, this work is rich in detailed information and observations on many points related to the text and history of the *Book of Enoch*. It marks no change, however, in Milik's position on the two central issues dealt with in our article which has consequently been left unchanged. At its end, a Postscript has been added discussing the points at which the new publication bears upon our argument.

[1] J. T. Milik, "Problèmes de la littérature hénochique à la lumière des fragments araméens de Qumrân," *HTR* 64 (1971) 333-78.

[2] J. T. Milik, "Turfan et Qumran, Livre des Géants juif et manichéen," in G. Jeremias, H.-W. Kuhn, and H. Stegemann, eds., *Tradition und Glaube: Das frühe Christentum in seiner Umwelt* (K. G. Kuhn Festschrift; Göttingen: Vandenhoeck & Ruprecht, 1971) 117-27.

[3] W. B. Henning, "The Book of Giants," *BSOAS* 11 (1943) 52-74.

Consequently, he claims that these five Enochic works could not have been written in one scroll.[4]

The parts of the Enochic corpus represented in the extant Qumran manuscripts are set forth schematically below:

Chapters   Manuscripts containing fragments of section

1-36	4QHen	a	b	c	d	e				
72-82	4QHen^{ast}						a	b	c	d
83-90	4QHen			c	d	e	f			
91-107	4QHen			c				g		

This Table is based on Milik's information,[5] as are the dates of manuscripts which are given below. It will be immediately observed that 4QHen^c contains the first, third, and fourth of the works here listed and that the first and third also are contained in 4QHen^d and 4QHen^e. Milik asserts that 4QHen^c probably also contained *The Book of the Giants*[6] and that 4QHen^d and 4QHen^e may also have contained this Enochic tetrateuch.[7] These four works, then, together with *The Book of the Luminaries* (which, however, was written on a separate scroll because of its length), supposedly formed the Qumran Enochic Pentateuch.

By the year 400 C.E., Milik maintains, a Greek Enochic Pentateuch had developed, now preserved in the Ethiopic version, which varied from the Qumran one in three respects. *The Book of the Luminaries* had been greatly reduced in scope and placed in the third position. *The Book of the Giants* had been replaced by the *Similitudes,* and chap. 108 had been appended at the end of the whole.[8] This, however, is all by way of hypothesis, unsupported by any solid evidence except for the following: three

---

[4] D. Dimant, *"The Fallen Angels" in the Dead Sea Scrolls and in the Apocryphal and Pseudepigraphic Books Related to them* (diss., Hebrew University, 1974 [in Hebrew]) 20, calculated that *The Book of the Luminaries,* even if twice as long as its preserved Ethiopic form, is still shorter than the *Similitudes*. However, in view of the length of scrolls like 1QIsa^a and the new Temple Scroll, one may ask whether it is impossible to conceive of a large Qumran scroll containing all the Enochic writings known there.

[5] *HTR* 64 (1971) 336-37.

[6] 4QHenGiants^a was copied by the same scribe as 4QHen^c but it seems to be a different manuscript; see Milik, "Géants," 124.

[7] *HTR* 64 (1971) 334-35. Milik adduces no evidence for this, and it seems most likely that the situation presented in the Table is the one that actually existed in the manuscripts.

[8] Ibid., 373-74.

Enochic works are copied together in one Qumran manuscript and two of these in two more; fragments of five or more Enochic works have been discovered at Qumran; and, finally, a differing selection of five works are combined in the Ethiopic version.

It is by no means evident that, because five works are combined in the Ethiopic version of *Enoch,* they were considered by the Greek or Ethiopic compiler to be a Pentateuch. If such a title is to be meaningful, presumably it implies that they were arranged as a Pentateuch based on the model of the Mosaic Pentateuch. Even if this were true for the Ethiopic book, nothing in the evidence adduced by Milik shows that it was true at Qumran. Were there five Enoch works at Qumran? If *The Book of the Giants* was part of the Enochic corpus, the answer is affirmative; but in the manuscripts, it occurs, it has been pointed out, quite separately from the Enochic works and has a separate literary history.[9] However, these five books are not the only works which could be considered part of Qumran's Enochic literature: one could claim this also for 1Q*19,* the so-called "Book of Noah," which then potentially constitutes a sixth Enoch book.

However, one cannot, merely by material arguments based on the number of Enochic books found at Qumran or the existence of several such works copied into a single scroll, demonstrate that these books were thought to be a "Pentateuch." An examination of the Qumran manuscripts of the Mosaic Pentateuch and the Mosaic apocrypha shows this clearly. It would be difficult from the copying of pairs of books of the Pentateuch in the same scrolls to demonstrate that these five books were intended to form a Pentateuch.[10] Moreover, *Jubilees* is a work clearly attributed to Moses which occurs at Qumran in a number of copies, bringing the number of Mosaic works there to six at least, without necessarily forming a Hexateuch.[11]

Rather, evidence to demonstrate that an Enochic Pentateuch existed (whether at Qumran or in Greek or in Ethiopic) should be sought either within the books themselves—and to the best of our knowledge none such exists—or in the witness of external authorities—again, not to be found. This point is significant: if

---

[9] Dimant, *Fallen Angels,* 20.

[10] Personal communication by John Strugnell.

[11] The Temple Scroll may also formally prove to be in this category, and still further Mosaic apocrypha may yet be identified. If *Jubilees* be maintained to be an angelic revelation (chap. 2) and not a Mosaic one (chap. 1), the pseudo-Mosaic character of 4QDibrêMošé is in no doubt. With it perhaps certain other 4Q documents should be associated (oral communication of J. Strugnell).

there was not a clear concept of an "Enochic Pentateuch" determining the number of works to be combined in the various forms of the *Book of Enoch* in the early centuries, the arguments about the date of the *Similitudes* are greatly weakened (see below).

A final observation should be made on this point. There is apparently a pattern in the occurrence of the various works, separately or together, in the Qumran manuscripts. The oldest manuscripts, 4QHen^a, ^{b}, ^{g}, each contain only one work. By the middle of the first century B.C.E., two or three Enochic writings were being copied in a single scroll (4QHen^c, ^{d}, ^{e}) and the scribe of one of these manuscripts at least also copied, though perhaps not in the same scroll, *The Book of the Giants.* Toward the end of the period when Qumran was inhabited, only 4QHen^{astr} and 4QHenGiants were still being copied, and that in separate manuscripts.[12] It would be interesting to know if a similar combination of other short, related works into a single scroll occurs at the same time. In any case, as was noted above, this is no evidence for the existence of an Enochic Pentateuch at Qumran.

An earlier attempt to see the *Book of Enoch* as a Pentateuch was made by G. H. Dix.[13] This is of interest, for he has tried to show a parallelism between the five constituent parts of the Ethiopic *Enoch* and the Five Books of Moses. Three comments seem to be in order. *(a)* While certain of the actual parallels are intriguing (pp. 29-31), others are somewhat farfetched. This is particularly true of those supposed to exist between *The Book of the Luminaries* and Leviticus, and between *The Dream Visions* and Numbers. *(b)* His Pentateuch theory is based on the inclusion of the *Similitudes*, thus standing in strong conflict with the views of Milik.[14] *(c)* His view is that the Enochic Pentateuch was created to provide a "Law of Righteousness" which was in deliberate and polemical contrast with the Mosaic Law. This was done by "a body of laity who, holding themselves aloof from the official religion of Judaism, set themselves to observe the moral and spiritual principles for which the prophets contended and made

---

[12] Dimant, *Fallen Angels,* 20. This does not indicate decisively that they did not belong to a Pentateuch. There are also more copies of Deuteronomy than of Leviticus.

[13] "The Enochic Pentateuch," *JTS* 27 (1926) 29-42.

[14] Milik's substitution of *The Book of the Giants* for the *Similitudes* and his rearrangement of the constituent parts of the "Enochic Pentateuch" would render Dix's theory obsolete, although it would be true, were there not other objections to it, for Ethiopic.

little of the demands of the Mosaic Torah."¹⁵ Such a view, even if it were acceptable in liberal theological circles in Dix's day, can no longer be held to reflect any sort of historical reality. The combination of spirituality, priestly ideology, and legal rigor at Qumran serves to highlight this, but it is clear on other grounds too. So it seems that Dix's theory (while showing one construction which can be put upon the evidence) is still far from being demonstrated. It fails to convince in detail and, moreover, loses cogency once the motive for the creation of the Enochic Pentateuch is seen to be spurious.¹⁶

II

The Enochic Pentateuch has proved to be a chimera, but the absence of the *Similitudes* from the Qumran corpus remains a problem. Milik has claimed, on the basis of this absence and also on the basis of certain internal criteria, that it is a late work.¹⁷ Some scholars have been convinced by his statements, but they have forgotten that the non-existence of a literary work during the period between 200 B.C.E. and 100 C.E. cannot be demonstrated merely by its absence from Qumran. Is the absence of Esther from Qumran an argument for its non-existence in this period? A variety of other explanations for the absence of Esther can be offered: *(a)* it existed but was not yet known at Qumran, *(b)* it was not yet accepted as canonical, *(c)* it was not considered worthy of study at Qumran, or *(d)* pure accident. On this basis, therefore, one cannot demonstrate that Esther, or indeed the *Similitudes*, was not composed by this period.

Again, if an argument for the late date of the *Similitudes* is based not on the absence of this writing from Qumran but rather on the supposition that it later replaced a rejected section of a

---

¹⁵Dix, *JTS* 27 (1926) 31-32.

¹⁶The new scrolls, of course, demand at least a drastic revision of Dix's theories on the literary composition of *Enoch*.

¹⁷Milik, *HTR* 64 (1971) 373-78. J. Coppens ("Le Fils d'Homme dans le Judaisme de l'époque néotestamentaire," *OLP* 6/7 [1975-76] 65-68) has examined Milik's views on the date of the *Similitudes*. He points out particularly that the pattern of usage of the Enochic literature at Qumran indicates a loss of interest in it from the Herodian period on. This would make Qumranite manipulation of the Enochic corpus, i.e., the introduction into it of the *Similitudes,* unlikely. This seems plausible, although one fails to see in what measure this refutation responds to Milik's argument. It rather seems to indicate the currency of the Enochic literature in non-Qumran circles. Coppens doubts the weight of early Christian usage as an argument and denies the validity of Milik's supposed historical references.

putative earlier Enochic Pentateuch, the observer may simply inquire why a rejected section could not have been replaced by another early work, a work which dealt with Enoch and which may have been part of an Enoch cycle, but which was not present at Qumran for any number of reasons.

The *Similitudes* may be considered to have been part of a larger body of Enochic literature. The developed legend of Enoch as heavenly scribe, sage, and seer was widespread in Jewish circles and was by no means limited to the Qumran sect. Such diverse sources as Ben Sira 44:6 and the Samaritan Hellenistic historian known as Pseudo-Eupolemus clearly knew the Enoch legend. Citations from writings or books of Enoch in the *Testaments of the Twelve Patriarchs* (and perhaps also in the *Mani Codex*) which do not occur in extant Enochic works also attest to this.[18] It is of course possible that such quotations were invented, but their very invention and attribution to Enoch would be itself indicative of the fecundity of Enoch's pseudepigraphic genius. The composition of at least some Enochic books outside the confines of the Qumran sect is clearly probable.[19]

We owe to David Flusser the observation that the *Similitudes,* even if known, would not have been acceptable to the sectaries of Qumran because of the manner in which the sun and moon are treated in chap. 41; their tasks and roles are equal—the sun does not receive the special place afforded it in the various Qumran writings. This factor alone would certainly have sufficed to effect the exclusion of the *Similitudes* from the Qumran Enochic corpus.[20] Yet a comparison of terminology used in the *Similitudes* with that familiar from the sectarian texts found at Qumran shows that the *Similitudes* too may have come from a sectarian (though not necessarily Qumran sectarian) milieu. Four items will suffice. (1) "Lord of the Spirits" found frequently in the *Similitudes*—*rwḥwt* is used throughout the Scrolls both for the

---

[18]Cf. for details A.-M. Denis, *Introduction aux pseudépigraphes grecs d'Ancien Testament* (SVTP 1; Leiden: Brill, 1970) 21-22. For Pseudo-Eupolemus see Eusebius, *Praep. ev.* ix.17. 419 d (= Jacobi 724 F 1) and the remarks of B. Z. Wacholder, *HUCA* 34 (1963) 97-99 and idem, *Eupolemus. A Study of Judaeo-Greek Literature* (Monographs of the Hebrew Union College 3; Cincinnati: Hebrew Union College—Jewish Institute of Religion, 1974) 74-77.

[19]Not to speak of the appearance of Enoch in non-Essene works found at Qumran like 1QapGen 2:22-26 or in later pseudepigrapha such as the *Testament of Abraham,* recension B, chap. 9. On the *Mani Codex,* see below, section V.

[20]Cf. for this and the following, J. C. Greenfield, "Prolegomenon" to the reprint of H. Odeberg, *3 Enoch* (New York: Ktav, 1973) xvii-xviii.

guiding spirits of man and also for the angels. Note particularly the phrase ᵓ*dwn lkl rwḥ* in 1QH 10:8. This is a sectarian usage even though, of course, a somewhat similar expression, ᵓ*l* ᵓ*lhy hrwḥt lkl bśr*, occurs twice in Numbers (16:22; 27:16). The sectarian character is clear from an examination of its occurrences in literature of the Second Temple Period; cf. also *Jubilees* 10:3. (2) *bḥyr, bḥyrym*—the use of the term *bḥyr* for the elect of God, especially in the role of one who will enact judgment (*Enoch,* chaps. 61-62) may be compared to the use of *bḥyr* ᵓ*lh*ᵓ in the fragment of the Aramaic "elect of God" text from 11Q. The term *bḥyrym* for the righteous is well known (see, e.g., 1QM 12:1). (3) *gwrl,* "lot," is a central term of the *yaḥad* and cf. *Enoch* 58:2. (4) Destructive angels (*Enoch* 63), cf. 1QM 13:12; 1QS 4:12; CD 2:6. These terms as well as others which could be adduced, in contrast to terminology of such mainstream books as Baruch or Ben Sira, hint at the circles in which the *Similitudes* were written and might serve to indicate the period in which the work was composed. The circles, though probably not part of the mainstream, still differ from the Qumran sectaries at least in calendar reckoning. The same general period as that of the composition of the Qumran documents seems probable.

A further corroboration of an early date is that, if the *Similitudes* are Jewish (and there is no reason to suppose they are not) they use the term "Son of Man." The role of the Son of Man—an old title in Jewish usage which had taken on new meaning—is already suppressed and reinterpreted by the author of 4 Ezra at the end of the first century C.E.[21] For Milik, however, this title serves as a sign of dependence on the New Testament. Yet it is difficult to see as a late, Christian work a book devoted largely to the prediction of the coming of a superhuman Son of Man, existent in the thought of God before creation, which does not make the slightest hint at his (from Enoch's viewpoint) future incarnation, earthly life, and preaching, or crucifixion (and perhaps their cosmic implications). Further, in chap. 71 (admittedly an appendix to the *Similitudes*) the Son of Man is identified as Enoch. This is rather unlikely in a Christian composition the appendix to which will undoubtedly be Christian.

---

[21]See Michael E. Stone, "The Concept of the Messiah in IV Ezra," *Religions in Antiquity: E. R. Goodenough Memorial Volume* (ed. J. Neusner; Leiden: Brill, 1968) 303-10.

III

Other attempts have been made to uncover Christian elements in the *Similitudes,* but Erik Sjöberg has convincingly demonstrated that the *Similitudes* were a unity and that the supposed Christian element is nothing more than a figment of scholarly imagination.[22] Still, the date of the *Similitudes* remains a crucial problem, and there are two historical references in the *Similitudes* which must be carefully considered in this connection. The first is in 56:5-7. Verse 5 reads:

> And in those days the Angels shall return and hurl themselves to the east upon the Parthians and Medes: They shall stir up the kings so that a spirit of unrest shall come upon them, and they shall rouse them from their thrones, that they may break forth as lions from their lairs, and as hungry wolves among their flocks.

Taken at face value, this and v 6 must refer to the invasion of Palestine by the Parthians in 40 B.C.E. The invaders are called "Parthians and Medes," a phrase reminiscent of the older "Persians and Medes" (this is the sequence familiar from Esther), and may very well be an "updating" of that phrase. But besides being a literary allusion, the problematic mention of "Medes" may have its roots in reality—the rulers of Media Atropatene were vassals of the Parthians during this period. The reference in v 7 to strife among the invaders, expressed in terms borrowed from the Hebrew Bible, may refer to the constant strife in the kingdoms adjacent to Parthia.

J. C. Hindley has recently endeavored to use the Parthian reference as a means of dating the *Similitudes.*[23] He argues against the date 40 B.C.E., on the basis of Josephus' report that the Jews welcomed the Parthians, and therefore concludes that the "emphatically hostile" references to the Parthians in the *Similitudes* would not fit this date. However, Hindley has forgotten that the author of the *Similitudes* may well not have been an ordinary Jew but a sectarian (of some sort) who could not but see the Parthians as foreign invaders whose presence in Jerusalem was an abomination. Indeed, for many Jews at that time, any foreign occupation of Jerusalem, Roman or Parthian,

---

[22] See the discussion in detail in his *Der Menschensohn im äthiopischen Henochbuch* (Lund: Gleerup, 1946). See, too, G. Widengren, "Iran and Israel in Parthian Times with Special Regard to the Ethiopic Book of Enoch," *Temenos* 2 (1966) 139-77.

[23] J. C. Hindley, "Toward a Date for the Similitudes of Enoch, an Historical Approach," *NTS* 14 (1968) 551-65.

would be an abomination.[24] But it may be futile to try to seek detailed historical references, for the use of biblical verses and the contrast between the sinners and the elect in v 8 clearly mark the section 56:5-8 not as objective history but as highly subjective interpretation of history.

Hindley's attempt to refer 56:5-7 to Trajan's Parthian campaigns is rather farfetched. Hindley admits that we have few solid facts to go by and at the most one has the Parthians in 113 C.E. moving toward Antioch. Although "Antioch is 300 miles from Jerusalem," he insists that "the progress of the Parthian Army might well have given rise in apocalyptic circles to fresh speculation that the eschatological invasion was on the way. . . ." Suffice it to say that this sort of reasoning is unacceptable as a means of dating a literary work, for it is based on a construct rather than on fact and it totally disregards other aspects of the *Similitudes*.

Even more farfetched is J. T. Milik's attempt to pinpoint the historical reference in 56:5-7.[25] Milik believes that the events behind our verses are "the terrible years of anarchy and invasions in the middle of the third century, and in particular the victorious campaigns of Sapor I which brought him as far as Syria and which culminated in the capture of Valerian in September 260." The Parthians and the Medes of 56:5, then, are not the nations called by those names but rather the Palmyrenes under Odenath who were victorious *against* the Persians. Milik's identification of the Parthians and Medes with the Palmyrenes seems to be based on two disparate "facts." The first is the identification of *mdy* and *md̲* of certain Safaitic inscriptions with the Palmyrenes; the second is the supposed sparing of Jerusalem by the Palmyrenes under Zenobia when they marched through Palestine toward the Nile. The reason given for this is that "Zenobie était bien connue pour ses sympathies juives et chrétiennes."

All of this is pure fiction. The identification of *md̲y* with the Palmyrene legions cannot be taken seriously by an epigraphist; the forces of Zenobia did indeed conquer Egypt, but we know next to nothing about their route, their conduct in Palestine, or their treatment of Jerusalem; furthermore, Zenobia's attraction

---

[24]The Ethiopic word *mā^cqafa* in 56:7a is unclear. It is rendered "hindrance" by Charles; Ch. Rabin has suggested "stumbling block" to the writers; MS Q, of the sixteenth century, reads *mawāqéfa,* "standing place." None of these permits the drawing of precise historical conclusions as to what happened or did not happen to the Parthians in Jerusalem.

[25]Milik, *HTR* 64 (1971) 377.

to Judaism is based on unverifiable reports. Granted that the Palmyrene cavalry was something to be reckoned with by the Romans under Aurelian, it is nevertheless impossible to read any of this into *Enoch* 56:5-8.[26] One returns to the simple interpretation of the mention of "Parthians and Medes" in relation to Jerusalem—that it refers to the year 40 B.C.E. when the Parthians and their allies actually conquered Jerusalem and held it for a few years.

The second historical reference is found in chap. 67:8-9. The waters of Callirhoe and their curative effects are referred to, and it is said that for the wicked these waters can have the opposite effect on both the body and the mind. This has long been seen as a reference to the attempt by Herod to cure himself in the waters of Callirhoe and to his increased psychological disturbance before his death (Josephus, *Ant.* 17.6.5 §§171-73; *J.W.* 1.33.5 §§657-58).[27]

These two references indicate that the final composition of the *Similitudes* took place at some time during the first century C.E. They may be a part of the original composition, or they may very well have been added to an already extant composition to give the reader historical instances of God's judgment. They strengthen the view that the *Similitudes* is a contemporary of the Qumran texts.

IV

A further matter that impinges on the dating of the *Similitudes* and its place within the Enochic corpus is the important fact mentioned by Nathaniel Schmidt, but not given enough attention by subsequent writers, that no Byzantine writer quotes from the *Similitudes* and that not a scrap of the Greek text has reached us to date. Milik has used this as an argument for the late date of the composition of the *Similitudes* and has even called it "une composition grecque chrétienne." But one can easily turn the tables on him, for if it were really a late composition in Greek, one would have expected later writers to make extensive use of it; indeed, one would have expected Syriac or other daughter

---

[26] To judge by *y. Terumot* 8,10 (46b) Zenobia was far from friendly to the Jews. It should be remembered that the oldest text which refers to Zenobia and her Jewish sympathies is that of Athanasius, *Historia arianorum ad monachos* = *PG* 25. 777 B, and that his purpose is to condemn Paul of Samosata; cf. G. Downey, *A History of Antioch in Syria* (Princeton: Princeton University, 1961) 262-71, 312.

[27] See A. Schalit, *König Herodes* (Berlin: de Gruyter, 1969) 640, n. 200.

translations to be in circulation and at least partially preserved, for they would have served well to bolster the New Testament's use of the "Son of Man" imagery. One may make the claim, admittedly based on an argument from silence, that since a Greek version of the *Similitudes* is not known to have circulated freely, it may perhaps never have existed. Schmidt's claim that the Ethiopic stems from a direct translation of an Aramaic text has never been refuted and has been strengthened by the recent arguments of Edward Ullendorff to the same effect.[28] Ullendorff accepts Schmidt's view as to the *Similitudes* but would extend the thesis to the whole of *Enoch.* He provides a nuance, saying that possibly the translators had recourse to a Greek translation in the course of their work, but this would not necessarily be relevant to the *Similitudes.* Other Ethiopic scholars with whom we have discussed this problem have also been of the opinion that the Ethiopic version of the *Similitudes* was a direct translation from an Aramaic source. Matthew Black, who has attempted to counter the Aramaic origin of the Ethiopic *Enoch,* has not provided any further convincing arguments since he compared the Ethiopic texts with the Aramaic texts known from Qumran.[29] But the one fact that emerges clearly from the Enoch material published and reported on by Milik is that the Ethiopic text (or the Greek, which Milik and most others assume to intervene between the two) is based on a text differing in many ways from the Qumran text. One must await the full investigation of the Qumran Aramaic text to form an independent judgment of its relationship to the Ethiopic text. The language of the *Similitudes* must be treated separately; if the opinion of competent Ethiopic scholars is properly considered, then an Aramaic original, and consequently an early date, seems probable.

V

Milik's assumption is that the *Similitudes* replaced *The Book of the Giants* in the Enochic corpus. A case may be made for the

[28] See N. Schmidt, "The Original Language of the Parables of Enoch," *Old Testament and Semitic Studies in Memory of W. R. Harper* (Chicago: University of Chicago, 1908), 2. 329-49. R. H. Charles, *The Book of Enoch* (Oxford: Oxford University, 1912) lxi-lxviii, made a feeble attempt in this direction. He argued for a Hebrew original. E. Ullendorff, "An Aramaic 'Vorlage' of the Ethiopic Text of Enoch?" was published in *Atti del convegno internazionale di Studi Etiopici* (Rome: 1960) 259-67.

[29] M. Black, "The Fragments of the Aramaic Enoch from Qumran," *La littérature juive entre Tenach et Mischna* (ed. W. C. van Unnik; Leiden: Brill, 1974) 15-28.

existence of different corpora in some of which material such as *The Book of the Giants* was not included. Nevertheless, we are now better informed about *The Book of the Giants* and related texts and can trace the reasons for such a substitution with greater accuracy. Scholarship is indebted to Milik for drawing attention to the close parallel between the Qumran Enochic fragments of *The Book of the Giants* and the related Manichean *Book of the Giants.* Milik did not deal with the mode of transmission of such writings, but this has been clarified by the recently discovered Cologne *Mani Codex.*[30]

This document shows that Mani was raised in an Elchasaite camp and was indoctrinated at an early age in a Jewish-Christian tradition which had its origins in Palestine. The *Mani Codex* also contains some excerpts from an "Apocalypse of Enoch." Enoch the righteous is in great sorrow and distress. He sees seven angels descending from heaven. Michael, one of them, addresses him and relates that he was sent to reveal to Enoch the place of the righteous and of the punishment of the wicked. They seat him in a "chariot of wind" ($\dot{\epsilon}\pi\grave{\iota}\ \ddot{\alpha}[\rho]\mu\alpha\tau\sigma\varsigma\ \dot{\alpha}\nu\acute{\epsilon}\mu\sigma\upsilon$) and bring him to the far parts of heaven. He goes through the worlds, that of death and that of darkness and that of fire. Then he is brought to a beautiful world of light and luminaries. Then, the Codex continues, Enoch saw all and recorded what the angels told him in books.

These citations are quite distinctive and clearly draw upon a source rather than being pure invention. Although the seven archangels are mentioned in the Ethiopic *Enoch* 20:7, in that book the extensive revelation is in the hands of a group of four archangels. The revelation of, or visit to, the "worlds" of darkness, of death, and of fire have no parallel in the Ethiopic *Enoch,* though of course chap. 22, etc., show the place of punishment. The "chariot of the wind" is equally missing from the Ethiopic *Enoch* (cf. the parallels cited by Henrichs and Koenen, p. 83).[31] Yet this "Apocalypse of Enoch" has clear affinities with

---

[30] The first report on this important document was given by A. Henrichs and L. Koenen, "Ein griechischer Mani-Codex," *Zeitschrift für Papyrologie und Epigraphik* 5 (1970) 97-216. The first part of the edition has now been published by them in the same journal, 19 (1975) 1-85. We are grateful to Professor Henrichs for making this text available to us early in the process of publication.

[31] Professor Ephraim Isaac informs us that MS Kebrān 9 of Ethiopic *Enoch* from Lake Ṭānā (see E. Hammerschmidt, *Äthiopische Handschriften vom Tānāsee* [Wiesbaden: Steiner, 1973] 107) of the early fifteenth century reads "chariot" or "vehicle of wind" at *Enoch* 52:1, resembling Charles's MS 9x *q* at this point. The other features of the work referred to in the *Mani Codex* are not to be found, however, in this new manuscript of Ethiopic *Enoch*.

the Ethiopic work which certainly indicate that this work belonged somewhere within the Enochic corpus of writings.

A similar conclusion, that Mani consulted an Enoch book different from the Ethiopic and Slavonic works but close in character to the former, was reached by W. B. Henning on the basis of two Middle Persian Turfan fragments. The first of these contains a list of names of ancient prophets, "Šem, Sem, Enōš, Nikotheos (?) . . . and Enoch." The other refers to Watchers and Giants and to Enoch's interpreting someone's dream.[32] The fragments published by Henning do not overlap with those quoted by the *Mani Codex,* but there seems to be no good reason to doubt their belonging to the same writing. Henning does not think that this *Book of Enoch* was identical with *The Book of the Giants,* nor do the new citations from it in the *Mani Codex* give the lie to his judgment. Furthermore, there is no reason to assume that this *Book of Enoch* was a Manichean composition; Mani may well have read it when he was in the Elchasaite camp, among which group Jewish sectarian writings might well be at home. Like *The Book of the Giants,* however, this *Book of Enoch* became an integral part of Manichean literature.

It is instructive to see how a particular text can be detached from one tradition and absorbed by another. If *The Book of the Giants* were acceptable at Qumran, it need not have been acceptable elsewhere to mainstream or to other, related or differing, sectarian groups. The fact that it appealed to those like the Manicheans who carried dualism to its extreme might argue for its not being acceptable to the more moderate. It is, therefore, not implausible that diverse Enochic corpora were current in first-century C.E. Palestine, some containing the *Similitudes* and others containing *The Book of the Giants* and still others containing material known to us only from random quotations.[33]

---

[32]W. Henning, "Ein manichäisches Henochbuch," *SPAW,* Philosophisch-historische Klasse 1934, 5. 2-11. The series of names matches that in the *Mani Codex:* Adam (49), Sethel (50), Enos (52), Sem (54), and Enoch (57), to each of whom apocalypses are attributed. It is instructive to compare these verses with Ben Sira 49:14, 16: there Enoch, Shem, Seth, and Enosh are mentioned, culminating in Adam.

[33]Cf. the reference to Enoch in Barnabas 4:3, also unknown in any extant Enoch work. For some reflexes of *The Book of the Giants* in Jewish tradition, see J. C. Greenfield, "Notes on some Aramaic and Mandaic Magic Bowls," *JANESCU* 5 (1973; T. H. Gaster Festschrift) 150-54.

Postscript

"Milik" throughout this Postscript refers to J. T. Milik with M. Black, *The Books of Enoch* (Oxford: Clarendon, 1976). The present writers have restricted their observations to those points at which Milik has supplemented or changed those arguments in his previous writings which touch directly upon the subject of this article. There are, of course, many other matters in this intriguing book upon which the writers could comment, but these would lead us beyond the proper limits of the present essay.

1. *Qumran Manuscripts of Enoch.* The information on the extant Qumran manuscripts presented in the Table above is now confirmed by Milik, pp. 5-7.

2. *Qumran and Enochic Writings.* Another such Enochic writing is the Hebrew fragment 4Q*227,* published by Milik, p. 12. This resembles the Enoch passage in *Jubilees* 4. On pp. 59-69, Milik also discusses this issue. Naturally any proof of the existence of more than five works associated with Enoch at Qumran weakens the argument for the Pentateuch hypothesis, but the only serious claimants are 1Q*19* and 4Q*227.* P. Grelot ("Hénoch et ses Ecritures," *RB* 82 [1975] 481-500) examines the knowledge of books of Enoch by the author of *Jubilees* 4:16-26. He knew, Grelot concludes, *The Book of Luminaries, The Dream Visions,* and *The Book of the Watchers.* The *Similitudes* and the *Epistle* (including the Apocalypse of Weeks) were unknown to him (pp. 481-88). Grelot provides a new edition of 4QMess ar, suggesting *inter alia* that this text is part of the discourse of Enoch to Methusaleh referred to in *Enoch* 106 and 1QapGen 2-3 and that the three works to which it refers in line 5 are the three Enochic works—dare we say the Enochic Triateuch—known also to the author of *Jubilees.* This work, if he is correct, might also belong to the Enochic literature: he raises other possibilities, however, and it remains hypothetical. Grelot puts forward some interesting suggestions about the growth of the Enoch literature at Qumran not easily reconciled with the Pentateuch theory. 6Q*8,* the Barakiel text, is also cognate with the above writings, but the exact definition of the relationship between these documents is unclear.

3. *The Book of the Giants in Manuscripts of the Enochic Pentateuch.* Milik now suggests (1) on p. 310, cf. pp. 58 and 76, that 4QHenGiants[a] occurred in 4QHen[c], following *The Book of the Watchers;* (2) on pp. 317-20, that the Syncellus quotes *The Book of the Giants* following *The Book of the Watchers,* which supposedly indicates that his source, Panodorus or Annianus,

knew the sequence *Watchers-Giants* in a Greek codex in the fourth century. Point (1) is pure supposition. Point (2) is specious since the supposed source of the Syncellus' quotation in *The Book of the Giants* cannot be proved. This is, moreover, against the Syncellus' own witness. Further, even if the quotation were from *The Book of the Giants*, its place in the Greek Chronicles might be dictated by the order of the events they relate rather than by the supposed order of writings in a hypothetical Enochic Pentateuch manuscript. Milik also adds, as a declaration of faith, that the codex of Panodorus also contained *The Book of Dreams* and *The Epistle of Enoch*. In such matters the accumulation of undemonstrated and unprovable hypotheses carries no more conviction than does the strongest single one of them.

4. *Deuteronomy and the Epistle of Enoch*. Milik, pp. 54-55, 183-84, does pick up the idea that *The Epistle of Enoch* was written as a "Second Law" like Deuteronomy. Both, he claims, contain the last words of patriarchs and increase the precision of, or modify, the teachings of earlier writings. Dix already tried to draw such a parallel (*JTS* 27 [1926] 31—not cited by Milik). Note, however, that the Enochic writing is an *epistle* while Deuteronomy is emphatically not such. 4 Ezra 14:28-36 is in many ways a clearer, if succinct, deliberate parallel to Deuteronomy. Like the latter, it is set forth as paraenesis, not as an epistle. The revisionary character of the *Epistle* is, likewise, not particularly striking.

5. *Extra-Qumran Enoch*. Milik, p. 9, assumes, with no basis other than his attribution of astrological knowledge to Enoch, that pseudo-Eupolemus knew *The Book of the Luminaries*. This is also proposed, hesitantly, by P. Grelot (*RB* 82 [1975] 484). Unproved! Perhaps both knew a common tradition.

6. *Winged Angels*. The most striking of the new arguments adduced by Milik for the late date of the *Similitudes* is that in *1 Enoch* 61:1 "the angels take wing and fly away" and, he observes, except for cherubs and seraphs, angels are always wingless until the time of Tertullian (p. 97). Yet a careful reading of the text of the verse shows that the angels did not take wing (i.e., take off using their own wings); instead it says that they *took on* wings, i.e., used borrowed pinions for flight, just as elsewhere clouds, winds, or even chariots serve as means of transportation for angelic or human travellers.

THE SO-CALLED OINTMENT PRAYER IN THE COPTIC VERSION OF THE DIDACHE: A RE-EVALUATION*

Stephen Gero

Brown University
Providence, RI 02912

In the extant fragment (corresponding to 10:3-11:2 of the Greek text) of the Coptic translation of the *Didache*,[1] after the prayer over the bread and the permission for "prophets" to improvise the benedictions if they so wish (10:7), there is a passage which has no parallel in the Greek.[2] It has much potential importance for the early history of the liturgy; however, none of the several interpretations which have been offered to date is entirely satisfactory.[3] The text and a provisional translation of the

---

*I wish to express my appreciation to my colleagues, Professors H. R. Moehring, J. Neusner, and R. Mathiesen, for reading the manuscript and for their comments. The unfailingly prompt and efficient help of the Brown University Library staff has expedited greatly the completion of the documentation for the paper.

Abbreviations: *Ap. Const.* = *Apostolic Constitutions*; Baumstark, *Geschichte* = Anton Baumstark, *Geschichte der syrischen Literatur* (Bonn: Marcus & Weber, 1922); Brightman, *Liturgies* = Frank Edward Brightman, *Liturgies Eastern and Western,* vol. 1 (London: Clarendon, 1896); Graf, *Geschichte* = Georg Graf, *Geschichte der christlichen arabischen Literatur,* vol. 1 (Vatican: Bibliotheca Apostolica Vaticana, 1944).

[1] *Editio princeps* of Br. Mus. Or. 9271 by George Horner, "A New Papyrus Fragment of the *Didaché* in Coptic," *JTS* 25 (1924) 225-31; the manuscript was collated again and published in a more satisfactory manner by Carl Schmidt, "Das koptische Didache-Fragment des British Museum," *ZNW* 24 (1925) 81-99, and, more recently, by Louis-Théophile Lefort, *Les Pères apostoliques en copte* (CSCO 135; Louvain: 1952) 32-34 (text; translation in CSCO 136, 25-28).

[2] For a thorough survey of the problems connected with the text and the interpretation of the *Didache*, see Jean-Paul Audet, *La Didachè: Instructions des apôtres* (EBib; Paris: Gabalda, 1958); on the Coptic text, cf. pp. 28-34. The recent full-length study of the *Didache* by Stanislas Giet (*L'énigme de la Didachè* [Paris: Ophrys, 1970] 213, n. 76) dismisses the problem of the fragment in a brief note opting, following Audet, for the inauthenticity of the passage in question.

[3] For a recent detailed discussion of the "ointment" prayer, with critical evaluation of earlier literature, see Arthur Vööbus, *Liturgical Traditions in the Didache* (Stockholm: Estonian Theological Society in Exile, 1968) 41-60. See also Audet, *La Didachè,* 67-70.

passage will be first presented, followed by our own analysis and interpretation.

> *Etbe pseği de nmpe[st]inoufi šephmat ñteihē etetnğō mas . ğe [te]nšephmat ñtaatk piot etbe [p]ectin[ou]fi etehaktaman elaf [e]bal [hi]tñ īēs pekš[eri].pōk p[e p]aou nšaeneh amēn.*[4] ("Concerning the matter[5] of the *stinoufi*[6] give thanks thus, as you (pl.) say: We give thanks to you, Father, concerning the *stinoufi* which you made known to us through Jesus, your child. Yours is the glory which is for ever. Amen.")

It is obvious that the exegesis of this passage depends entirely on the interpretation one gives to the word *stinoufi*. The first editor, Horner,[7] followed by Schmidt,[8] identified *stinoufi* with *myron*, ointment, both clearly being influenced by the wording of

---

[4]Schmidt, "Didache-Fragment," 84-85, lines 15-20; ed. Lefort, *Pères apostoliques* (CSCO 135) 32, lines 16-20. I have personally collated the papyrus in the British Library on May 24, 1976, and transcribed the passage which is quoted here. Only the clearly necessary editorial emendations are indicated. There is no need to emend *mas* to *mmas* as Lefort does, since the text is in fact characterized by the omission of the particle *n* as the sign of the accusative (see Schmidt, "Didache-Fragment," 83, for examples).

The dialect in which the text is written is similar to Fayyumic, but has some interesting features which cannot simply be dismissed as due to careless copying. According to Paul Ernst Kahle, Jr. (*Balaʾizah: Coptic Texts from Deir El-Balaʾizah in Upper Egypt*, 1 [London: Oxford University, 1954] 224), we have here a text in a sort of proto-Fayyumic, or more precisely "Middle Egyptian, with Fayyumic influence." It should be noted that what Kahle isolates and describes as a new "Middle Egyptian" dialect of Coptic is the language of a relatively small number of texts (several of which have not been published yet) which were previously regarded as written in a Sahidicized Fayyumic. Kahle's discovery of the new dialect has met with the weighty approbation of Jozef Vergote ("Les dialectes dans le domaine égyptien," *Chronique d'Egypte* 26 [1961] 243). Kahle is of the opinion that "the manuscript of the Didache is probably the latest text in this dialect [i.e., "Middle Egyptian with Fayyumic influence"] being written about the beginning of the fifth century" (*Balaʾizah*, 226). Kahle's study of the language of the Didache fragment shows that it has in certain respects more similarities with Bohairic than with pure Fayyumic (*ibid.*). In view of this sophisticated dialectological analysis, Lefort's earlier view (*Pères apostoliques* [CSCO 135] xiii-xiv) that the peculiarities of the text can be accounted for simply by the hypothesis that it is not directly translated from Greek but is the transposition of an older Sahidic translation into Fayyumic cannot be sustained.

[5]Or "word" (*seği*, which corresponds more closely to Bohairic *saği* than to either Fayyumic *šeği* or Sahidic *šağe*). The reference is perhaps only to "the manner in which," but could also indicate a more precise directive for the actual wording, *peri tou logou*, of the prayer which follows.

[6]We shall presently comment at length on the meaning of this crucial term and therefore leave it for the moment untranslated.

[7]"New Papyrus Fragment," 230: "The aroma (ointment)."

[8]"Didache-Fragment," 85: "Salböl."

the parallel passage in the *Ap. Const.*[9] This interpretation was not questioned by scholars for several decades. But the latest editor, Lefort, has pointed the way to a more correct interpretation by showing that the usual equivalent of *myron* is not *stinoufi*, but rather *sočn*;[10] therefore, whatever its correct interpretation, this is *not* a prayer over ointment. Lefort himself opts for the rendering "parfum."[11] But, though the translation "fragrance," "perfume" is even etymologically quite possible,[12] it must be emphasized that we are dealing with a passage clearly cast into the form of *a precise liturgical directive*, which follows upon and patently imitates the wording of part of the blessings over the cup and the bread.[13] What then is the meaning of the "good smell" if on lexicographical grounds alone we must reject the interpretation as the fragrant oil, the *myron*,[14] and hence any putative baptismal associations?[15] In the subsequent discussion we will attempt to give some cogency to an alternative solution, that—whatever

[9] Schmidt, "Didache-Fragment," 85. On the *Ap. Const.* text see below, p. 71.

[10] *Pères apostoliques* (CSCO 136) 26, n. 13. In the Sahidic NT *sočn* translates *myron* 12 times (Michel Wilmet, *Concordance du Nouveau Testament sahidique* [CSCO 183; Louvain: 1958] 898), whereas *stinoufe* renders the expression *osmē euōdias* twice (Wilmet, *Concordance,* 827) and *euōdia* by itself once (2 Cor 2:15). Once, to be sure, it renders *myron* in the Sahidic NT (Luke 23:56), and in the Bohairic version of Ezek 27:17 (Crum, *Coptic Dictionary*, 363a). But Lefort is clearly correct in saying that a Coptic translator normally would not have chosen *stinoufi* to render *myron*.

[11] *Pères apostoliques* (CSCO 136) 26, line 6.

[12] *Stinoufi* can be analyzed as *sti*, "smell," plus *noufi*, "good." As Crum points out (*Coptic Dictionary*, 240a), this form of the adjective is usually found only in compounds.

[13] Compare the Coptic text just cited with *Did.* 9.2-3.

[14] It should be noted that some scholars, while accepting Schmidt's *myron* interpretation, do not regard the text as having a *baptismal* connotation, but rather take it as a reference to the oil of healing and as providing a proof text for what was later called the sacrament of extreme unction (so Bernhard Poschmann, *Penance and Anointing of the Sick* [New York: Herder & Herder, 1964] 237, following E. Riebartsch).

[15] Insistence on a "baptismal" interpretation fundamentally vitiates Vööbus' lengthy analysis. Though he accepts Lefort's comments on *stinoufi*, Vööbus concludes: "The papyrus fragment in Coptic does not go beyond the term 'aroma.' No explanation of its meaning is given and there is nothing to help here" (*Liturgical Traditions*, 45). Then, simply on the basis of the reference to the "immortal aeon" in the parallel text in the *Ap. Const.* (where in any case the "aroma" is unambiguously identified as "myron": see below, p. 71), he concludes that we are dealing with "the imagery of the baptismal rite and experience" (p. 46). This of course assumes that the *Ap. Const.* provide the correct interpretation of the *Didache aucta* text; even more crucially, the argument ignores that *stinoufi* is not merely "imagery" but is as concrete, as material, as the cup and the bread!

particular Greek word underlies *stinoufi*[16]—the reference is specifically to *incense,*[17] and the text is *a prayer over incense burned at the solemn communal meal* described in *Didache* 9 and 10.

We will be much concerned with the date and origin of the Greek text underlying the Coptic; therefore very briefly some pertinent facts about the Coptic MS and external attestation for the *Didache* should be noted for reference. The MS, on paleographical grounds, is not to be dated any later than the fifth century, according to the expert opinion of all three editors. The *Didache* was known in Egypt in the fourth century: it is mentioned in Athanasius' famous *Festal Letter* of 367,[18] and the existence of the first part of the work, the so-called "Two Ways" catechism, in Sahidic, is attested in the literature of early Pachomian monasticism.[19] The liturgical portion of the work, however, is not attested independently in Coptic otherwise, and, as we have seen, the argument for the existence of a Sahidic *Vorlage* for the extant Coptic fragment is precarious.[20] The literary and liturgical affinities of the Coptic text can be further elucidated only by reference to the parallel text from the *Apostolic Constitutions*, to which we shall turn now.

The composite nature of the *Ap. Const.* should be kept in mind when we discuss the specific passage of interest.[21] Books I-VI of the *Ap. Const.* are a reworking of the Greek *Didascalia* (extant

---

[16] *Euōdia* is the most obvious but not the only possibility (see n. 17). The word *euōdia* of course basically just means "good scent," and can be connected with ointment as well as incense (cf. A. Stumpff, "εὐωδία," *TDNT* 2 [1964] 809).

[17] *Stinoufi* or its equivalents in other Coptic dialects *can* stand for *thymiama* (in the Bohairic version of Ezek 16:18) and *thymiasma* (in both Bohairic and Sahidic versions of Isa 43:24), terms which can only refer to burning incense proper, as well as for the more general *arōma* and *euōdia* (Crum, *Coptic Dictionary*, 363a). *Stinoufi* is not the only expression for incense; *šouhēne* is another, even more common one; it renders *thymiama* uniformly in the Sahidic NT, and is used in the Sahidic text of Ezek 16:18. In some liturgical texts *stinoufe* is used interchangeably with *šouhēne*. Our initial contention merely is that *stinoufi* = "incense" is lexically *possible*; but, as we will presently show, it also yields the most plausible interpretation of the text.

[18] Greek text cited and discussed in Audet, *La Didachè*, 83-85.

[19] E.g., "Instruction of Apa Pachomius," ed. Ernest Alfred Wallis Thompson Budge, *Coptic Apocrypha in the Dialect of Upper Egypt* (London: Longmans, 1913) 146-76.

[20] See above, n. 4.

[21] The fundamental investigation is, despite some needed rectifications, still Franz Xaver Funk, *Die apostolischen Konstitutionen: Eine litterar-historische Untersuchung* (Rottenburg: 1891; reprint Frankfurt / Main: Minerva, 1970) 28-179.

only in Syriac and Latin).²² The first part of Book VII is textually dependent on the *Didache*.²³ The influence of Jewish synagogue prayers on the prayers of Book VII. 33ff. and of several in Book VIII has been long recognized.²⁴ Much of Book VIII has close affinities with the third-century *Apostolic Tradition* of Hippolytus,²⁵ though the liturgy described in Book VIII is generally, and rightly, regarded as reflecting the Syrian (Antiochene?) liturgy of the fourth century.²⁶ The so-called *Apostolic Canons*, which form the concluding portion of Book VIII, depend on the disciplinary canons of fourth-century councils but as a whole are the composition of the last, Syrian, redactor of the eight books working in the latter part of the fourth century.²⁷

The Coptic *Didache* passage with which we are concerned here is closely related to a prayer in the first part of Book VII of the *Ap. Const.*, the reworking of a Greek *Didache*. *Ap. Const.* VII.27 is as follows: "Concerning the *myron*, give thanks thus: We give thanks to you, O God, creator of all *(thee, dēmiourge tōn holōn)*, and for the good smell of the myron *(hyper tē euōdias tou myrou)*, and for the immortal aeon *(hyper tou athanatou aiōnos)* which you made known to us through Jesus your child, because yours is the glory and the power forever. Amen."²⁸

A comparison of this Greek text with the Coptic makes clear the dependence of the *Ap. Const.* text on a Greek *Vorlage* which

---

²²See R. Hugh Connolly, *Didascalia apostolorum* (Oxford: Clarendon, 1929) xx-xxi.

²³Cf. Adolf Harnack, *Die Lehre der zwölf Apostel* (TU 2; [1884]) 170-92.

²⁴Wilhelm Bousset, "Eine jüdische Gebetssammlung im siebenten Buch der apostolischen Konstitutionen," *Nachrichten von der Königlichen Gesellschaft der Wissenschaften zu Göttingen*, Philologisch-historische Klasse aus dem Jahre 1915 (Berlin: Weidmannsche Buchhandlung, 1916) 435-89.

²⁵Gregory Dix, *The Treatise on the Apostolic Tradition of St. Hippolytus of Rome* (London: Society for Promoting Christian Knowledge, 1937) lxxi-lxxvi.

²⁶Brightman, *Liturgies*, xxix-xlvi; the text of the reconstructed liturgy is printed, with conventional rubrics added, on pp. 3-27. For a study of the materials to be used for a reconstitution of the fourth-century Antiochene liturgy, with a careful estimate of the evidence of the *Ap. Const.*, see Massey H. Shepherd, "The Formation and Influence of the Antiochene Liturgy," *Dumbarton Oaks Papers* 15 (1961) 23-44.

²⁷Funk, *Konstitutionen*, 180-206. For an attempt at a more accurate dating (the 380's) see Eduard Schwartz, *Über die pseudapostolischen Kirchenordnungen* (Strassburg: Trübner, 1910) 12-27.

²⁸Ed. Franz Xaver Funk, *Didascalia et constitutiones apostolorum* (Paderborn: Schoening, 1905) 414, lines 10-14.

is very close to that which underlies the Coptic.[29] Some of the redactorial touches are quite evident: replacement of the simple address "Father" by the ceremonious *thee dēmiourge tōn holōn*, and the amplification of the closing doxology. Also, though the exact meaning of the phrase *hyper tou athanatou aiōnos* is not clear,[30] it has no parallel in the Coptic, and seemingly one is confronted again by a redactional interpolation.[31] In the expression *hyper tēs euōdias tou myrou* the qualifier *tou myrou* is seemingly a redactional gloss on *euōdia*. In the introductory

---

[29] Some comment is in order here on the potentially important argument which Alfred Adam adduces in favor of his hypothesis of a Syriac original for the Coptic text from the *stinoufi* passage ("Erwägungen zur Herkunft der Didache," *ZKG* 68 [1957] 8-11). Adam reasons in the following way: The entry in Crum's *Coptic Dictionary* on *stinoufi* shows that the word is a usual equivalent of *euōdia*, and in particular for the OT expression *ryh hnyhwh*, which in the Peshitta "in den alttestamentlichen Stellen mit *rēhā danjāhā* oder *rēh njāhā* an den neutestamentlichen Stellen mit *rēhā* 'Duft' wiedergegeben ist." Thus *nyāhā* is the equivalent of *euōdia*. Therefore, Adam concludes, "Auf Grund des älteren Sprachgebrauchs, wie er in der Peschitta des Alten Testaments vorliegt, darf wohl die Schlussfolgerung gezogen werden, dass in der syrischen Vorlage des koptischen Fragments *njāhā* gestanden hat" ("Erwägungen," 9). This, in Adam's view, provides the clue to the *stinoufi* passage. He notes that *nyāhā* has a variety of meanings, *inter alia* that of *anapausis*, "refreshment," and that the feminine form *nyāhtā* is used as a terminus technicus for the *agapē* feast. Therefore, the *stinoufi* prayer is simply a "Schlussgebet das den Dank für die ganze Feier in den einfachsten Worten ausspricht" (p. 10)—that is, *stinoufi* is the whole *agape* feast! Now, though the reasoning is ingenious, it cannot be sustained upon closer examination. First, Adam does not even note that *stinoufi* can stand for words other than *euōdia*. Moreover, the employment of the word *nyāhtā*, "repose," is not common in early Syriac as an expression for the *agapē* feast—it is so used first by Rabbula (5th century) for funerary feasts, and in the 6th-century Philoxenian translation in 2 Pet 2:13, Jude 13. Even more crucially, the whole argument again ignores the liturgical specificity of the prayer: the blessing is made over some actual substance, not simply for "the good cheer," so to speak! But Adam rightly recognizes the secondary nature of the *Ap. Const.* "myron" text, and that it represents a misunderstanding of "das Hinweisen auf den wohlgefälligen 'Duft' der Agapefeier" (p. 10). Adam, with commendable reserve, does not commit himself on the question of the relationship of the hypothetical Syriac text to the Greek of the Constantinople MS. A detailed analysis of his other arguments for a Syriac *Vorlage* would take us too far afield, but they have little cogency either. Cf. Vööbus' brief critique of Adam's hypothesis (*Liturgical Traditions*, 44-45).

[30] Vööbus (*Liturgical Traditions*, 45-46) opts for a baptismal interpretation. But the wording is strange indeed, and has no affinity with the definitely baptismal *peri tou mystikou myrou eucharistia* in VII.44.

[31] The Greek MSS used by Funk all have the phrase in question; but the Ethiopic *Didascalia* (a reworking of Books I-VII of the *Ap. Const.*, not to be confused with the old Greek *Didascalia* which is the *Vorlage* of Books I-VI!) has the following wording: "Thou shalt give thanks thus: We give thanks to Thee,

rubric I surmise that the redactor replaced *euōdia* or some other word by *myron*; it is possible, though direct proof cannot be offered, that *myron* stands for a more unambiguous word for incense, e.g. *thymiama,* rather than *euōdia.* However, it is quite clear that —whatever the intent of the prayer in the *Vorlage*—the amplified Greek text of the *Ap. Const.* has no reference to incense, but is intended to be an ointment prayer, whereas, as we have seen, the Coptic text has a strong claim to be referred to incense but almost none to *myron.* Which text represents the wording of the Greek *Vorlage* at the crucial point of the intention of the prayer? Was the prayer, in any form, part of the primitive *Didache,* or does it represent a liturgical updating[32] of the text as preserved in the Constantinople MS? Answers to these questions can be given only in the context of a close study of the place and date of the relevant portions of the *Ap. Const.,* and of the evidence for the use of incense in early Christianity, particularly in the fourth and fifth centuries.

First, though the "Clementine" liturgy of Book VIII is clearly of Syro-Palestinian provenance, much liturgical material in Book VII, as has been demonstrated, quite convincingly in my opinion, by Anton Baumstark, is rather of *Egyptian* origin.[33] In particular the *myron* prayer of VII.27 after the "eucharistic" prayers is in agreement with the arrangement of early and indisputably Egyptian material, specifically the Euchologium of Serapion.[34]

Creator of all things, for the savour of this chrism, *and for this oil of immortality,* which Thou hast revealed to us by Jesus Christ Thy Son. For Thine is the glory, and the kingdom, and the power for ever and ever. Amen." (transl. from Br. Mus. Or. 752, by John Mason Harden, *The Ethiopic Didascalia* [London: S.P.C.K., 1920] 172). The Ethiopic is based on an Arabic version of the *Ap. Const.,* but neither the Arabic nor the Ethiopic has been investigated with any thoroughness.

[32]Since we have accepted Lefort's argument that *myron* would have been rendered by *soĉn* rather than *stinoufi,* it is not necessary to review at length the various opinions concerning authenticity which have been based on the older *myron* interpretation. Incidentally, Erik Peterson's provocative hypothesis that the *myron* prayer is authentic, and that its suppression in the Bryennios text of the *Didache* is a sign of Novatian heresy which, *inter alia,* opposed post-baptismal anointing ("Über einige Probleme der Didache-Überlieferung," in his *Frühkirche, Christentum und Gnosis* [Freiburg: Herder, 1959] 166; reprinted from *Rivista di archeologia cristiana* [1951] 37ff.) has been thoroughly refuted and needs no further comment. See Audet, *La Dīdachè,* 68, n. 3, and Vööbus, *Liturgical Traditions,* 31-33.

[33]Anton Baumstark, "Aegyptischer oder antiochenischer Liturgietypus in AK I-VII?" *OrChr* 1, 7 (1907) 388-407.

[34]Ibid., 395. The prayer in question is clearly a blessing over the water and oil of exorcism and healing (ed. Georg Wobbermin, *Altchristliche liturgische*

Though some details of Baumstark's argument are precarious,[35] his conclusion that the first part of Book VII reflects Egyptian liturgical usages not later than ca. 400 has great cogency, and, as we shall presently see, is very significant for the purposes of our investigation.

The second point requires rather extensive analysis of the documentation. It is generally recognized that the use of incense in the eucharistic ceremony as described in the developed liturgies is a post-Constantinian phenomenon.[36] Second and third-century Christian writers either refer to incense (prominent, of course, in temple ritual as described in the OT) in a metaphorical fashion or reject its use outright as a sign of paganism.[37]

Stücke aus der Kirche Ägyptens (TU 17, 36 [1898] 7-8). There is a similar prayer at a later point which, however, does not seem to be connected with the eucharistic prayers (ibid., 13-14). See also Frank Edward Brightman, "The Sacramentary of Serapion of Thmuis," *JTS* 1 (1900) 108, 267-68.

[35]Thus the application of the expression *antitypa* (*Ap. Const.* VII.25) to the eucharistic elements is not peculiarly Egyptian (so Baumstark, "Liturgietypus," 398): cf. my article, "The Eucharistic Doctrine of the Byzantine Iconoclasts and Its Sources," *Byzantinische Zeitschrift* 68 (1975) 13, n. 46. Baumstark notes ("Liturgietypus," 395) that the *Testamentum Domini* has a prayer over oil and water after the eucharistic prayers proper (I.24-25); (ed. Ignatius Ephraem Rahmani, *Testamentum domini nostri Jesu Christi* [Mainz: Kirchheim, 1899] 48). But that this work (written in Greek, but [apart from some Latin fragments] extant only in oriental translations [Syriac, Arabic, Ethiopic]) is of Egyptian origin is by no means as certain as Baumstark assumes ("Liturgietypus," 389-90). Thus, though transmission in Arabic (via Coptic) and in Ethiopic argues for Egypt, Baumstark himself ("Überlieferung und Bezeugung der διαθήκη τοῦ κυρίου ἡμῶν'Ἰησοῦ Χριστοῦ," *RQ* 14 [1900] 39) accepted earlier tne hypothesis of Syrian origin. Franz Xaver Funk (*Das Testament unseres Herrn und die verwandten Schriften* [Mainz: Kirchheim, 1901] 87 opts for Syria; A. J. MacLean, though with many misgivings, even proposes Asia Minor (in James Cooper and Arthur John MacLean, *The Testament of Our Lord* [Edinburgh: Clark, 1902] 42-45). But Theodor Schermann's refusal *(Ägyptische Abendmahlsliturgien des ersten Jahrtausends* [Paderborn: F. Schöningh, 1912] 97-98) to grant *any* cogency to Baumstark's arguments depends on an all too ready assumption of Syrian influence on well nigh all aspects of early Egyptian liturgical usage.

[36]The fundamental work on the whole subject is still Edward Godfrey Cuthbert Frederic Atchley, *A History of the Use of Incense in Divine Worship* (London: Longmans, 1909). Another valuable collection of the material (even though one must dissent from some of the hypothetical constructions imposed upon it) is Carl Schneider's "Studien zum Ursprung liturgischer Einzelheiten östlicher Liturgien, 2. ΘΥΜΙΑΜΑΤΑ," *Kyrios* 3 (1938) 149-90, 293-311. See also E. Fehrenbach, "Encens," *DACL* 5. 1, cols. 2-22, esp. cols. 6-11, and Jean Michel Hanssens, *Institutiones liturgicae de ritibus orientalibus,* Tom. III (Rome: Gregoriana, 1932) 70-91.

[37]See Atchley, *History*, 81-96. The material is also collected in Frederick Edward Warren, *The Liturgy and Ritual of the Ante-Nicene Church* (London:

The employment of incense in Christian funerary ceremonies is attested earlier than a connection of censing with the eucharistic liturgy.[38] Apart from a hardly trustworthy reference in the *Passio* of the bishop Peter of Alexandria (died A.D. 311),[39] the earliest pertinent material is of *Syrian* provenance. Ephrem in his *Testament* expresses his wish not to be honored with the burning of incense at his funeral.[40] John Chrysostom refers to incense used in Christian funerary processions.[41] The pilgrim Etheria's[42] mention of incense at the Sunday services of the Church of the Anastasis in Jerusalem[43] probably should be classified here, as a "passion play" type imitation of a (supposed) detail of the burial of Jesus,[44] rather than as a eucharistic censing proper.

Of more direct relevance to our problem seem to be texts which connect incense with prayer and propitiation. Ephrem, in an undoubtedly genuine poem, refers to the prayer, the *censer*, and the sacrifices of Abraham, bishop of Nisibis.[45] There are other,

---

S.P.C.K., 1897) 129-31. See also W. H. Frere, "Notes on the Early History of the Use of Incense," in Henry Westall, ed., *The Case for Incense* (London: Longmans, 1899) 43-86.

[38]Cf. Atchley, *History*, 97-116.

[39]Only one 9th-century Latin version of the *Acta* of Peter, but none of the older Greek, Coptic and Arabic recensions mentions that, after the preparation for burial *(odoriferis condientes aromatibus induerunt illum sericis indumentis)*, the saint was carried to his final resting place *flammantibus cereis, concrepantibus hymnis, flagrantisque thymiamatibus* (*PG* 18. 465C).

[40]"Burn incense [*besmē*] in the sanctuary; as for me, accompany me with prayer. . . . Go and burn [the incense] in the sanctuary, so that there may be good smell for those who go there" (ed. Edmund Beck, *Des heiligen Ephraem des Syrers Sermones* IV [CSCO 334; Louvain: 1973] 51, lines 9-11). At an earlier point the text makes a very realistic reference to the corpse and "the stinking smell of Ephrem," *riḥeh saryā dAphrem* (ibid., 48, lines 9-10). In this work the fumigatory use of incense seems to have as its pendant the (habitual?) use of incense in churches, though no connection is made with the eucharistic liturgy.

[41]E.g., *Hom. xli: de S. Pelagia* (*PG* 50.585).

[42]Late fourth or early fifth century; see John Wilkinson, *Egeria's Travels* (London: S.P.C.K., 1971) 27-30 for an attempt at an exact chronology.

[43]*Dictis ergo his tribus psalmis et factis orationibus tribus ecce etiam thiamataria inferuntur intro spelunca Anastasis, ut tota basilica Anastasis repleatur odoribus* (*Itinerarium Egeriae* XXIV. 10, ed. A. Franceschini and R. Weber, in *Itinerariae et alia geographica,* CChr Series latina 175.69, lines 81-84).

[44]This suggestion was first made by Juan Mateos, "La vigile cathédrale chez Egérie," *Orientalia Christiana Periodica* 27 (1961) 292: the resurrection theme explains, *inter alia,* "l'encensement du tombeau que rappellent les parfums portés par les femmes." The explanation is accepted by Wilkinson, *Egeria's Travels*, 65, and Rolf Zerfass, *Die Schriftlesung im Kathedralofficium Jerusalems* (Münster: Aschendorff, 1969) 27.

[45]"May your fasting be armor for our land, your prayer a shield for our city, may your censer [*piromāk*] purchase reconciliation [*tarʿutā*]. Blessed be he

somewhat later texts which indicate that supplication of one form or another was often accompanied by the burning of incense.[46] In fact, in some texts censing is used as a synonym for supplication, in contexts where literal burning of incense was quite unlikely.[47]

This brings us to the evidence for the use of incense during the eucharistic liturgy proper. Censing at various stages of the service characterizes all the "classical" eastern liturgies,[48] but the evidence of these, based on MSS which do not antedate the ninth century, cannot be retrojected into the fourth century.[49] The datable early extant evidence is again of Syrian provenance. We have just referred to a passage from Ephrem's *Carmina Nisibena* which has been taken by some scholars to allude to censing in the liturgy. A passage from John Chrysostom *can* also be interpreted, despite the lack of precision, as referring to the use of incense prior to and/or during the eucharistic liturgy.[50] But the earliest unambiguous fourth-century evidence comes from the *Apostolic Canons* (if, as it seems most likely, their author is to be identified with the final redactor of the *Ap. Const.*[51]). The third Canon prescribes that "At the fitting time, it is not lawful to bring forth to the altar anything but fresh ears of corn or grapes, and oil for the lamp and incense *(thymiama)* at the time of the holy offering."[52] The incense, which is to be used "at the time of the holy offering,"

---

who sanctified your sacrifices" (ed. Edmund Beck, *Des heiligen Ephraem des Syrers Carmina Nisibena* 1 [CSCO 218; Louvain: 1961] 46, lines 18-19). Hans Lietzmann (following the suggestion of the earlier editor, Bickell) sees in the passage a reference to the sequence of liturgical activities: fasting, prayer, censing of the eucharistic elements and the eucharistic sacrifice (*Messe und Herrenmahl* [Bonn: Marcus & Weber, 1926] 86-87). However, other evidence which merely associates the offering of incense with supplication (see note 46) makes this reasoning somewhat doubtful.

[46]Cf. Atchley, *History*, 118-19.

[47]Thus, in one recension of a Syriac collection of the miracles of the Virgin, some of her devotees, threatened by imminent shipwreck in a storm "remembered her, and placed incense on the fire [$sāmu\ besmē^y\ al\ nurā$] and immediately the sea became calm . . ." (ed. Ernest Alfred Wallis Thompson Budge, *The History of the Blessed Virgin Mary . . .* [London: Luzac, 1899] 138, n. 1).

[48]The evidence is collected and subjected to an incisive, but not entirely convincing, analysis by Lietzmann, *Messe und Herrenmahl*, 86-93.

[49]Cf. R. Taft, "Evolution historique de la liturgie de saint Jean Chrysostome . . . L'encensement et le lavabo," *Proche Orient Chrétien* 25 (1975) 275-86.

[50]*PG* 58.781, cited by Atchley, *History*, 200. Chrysostom contrasts the censing of the church to produce a pleasant odor with the reluctance to banish the evil smell of spiritual uncleanliness.

[51]See Funk, *Konstitutionen*, 180-206, for detailed proof.

[52]Funk, *Didascalia et constitutiones apostolorum*, 564, lines 8-10.

is to be blessed at the altar, as are the oil for the lamp, fresh corn, and grapes. The textual evidence is quite secure: the phrase concerning incense is found in all the Greek MSS and in both recensions of the Latin translation of the Canons by Dionysius Exiguus (early sixth century).[53] The oriental evidence is quite concordant; the Coptic (Sahidic and Bohairic[54]), both Syriac versions,[55] the Arabic[56] and Ethiopic[57] renderings all support the Greek. It should be noted, again, however, that, despite the literary unity of the work, the "Clementine" liturgy of Book VIII does not explicitly mention censing. A sacrificial interpretation of incense in close connection with the eucharist is found in an exegetical work of Theodoret of Cyrrhus (middle of the 5th cent.): "We offer to God incense *(thymiama)* and the light of the lamp, and the sacred rite of the holy table."[58] In one of the homilies (No. 17) ascribed to the great Nestorian theologian Narsai of Nisibis (latter half of the fifth century) the sumptuous

---

[53]Dionysius' *Interpretatio prima* has *timiama (id est incensum) tempore quo sancta celebratur oblatio* (ed. Cuthbert Hamilton Turner, *Ecclesiae occidentalis monumenta iuris antiquissima* 1.1 [Oxford: Clarendon, 1909] 10, col. 1, lines 3-5). The *Interpretatio altera* differs only in giving the more correct transliteration *"thymiama"* (col. 2, line 2).

[54]The Sahidic version has *oušouhēne mpnau nte prosphora etouaab* ("incense at the time of the holy sacrifice"), ed. Paul Anton de Lagarde, *Aegyptiaca* (Göttingen: Dieterich, 1883) 210. The Bohairic text (ibid.) uses *ousthoi-noufi* for "incense"; this text, according to the colophon translated from Sahidic (de Lagarde, *Aegyptiaca* 238; see also Henry Tattam, *The Apostolic Constitutions or Canons of the Apostles in Coptic* [London: Oriental Translation Fund, 1848] 213) may reflect a Sahidic *stinoufe* as the word for incense. Rather interestingly, the marginal gloss in the Bohairic MS, *nem ousoug̃en*, "with myron," shows an evidence of wanting to bring the work liturgically up to date.

[55]The version in the Epitome of Ebedjesus (cf. Baumstark, *Geschichte*, 324) has *besmē bᶜedānā dqurbānā ʾalahāyā*, "incense at the time of the divine offering" (ed. Angelo Mai, *Scriptorum veterum nova collectio . . .* tomus X [Rome: Apud Burliaeum, 1837] 175). The version incorporated in an older Syriac pseudo-Clementine canonical collection has only *besmē bᶜedānā dqurbānā* (ed. P. de Lagarde, *Reliquiae iuris ecclesiastici antiquissimae* [Leipzig: 1856; reprint Osnabrück: Zeller, 1967], p. *mh*, lines 5-6). Cf. Baumstark, *Geschichte*, 82, and Ignazio Ortiz de Urbina, *Patrologia syriaca* (Rome: Pont. Institutum Orientalium Studiorum, 1958) 224-25.

[56]*baḫūr fī waqt al-quddās al-ṭāhir*, "incense at the time of the pure consecration," from the version of the *Apostolic Canons* proper incorporated in the "127 Canons of the Apostles" (ed. Jean Périer and Augustin Périer, PO 8 [1912] 655). On this compilation, which with most likelihood is translated from Coptic, see Graf, *Geschichte*, 572-77.

[57]*ᶜeṭān bagizē qʷerban neṣuḥ* "incense at the time of the pure offering" (ed. Winand Fell, *Canones apostolorum aethiopice* [Leipzig: Brockhaus, 1871] 13).

[58]*PG* 80, 284C.

ritual is described just before the consecration: "the mysteries are set in order, the *censers are smoking*, the lamps are shining . . ."[59] It is significant that a preliminary censing of the church is not noted. But the earliest detailed description of censing, at the beginning of the liturgy, is found in the pseudo-Dionysian corpus, which reflects the Syrian liturgy of the late fifth or early sixth century.[60] According to pseudo-Dionysius, "The hierarch . . . having accomplished the holy prayer at the sacred altar, begins to cense, having started from there, and comes around the whole circuit of the holy choir."[61]

All of the foregoing evidence for censing used in the eucharistic liturgy is significantly of *Syrian* provenance. Apart from one very doubtful text, the *Canons of Athanasius*,[62] there is no evidence for eucharistic censing in Egyptian liturgical practice in the extant

---

[59]Trans. R. Hugh Connolly, *The Liturgical Homilies of Narsai* (TextsS 8.1; Cambridge: Cambridge University, 1909) 12 (= ed. Alphonse Mingana, *Narsai doctoris syri homiliae et carmina primo edita*, vol. 1 [Mosul: Typis Fratrum praedicatorum, 1905] 281). There has been much doubt expressed about the authenticity of the homily, on stylistic and liturgiological grounds, and because of the attribution in some MSS to the thirteenth-century writer Ebedjesus of Elam (Connolly, *Liturgical Homilies*, p. xii). Cf. Baumstark, *Geschichte,* 112 and 348 (opting for inauthenticity!). See also Willem Cornelis van Unnik (*Nestorian Questions on the Administration of the Eucharist* . . . [Amsterdam: 1937; reprint Amsterdam: Grüner, 1970] 422ff.) who concludes that the question is still *sub judice* (p. 57).

[60]For a tentative reconstruction of the pseudo-Dionysian liturgy see Brightman, *Liturgies*, 487-88.

[61]*De ecclesiastica hierarchia* 3, *PG* 3. 425B.

[62]Ed. Wilhelm Riedel and Walter E. Crum, *The Canons of Athanasius of Alexandria* (London: Williams and Norgate, 1904). Though originally composed in Greek, the work is extant only in Sahidic and Arabic. The Sahidic version, though relatively old (one MS has been dated by Crum to ca. A.D. 600), is, however, fragmentary, and in particular these sections where the Arabic version mentions incense are missing. The Arabic text is not translated from the Sahidic, but rather, as Crum suggests, from a lost Bohairic version made independently from the Greek (ibid., 81). Though Riedel, with some hesitation, accepts the Athanasian authorship of the lost *Grundschrift* (ibid., pp. xiv-xxvi), it is quite clear that the translation into Arabic and the division into paragraphs is the work of Michael of Tinnīs (according to Graf [*Geschichte*, 605] perhaps to be identified with the 11th-century redactor of the *History of the Patriarchs* of Severus ibn al-Muqaffaᶜ). At any rate, the final portion of the Arabic (which includes [par. 106] a detailed description of the censing of the gospel book) has, as Riedel himself notes "almost the appearance of a subsequent edition" (Riedel and Crum, *Canons of Athanasius,* p. xxvi). In view of the silence of Athanasius and other early Egyptian fathers concerning liturgical censing (cf. note 63) I hesitate to ascribe the two passages concerned with incense (par. 7 *fin.*, par. 106) to Athanasius, whatever else in the work may be of early provenience.

fourth- and fifth-century material.[63] One finds, of course, use of the well-known metaphorical language of the odor of sanctity,[64] even symbolizing divine presence[65] or gnosis in Christian Egyptian texts.[66] But, as we have emphasized from the outset, the

[63] For a convenient collection of liturgical allusions in this patristic literature, see Brightman, *Liturgies*, 504-09. The earliest explicit mention of liturgical censing, to my knowledge, in a datable narrative Egyptian text is from the 11th-century recension of the Arabic biography of the patriarch Shenouti I (A.D. 849-80), according to which in a nocturnal liturgy "while he went around the sanctuary *(haikal)* with incense, his eyes shed bitter tears" (trans. Yassā ᶜAbd-al-Masīh and Oswald Hugh Ewald Burmester, *History of the Patriarchs of the Egyptian Church*, 2.1 [Cairo: L'institut français d'archéologie orientale, 1943] 55; Arabic text not published). To be sure, a number of censers from Egypt have been dated, in particular by Josef Strzygowsky (*Catalogue général des antiquités égyptiennes du Musée du Caire . . . Koptische Kunst* [Vienna: Holzhausen, 1904] 280ff.) as coming from the pre-Islamic period; he even dates two standing censers to the 2d to the 4th century (Nos. 9122-23). Though it is not within my competence to control the datings, they seem to be on the whole rather arbitrary, especially where one is dealing with objects acquired by purchase from private individuals or from antiquities dealers. In any case, there is no indication of the *function* these censers had, and for several there even seems to be no clear indication that they are of Christian origin. The archeological evidence is therefore of little moment, it seems to me, compared to the silence of the literary sources on censing in the eucharistic liturgy. Cf. Henri Leclercq, "Encensoir," *DACL* 5 (1922) cols. 21-33, and Schneider, "Studien," *Kyrios* 3 (1938) 171-74.

[64] For an example from "orthodox" Coptic literature, cf. the encomiastic *Vita* of bishop Pisentius (7th century), in which the saint is described as "one who was full of light and who spread forth *stinoufe* all the time" (ed. Ernest Alfred Wallis Thompson Budge, *Coptic Apocrypha in the Dialect of Upper Egypt* [London: Longmans, 1913] 74).

[65] See Ernst Lohmeyer's classic monograph, *Vom göttlichen Wohlgeruch* (Sitzungsberichte der Heidelberger Akademie der Wissenschaft, Phil-hist. Klasse 9; 1919), particularly pp. 15-22 on ancient Egyptian material; the latter is also discussed by the Egyptologist Hans Bonnet, "Die Bedeutung der Räucherungen im ägyptischen Kult," *Zeitschrift für ägyptische Sprache und Altertumskunde* 67 (1931) 20-28. See also Waldemar Deonna's more comprehensive study, "ΕΥΩΔΙΑ, Croyances antiques et modernes: l'odeur suave des dieux et des élus," *Genava* 17 (1939) 167-263.

[66] In the Coptic Gnostic *Gospel of Truth* "the smell" *(pstaei)* is identified with the Spirit and is described as an attribute of the Father (ed. Michel Malinine et al., *Evangelium Veritatis* [*Supplementum*; Zürich and Stuttgart: Rascher, 1961] 34). Much of the Gnostic material, and the classical background, is discussed à propos this passage in Jacques-É. Ménard, *L'Evangile de Vérité* (Leiden: Brill, 1972) 158-63. In the *Gospel of Philip*, the "odor" *(stoei)* occurs, but only in connection with "ointment" *(sočn)* (ed. Walter C. Till, *Das Evangelium nach Philippos* [Patristische Texte und Studien 2; Berlin: de Gruyter, 1963] 55, lines

Coptic *Didache* provides a concrete liturgical directive for the prayer over incense; not only is a liturgical parallel lacking in fourth- and fifth-century literature from Egypt,[67] but also the very practice of censing at the liturgy, which was introduced at an undetermined time (seventh or eighth century?),[68] and came to be prominent in the Coptic liturgy and penitential practice in the Middle Ages,[69] cannot be documented in the pre-Islamic period.

On the basis of the foregoing evidence one can now answer with some assurance the question whether the Coptic text represents a liturgical updating of the *Didache* or whether indeed it reflects a

36ff.). Incense specifically does not seem to have played a demonstrable role in the sacramental system of the Gnostics, judging by both the patristic accounts and the Coptic texts.

[67] It should be noted here that ch. 38 of the "vulgate" recension of the Arabic *Didascalia* (cf. note 31) has a detailed description of the liturgy, with a preanaphoral triple circumambulatory censing of the altar "in honor of the Holy Trinity" by the bishop, with a subsequent censing of the congregation by a presbyter (translated, with conventional rubrics added, in Brightman, *Liturgies*, 510-11; for another translation, see Funk, *Konstitutionen*, 233-34). The "Abū Isḥāq" recension, represented by *Borg. ar.* 22 and the Ethiopic translation, though lacking this particular chapter along with others (cf. Graf, *Geschichte*, 565), does assume a liturgical use of incense. The Ethiopic text (tr. John Mason Harden, *The Ethiopic Didascalia* [London: S.P.C.K., 1920] 92) says, "We command you, then, that no layman execute the office of the priesthood, neither offer incense, nor baptize, nor lay on hands, nor give the bread of blessing"—a reworking of *Ap. Const.* III.10, which does not mention the offering of incense as part of the sacerdotal duties. This Egyptian *Didascalia* tradition does attest the use of incense, but still there is no cogent reason to assume that it preserves fourth- or fifth-century usage. MacLean's statement that the censing in the Arabic *Didascalia* text is consistent with a fourth-century date for the work, simply because "incense is mentioned in the Pilgrimage of Silvia, about 385 A.D." (James Cooper and Arthur John MacLean, *The Testament of Our Lord* [Edinburgh: Clark, 1902] 34) is a misleading simplification, in view of the material we have presented earlier.

[68] One can only speculate about the time of and motives for the introduction of liturgical censing in Egypt; however, in view of the relatively early Syrian evidence and the strong influence of Syrian liturgical usages, especially after the monophysite schism (cf. Schermann, *Ägyptische Abendmahlsliturgien*, 97ff.), it seems that liturgical censing was such a Syrian import.

[69] By the twelfth century liturgical censing came to be extremely widespread in Egypt. The peculiar custom arose even of individuals confessing their sins before the censer carried around by the priest, at the time of the preliminary censing of the altar and nave (cf. n. 66), as a substitute for auricular confession. See Georg Graf, "Über den Gebrauch des Weihrauchs bei den Kopten," *Dem Prinzen Johann Georg Herzog zu Sachsen zum 50. Geburtstag gewidmet: Ehrengabe deutscher Wissenschaft dargeboten von katholischen Gelehrten* (hrsg. von Franz Fessler; Freiburg: Herder, 1920) 223-32, and idem, *Ein Reformversuch innerhalb der koptischen Kirche im zwölften Jahrhundert* (Paderborn: Schöning, 1923) esp. 55-59, 150-52.

primitive "long" recension. Following Baumstark, I argue for an Egyptian origin for much of the liturgical material in *Ap. Const.* VII. I surmise that the Egyptian redactor of Book VII already had a reference to incense in his Greek *Didache* text. But, in line with his very free and creative handling of his sources and his familiarity with *myron* prayers after the eucharist, and his "Egyptian" ignorance of, or penchant against, liturgical censing, he merely reinterpreted the *euōdia*—or *arōma* or *thymiama*—of his Greek *Didache*, as referring to the fragrant *myron* of the baptismal rite. The *final* redactor of the *Ap. Const.*—perhaps to be identified with the composer/interpolator of Book VIII and of the *Apostolic Canons*—no longer had access to the original text of the *Didache*, but knew it only in the form incorporated in Book VII. Though the final redactor of the *Ap. Const.*, judging by *Apostolic Canon* 3, was familiar with liturgical censing, he did not mention, perhaps by inadvertence, censing in the liturgy of Book VIII.[70] By contrast, the Coptic translator, working without the conscious purpose of the "Constitutor" of Book VII, rendered the Greek text quite literally,[71] not feeling it incumbent upon him, it seems, to harmonize the translation with the prevalent liturgical norms of Egypt.

Some comment is next in order on the possibility that the Coptic *Didache* text renders an interpolated Greek *Didache* text, revised in order to justify, by means of the fiction of apostolic institution, the introduction of incense in the eucharistic service of the Syrian rite. Though the probable Syro-Palestinian origin of the material in the *Didache* would argue in favor of the Syrian origin of the Greek *Vorlage* of the Coptic text,[72] the further conclusion that the Greek text reflects a fourth- or fifth-century

---

[70] Baumstark reduces the contribution of the final redactor to little more than that of arranger and compiler ("Die Urgestalt der 'arabischen Didaskalia der Apostel'..." *OrChr* 1, 3 [1903] 208).

[71] This can be easily seen by simultaneously comparing the Coptic translation and the relevant portion of the *Ap. Const.* with the Greek *Didache* text of chaps. 10-11.

[72] It should be pointed out, however, that a recognition of the Syrian element in the liturgical portion of the *Didache* is not incompatible with the view that the extant Greek recension (represented by the Bryennios MS and the Georgian version) is of Egyptian provenance. This is the opinion, for instance, of Cyril C. Richardson (*Early Christian Fathers* [Philadelphia: Westminster, 1953] 163) echoing in part Harnack's detailed arguments for an Egyptian *Heimat* for the *Didache* as a whole (*Lehre der zwölf Apostel* [TU 2; 1884] 15-18). If the final *redactor* of the Greek *Didache* was indeed Egyptian, then *a fortiori* the Greek *Vorlage* of the Coptic text would be an Egyptian MS, and the need to account for the influence of possible Syrian liturgical censing would disappear.

Syrian liturgy does not follow. The form of the incense prayer clearly imitates the archaic language of the prayers over the bread and the wine. There is no similarity with incense or *myron* prayers used in Egypt and elsewhere. Rather, in our view, the prayer over the incense is part of that liturgical archaism of the *Didache* which the interpolator of Book VII of the *Ap. Const.* strove to remedy.

This brings us finally to a discussion of the original character of the prayers in *Didache* 9 and 10. This is not the place to delve into details of the long controversy; I would merely register my agreement with those scholars who see in *Didache* 9 and 10 a reflection of a Christian "agape," without a "eucharistic" commemoration of the passion, an "agape" the structure of which was influenced by the ceremonial that surrounded solemn Jewish communal meals.[73] Literary evidence for the use of incense in Jewish *synagogue* services in early Christian times does not exist:[74] this would have provided, of course, the most natural stage of transition to account for incense in the *Didache* liturgy as a Jewish-Christian ceremonial peculiarity. The explanation is rather to be sought in the fact that *Didache* 9-10 in fact describe a communal meal.

The burning of incense during and after meals is well attested in Greco-Roman antiquity,[75] without any obvious religious overtones. The burning of incense is also attested for Jewish meals as these are described in the Talmud. Here we seemingly find the source for, or at least a striking analogue to, the apparently sacred aspect of the act of burning incense—but, to be sure, as just part of giving to minutiae of everyday conduct a religious dimension, which of course characterizes this entire literature. In the Mishnah (*m. Ber.* 6.6)[76] the requisite blessing

---

[73]See Joachim Jeremias, *Die Abendmahlsworte Jesu* (3rd ed.; Göttingen: Vandenhoeck & Ruprecht, 1960) 111, n. 6. Cf. Luigi Clerici, *Einsammlung der Zerstreuten: Liturgiegeschichtliche Untersuchung . . . der Fürbitte für die Kirche in Didache 9,4 und 10,5* (Münster: Aschendorff, 1965) 1-2, and the most recent discussion by Willy Rordorf, "Les prières eucharistiques de la Didachè," *Eucharisties d'Orient et d'Occident* (ed. Bernard Botte, et al.; Paris: Cerf, 1970) 1. 65-82.

[74]All the possibly pertinent material, literary, ethnographical, and archeological, on the Jewish use of incense is marshalled by Erwin Ramsdell Goodenough (*Jewish Symbols in the Greco-Roman Period* [New York: Pantheon, 1954] 4. 195-208).

[75]See Friedrich Pfister, "Rauchopfer," *PW* 2.1, col. 278; Atchley, *History*, 64-66.

[76]"If they were sitting down to eat, each individually, he says a blessing for himself; if they have a banquet, one says the blessing for all. If wine is brought to them in the middle of the meal, each one says the blessing for himself; if after the

over the incense *(mûgmār)*[77] which was burned at the meal is discussed,[78] but the *form* of the blessing is not yet given. Though the pertinent sections in both the Babylonian and the Palestinian Gemara begin with the blessing over burning incense proper,[79] for the most part the rabbinical opinions recorded are concerned with blessings over other fragrant oils and perfumes. The Babylonian Gemara does provide a form of the prayer over incense,[80] but this has nothing in common with the *Didache* formula. However, as we have noted, the *Didache* incense prayer imitates formulas of blessing over the cup and the bread, which are not of direct concern here.

The foregoing evidence makes it plausible that the *Didache* incense prayer is a reflection of a Jewish-Christian *(ḥaburah?)* meal practice.[81] The reference to the burning of, and blessing

---

meal, one says the blessing for all, and he says [the blessing] over the incense, also if they bring in the incense only after the meal" (ed. Chanoch Albeck, ששה סדרי משנה[Jerusalem-Tel Aviv: Mosad Bialik, 1958] 1. 25).

[77]The Mishnaic Hebrew word *mûgmār* is cognate to Jewish Aramaic *gûmrā*, "burning coal," and it refers to burning incense, unlike the word *bōsem* (pl. *bĕsāmim*), which has the broader connotation of aromatic materials, spices, perfumes, etc. On the subject, cf. Samuel Krauss, *Talmudische Archaeologie* (Leipzig: Fock, 1910) 1. 237-38. It is not at all certain that the *mûgmār* of *m. Ber.* 6.6 is to be identified with the aromas, *bĕsāmim*, in the disputed sequence in *m. Ber.* 8.5 ("light, food, *bĕsāmim, habdālāh*" [School of Shammai]; "light, *bĕsāmim*, food, *habdālāh*" [School of Hillel]). For a commentary on this passage, see Jacob Neusner, *Invitation to the Talmud* (New York: Harper, 1973) 49-50. That the burning of *mûgmār* was a routine part of the meal is made clear also by *m. ᶜEd.* 3.11, where R. Gamaliel [I?] allows that on a festival day the floor between the couches may be swept, and that "they may place the *mûgmār* [on the fire]" (ed. Albeck, *Mishna*, 4.297). The same ruling is found in *m. Beṣa* 2.7 (ed. Albeck, *Mishna*, 2.293).

[78]*Tosepta Ber.* 6.6 does not mention *mûgmār*, but does note a difference of the schools of Shammai and Hillel concerning the order of the benedictions of the light and the *bĕsāmim* (a dispute similar to *m. Ber.* 8.5 but different in detail). Is this a sign that at the time of the compilation of *Tosepta Ber.* the custom of burning incense has already fallen into desuetude?

[79]"Rabbi Zērā said [that] Rabba bar Jeremiah said, 'When do they say the blessing over the fragrance? When its column [of smoke] rises'" (*b. Ber.* 43a [bottom]). Since an objection from Zērā follows, and then a final solution from the master based on the *distinguo* of "intention," it seems that the text is in slight disarray; the initial question (When do they say the blessing?) must be in fact Zērā's. The parallel text in the Palestinian Gemara is briefer but more coherent: "Rabbi Zeᶜirā [said] in the name of Rab Jeremiah, '[Over] the *mûgmār*, as soon as the smoke rises, it is necessary to say the blessing'" (*y. Ber.* 6.6, p. 10b).

[80]Over all *mûgmārôt* the correct form of the benediction is "[Blessed be You], who do create fragrant woods" (*b. Ber.* 43a).

[81]This connection was surmised by Robert A. Kraft in his commentary *Barnabas and the Didache* (The Apostolic Fathers 3, ed. Robert M. Grant; New

over, incense was then simply not understood by the (fourth-century?) Egyptian redactor of *Ap. Const.* VII, who, to make some "liturgical" sense of it, turned it into a *myron* prayer. One can at least speculate that a similar lack of comprehension of an antiquated custom may have been the reason for the *excision* of the incense prayer from the common archetype of the eleventh-century Bryennios MS and the Georgian translation. Though admittedly the foregoing argumentation does not amount to actual proof that the incense prayer indeed formed part of the original *Didache*, one can assert with some probability that the Coptic fragment reflects the archaic Christian liturgical practice of burning incense at the end of the communal meal.

In closing, it should be noted that the acceptance of the foregoing interpretation of the Coptic *Didache* text does not imply that all the negative references with respect to incense in ante-Nicene Christian literature should be regarded as, so to speak, merely a literary smokescreen, and that the metaphorical *osmē euōdias*[82] from Paul onward *must* refer to the actual burning of incense at Christian cultic gatherings. Rather, as in other cases of liturgical and doctrinal development, one is simply led to recognize the diversity of early Christian usage and belief. After all, to paraphrase Paul, one man's *euōdia* may well be another's *dysōdia*!

York: Nelson, 1965), but not explored in detail. I will quote his comment in full: "An important clue . . . might be discovered if the significance of the 'ointment' or 'perfume' (fragrant oil) of 10:8 were known. It is not impossible that this too is a vestige from Christian Love Feasts, since the Jewish fellowship meal ritual included a blessing on the aromatic spices ('ointment'?) which usually were burned" (p. 167). As his source for Jewish usage Kraft refers only to Gregory Dix, *The Shape of the Liturgy* (Westminster: Dacre, 1945) 425-6. Dix alludes to the burning of spices at *ḥaburah* meals, and notes the section from *m. Ber.* which we have analyzed previously. However, then Kraft seems to retract his suggestion: "But ointment/oil was used in many connections in early Christianity" and lists various uses such as the oil of baptism, episcopal ordination, etc. In commenting on the text, Kraft does not seem to know Lefort's edition of the Coptic fragment and the important rectification of the translation of *stinoufi*; otherwise he would not be faced by the dilemma of "ointment" being burned, which forces him back to the *myron* interpretation.

[82] Cf. Gerhard Delling, "ὀσμή," *TDNT* 5 (1967) 493-96.

REFLECTIONS ON ASPECTS OF IMMORTALITY IN ISLAM*

Jane I. Smith

Harvard Divinity School
Cambridge, MA 02138

As many of you know, I have been engaged for some time in a study of Islamic conceptions of life after death. It was for purposes of research in this area that I spent last spring in Egypt and other parts of the Middle East. There I had the opportunity not only to consider contemporary writings on this subject but to talk with a number of persons who have been concerned with Qurʾānic exegesis and the formulation of Islamic theology.[1] With reference to this modern perspective I would like to think with you today about some aspects of the Islamic experience of the divine in relation to the human—in this world as well as in the world to come.

The Ingersoll lecture is specifically designed to consider the possibilities of human immortality. One might well question the justification for talking about immortality in a religious tradition which puts primary stress on the idea of death and resurrection, and in whose understanding only God, in absolute terms, is not subject to death. Certainly the Qurʾān is eminently clear in its assertion that all persons will die, and insofar as immortality suggests exemption from death it is clearly inappropriate to describe the human condition.

It could be argued, of course, that because God has breathed His spirit into human persons, and that spirit by virtue of its origin is deathless, we mortals are provided with a sufficient claim to immortality. And indeed a logical approach to the problem would be to view the nature of humanity in the Islamic conception, beginning with Qurʾānic descriptions of *rūh* and *nafs* (generally translated "spirit" and "soul"), the understanding of human beings as God's viceregents on earth, and what have you. This has been done on numerous other occasions, however, one of the most notable being the excellent piece by Duncan Black

---

*This essay was delivered as *Ingersoll Lecture on Immortality* on March 1, 1977, at Harvard Divinity School.

[1] My colleague in this research here and in the Middle East has been Yvonne Haddad of the Hartford Seminary Foundation.

MacDonald actually entitled "Immortality in Mohammedanism."[2]

I would prefer to approach the question from a somewhat different perspective, one which I feel is fully supported by the Qurʾān itself. This is the perspective of human accountability. It means that rather than moving from an initial consideration of the human condition we begin with an understanding of the nature of the divine—God's unique oneness and integrally related plan for creation. We humans will surely perish, but that is not the end of it. When God so pleases we will be resurrected and will again be returned to Him. And the condition of that return is one in which judgment will be rendered in terms of the way we have chosen to live our lives.

Now it is clear that the judgment which the Qurʾān affirms on almost every page is a judgment based on human responsibility (I will beg here the theologically engaging but practically sidetracking question of free will and predestination). What is it that we are responsible to do? I would like to suggest that the link between ethical responsibility in this world and accountability in the next itself provides a means for human immortality. Furthermore, it is precisely through the discharging of this responsibility that in one sense we can be said to reflect the immortality that finally is God's alone. That is to say that there is a direct and specific relationship between the recognition of God's oneness and unity (expressed by the Arabic word *tawḥīd*) and the living of an ethically responsible life. As W. C. Smith has so succinctly put it, "Tawhid is something that man does: It is the recognition of God's unity, at the lowest level, and in a series of ascending levels, it is the appropriation to one's self, also the proclamation, also the implementation of that unity: the living of a life that has integrity, because oneness is divine. . . ."[3]

The message, then, is quite simple: because God is one it is incumbent upon human beings to live lives of integrity (integratedness), of moral and ethical uprightness, and it is on the basis of the degree to which one does that that judgment is rendered and final felicity or purgation accorded. It is no coincidence that those who have earned a place in the Garden are often referred to as *"ahl al-tawḥīd,"* the people who affirm God's oneness.

---

[2]In E. H. Sneath, *Religion and the Future Life* (New York: Revell, 1922) 295-320.

[3]An unpublished personal communication from W. C. Smith, Harvard University, May 1969.

Christendom has long agonized over the relative importance of faith and works, and in commenting on the Qurʾānic imperatives in regard to the day of judgment orientalists have differed as to which is the crucial factor. What the Qurʾān really seems to be saying, however, is that the faith/works distinction is a useless dichotomy. *Īmān,* that response to God by which one earns eternal reward and most often translated as "faith," actually means conviction or affirmation of that which God has revealed. The *kāfirs,* those destined for the Fire, are not unbelievers as the term is commonly rendered so much as rejecters of God's signs. The content of one's affirmation or rejection is expressed specifically through one's actions, as the Qurʾān so clearly indicates in Sūrah 20:112, "And whoever does good works, is a *muʾmin* (a person of faith or conviction) and need fear no harm. . . ." It is interesting that one of the main concerns of contemporary Islamic theological writing about afterlife is to underline its intellectual plausibility, a clear and direct continuation of the understanding of faith as conviction and affirmation. "Thus the Qurʾān has explained the life hereafter in a manner which is acceptable to the intellect and called for faith in it," says Muḥammad al-Mubārak of the University of Mecca.[4] Such intellectual arguments for the existence of the afterlife, as he calls them, are characteristic of much of modern exegesis.

It is a common observation that two of the earliest and most important messages given to the Prophet Muḥammad were of the oneness of God, and the accountability of human beings at the last day or day of judgment. And it is certainly the case that the Qurʾān in many places talks about faith in God and the last day together. It seems to me that the very obviousness of this juxtaposition may tend to temper the force of what is being communicated: that faith in God *is* faith in the last day, the *yawm al-ākhirah,* that the two are inextricably related. Sūrah 57:3 says, "He is the first and the last *(al-ākhir).* . . ." One Western commentator has suggested that this is the only exception to *ākhir* being used in reference to the last day.[5] I think, however, that this is exactly the point—the eschatological reality of the day of resurrection is consonant with the return to God, return being essential to the completion of God's plan for all of creation. This theme is suggested in contemporary Muslim writings, as for example when Muḥammad Zafrullah Khan says, "Islam insists

---

[4] *Niẓam al-Islam* (Beirut, 1970) 148.
[5] Dalton Galloway, "The Resurrection and Judgment in the Korʾan," *The Moslem World* 12 (1922) 350.

on belief in the life after death. There are several matters of belief which Islam regards as essential, but belief in the life after death is concomitant with belief in the Existence of God. Failing belief in the life after death there is no faith at all."[6]

It is interesting to see in this connection that *tawḥīd*, the oneness to which we have been referring, has two dimensions. One is the recognition of that oneness by God's creatures and the appropriation of it in living lives of integrity. The second and related understanding is of a circle of oneness by which God draws back to Himself all of His creation. In the narrative of eschatological events, the great reunion of God and God's creatures follows an actual period of disintegration during which God alone remains and all of the creatures pass away. Before describing this final eschatological reunion, however, I would like to suggest several interesting instances of a kind of "temporary" drawing together of God and certain of His creatures. One of these instances is the prototypical *miᶜraj* of the Prophet, that mythical and mystical night journey during which Muḥammad ascended up through the seven heavens, witnessing the Garden and the Fire, and coming finally into the presence of God. This journey, from which he returned to the world of humanity, has served as a paradigm for two other such passages. One is the mystical journey undertaken by adepts on the Sufi path, the psycho-spiritual trip through the spheres of one's own existence into the presence of God. But as the mystics of all traditions have known, this kind of journey, too, usually requires a temporary return into the world of phenomenal existence.

A third journey based on the *miᶜraj* model is that on which individual souls are reported to be taken shortly after the moment of death. The Qurʾān says little about what happens to individuals between the time of bodily death and the resurrection at the eschaton, but Islamic tradition has willingly filled in a great many of the details, with varying degrees of authenticity and reliability. One of the most commonly accepted narratives, reiterated by some contemporary Muslim writers, is that describing the immediate events after death.[7] As a kind of "dry run" of the final journey to God, the good soul, which slips easily and painlessly from the body, is wrapped in perfumed coverings and taken by angels up through the seven successive layers of

[6]*Islam, its Meaning for Modern Man* (New York: Harper, 1962) 184.
[7]Versions of this, related in eschatological manuals, are based on traditions such as those cited in the following: *Ṣaḥīḥ Muslim* 51:75; *al-Sunan* (Nasāʾī) 21:9; *al-Sunan* (Ibn Mājah) 37:31; *Musnad* (Aḥmad ibn Ḥanbal) II:364, IV:287, 295, VI:139; *Musnad* (Tayālisī) Nos. 753, 2389.

heaven. At each of the seven gates the soul is asked, "Who are you?" and Gabriel answers "This is so-and-so," who did various kinds of good deeds during his life. The end of the journey is a vision of God, after which the soul returns to the grave to be reunited with the body. Souls of the less fortunate, those who rejected the signs of God and wreaked corruption on earth, have to be pulled forth from their bodies painfully, "like skewers out of wet wool." They are evil-smelling and noxious, and upon reaching the lowest of the seven heavens are forced to turn back, as the angels therein will not grant them admittance. In a sense one can say that here the analogy of the return to God, the completion (though temporary) of the circle of unity, falls short. For at that final day even the *kāfirs* will be returned directly to Him for the judgment, though they will be denied (perhaps only temporarily) the final and lasting vision of the Lord.

To the best of my understanding, most of the elaboration of detail concerning the various modes of dispensation of justice in the hereafter is not intended to be descriptive as much as instructive. One senses in reading through the literature of Islam concerning the afterlife that there is a real sense in which eschatology is *now*—not so much the realized eschatology of the kingdom of God being actualized as the idea of the *now*-ness of human ethical responsibility. Much contemporary theological writing concentrates on this aspect of Islam as the *dīn al-wasāt̞*, the religion which occupies the central position in tying together this world and the next, *al-dunyá* and *al-ākhirah*. Khalaf al-Sayyid ᶜAlī, head of the Islamic Research Center at Azhar, told us last spring when we asked him about conceptions of life after death in Islam: "Islam tries to fight materialism and rationalism in the attempt to keep *dīn wa-dunyá* from being separated."[8] Affirming the resurrection, recompense and accountability, he said that the hereafter is necessary because it is involved in the way man lives his life in this world. It is essential that human deeds in this world and working for the world be by the *dīn*—we participate in the world by implementing God's plan for creation, awaiting recompense in the end.

Through various of the approaches I have been proposing for an understanding of human immortality, there runs a theme that

---

[8]Cf. Sayyid Quṭub, *Mashāhid al-Qiyāmah fīʾl-Qurʾān* (Cairo: Dār al-Maᶜārif, 1961) 37: "Between the two worlds there is little distinction and at times there is no distinction at all. Sometimes God will show you that this world and the next are co-existent. At times the story takes place in this world and then it continues in the hereafter. . . ."

suggests the rich potential of the Islamic worldview—it is what I call a kind of bi-dimensionality. Recognizing on one hand the certainty of human fallibility and the limitations of human understanding, it nonetheless suggests, in fact promises, that which moves beyond this into the sphere of God's possibility. We have already seen this bi-dimensionality illustrated in the conjunction of faith and works in the human response of *īmān,* in the relation of *dunyá* and *ākhirah,* and in *tawḥīd* itself as both God's singleness and God's drawing back to Himself all of creation in a circle of unity.

There seems to be something in (modern) Western mentality that urges us to dichotomize, to see things as either/or. Thus we persist in asking such questions as: Are Islamic descriptions of the Garden and the Fire to be taken literally or figuratively? Is the often-discussed punishment of the grave physical or spiritual? While these questions have been debated by many generations of Muslims too, it nonetheless seems to me that the totality of the Islamic understanding suggests that the answer to the either/or is actually *yes.* That is, in considering whether certain eschatological features are to be taken literally or symbolically one must take into consideration the possibility that both are true. The *ḥūr,* the black-eyed maidens of paradise promised to the faithful,[9] may indeed be there for those who expect and want them. The bazaars to which the faithful can go daily to purchase new apparel in order to impress their mates waiting in tents made of pearl[10] for some may be a reality. Even the bridge over which the faithful and faithless alike must attempt to pass[11] and the basin where the Prophet Muḥammad waits to greet his community[12] can be seen as literal and/or as figurative without one interpretation necessarily negating the other.

There is another way in which the bi-dimensionality of Islam is expressed, and this, too, is a theme that has direct relationship to questions of afterlife and eternity. That is the fact that Islam itself

[9] See Qurʾān 54:44; 20:52; 72:55; 22:56.

[10] al-Baghawī, *Mishkat al-Masābīḥ* (trans. A. N. Matthews; Calcutta: Hindoostanee Press, 1809) 2. 621-26.

[11] See, e.g., *al-Jāmiʿ al-Ṣaḥīḥ* (Bukhārī) 81:48, 52; 97:24; *Ṣaḥīḥ Muslim* I:302; *Musnad* (Aḥmad ibn Ḥanbal) II:275, 368; III:11, 16, 25, 383; IV:14. The bridge is not specifically mentioned in the Qurʾān, but many commentators suggest it is that to which 19:71 refers.

[12] The basin *(ḥawḍ)* is also not mentioned in the Qurʾān but is referred to with great frequency in traditional materials and is attested to by such creeds as the *Fiqh Akbar II* (Art. 21) and the *Sharḥ al-ʿAqāʾid al-Nasafīyah.*

is both an individual and a communal phenomenon. The word *islām* signifies both the individual act of surrender by which one expresses the *tawḥīd* of God *and* the community of those who together recognize God's lordship over humanity. Implicit from the earliest days of Islam as a community has been the understanding that one cannot be a Muslim outside that community; such statements are being articulated explicitly in contemporary Muslim writings. One of the most interesting of the stories related in the eschatological manuals is that of the community of the faithful on the day of resurrection moving together for a prophet to act as intercessor with God. One by one they go to Adam, Noah, Abraham, Moses, and Jesus, but each has to proclaim himself inadequate to intercede. Finally they reach the Prophet Muḥammad who confesses that he is able to intercede *for his community* with God.[13] This very emphasis on community suggests another aspect of bi-dimensionality —immortality in Islam is not simply an individual human possibility, if indeed we can permit the term at all, but must be seen as related on one dimension to the group of which one is a member and on the other dimension to God.

Recognizing that the final return to God suggests a breaking out of the bounds of time, a return, if you will, to the absolute timelessness of immortality, we must nonetheless take into account the obvious fact that there is a sense of historical progression in Islam in relation to eschatology. A kind of time-frame can be constructed in which events of individual destiny after death as well as the cataclysmic events of the eschaton will take place.

We noted earlier that there is little mention in the Qurʾān of what happens to persons who have died during the period between immediate death and resurrection. The Holy Book picks up the story with the tremendously exciting descriptions of the reversal of the natural order that will occur just preceding the coming of the final hour of resurrection and judgment. From early on, however, questions were inevitably raised about the intermediate or waiting period: are we asleep? are we in communion with our family and friends? do we receive reward or punishment? The name generally given to the period and / or the place of this intermediate stay is *barzakh*, mentioned three times

---

[13]Many traditions attest to the intercession of the prophet Muḥammad; see, e.g., *al-Jamiʿ al-Ṣaḥīḥ* (Bukhārī) 8:56; 24:50; 60:3, 8; *Ṣaḥīḥ Muslim* 1:322, 326-29; *Musnad* (Aḥmad ibn Ḥanbal) I:4, 281, 295; III:116, 247; IV:416.

in the Qur³ān but subject to several possible interpretations.¹⁴ Tradition has come to assign to that place or period a series of clearly-defined events, some of which are confirmed by the orthodox creeds of Islam. I mentioned before the kind of *mi^crāj* journey on which souls sometimes are said to be taken immediately after death. Upon return from that journey, and after having been reunited with the body, the soul is visited by several personages. The angels Munkar and Nakīr, fearsome of visage and with fangs rending the ground, come with the questions: Who or what is your God, your prophet, your religion, your scripture and your prayer-direction?¹⁵ For those who can answer the questions, a window is opened in the top of the grave for sweet breezes to waft in from the Garden of eternity, reminding the faithful of what awaits him or her on the day of resurrection. For the one so conditioned by past deeds that the answers do not easily come, the punishment of the grave sets in. To every person a personification of his or her deeds done while on the earth appears as another reminder of the relationship of one's actions to the final punishment or reward.¹⁶

The question of the punishment of the grave is one which has occupied Islamic theologians through the centuries. Again the orthodox conclusion has been that this punishment is a reality,¹⁷ and elaborate details have been given in the traditions about the tomb itself tightening around the poor unfortunate being inside

---

¹⁴Found in Qur³ān 23:100, 25:53 and 55:20, *barzakh* has been interpreted to mean, among other things, the physical barrier between the Garden and the Fire or between this world and the life beyond the grave, as well as the period of time separating individual death and final resurrection. The most comprehensive English work on the subject is Ragnar Eklund, *Life Between Death and Resurrection According to Islam* (Uppsala: Almqvist and Wiksell, 1941).

¹⁵Non-Qur³ānic and seldom mentioned by name in the canonical traditions, these angels are referred to frequently in the medieval Islamic texts and are part of such credal statements as the *Waṣīyat Abī Ḥanīfah,* the *Fiqh Akbar II* (see note 17 below) and the *Sharḥ al-^cAqā³id al Nasafīyah.*

¹⁶Reminiscent of the female *daena* of Zoroastrian mythology, the personification of one's deeds who visits the third day after death in the form of a beautiful maiden or ugly hag, this figure in Islamic lore is portrayed as a male personage whose appearance corresponds to the quality of the deeds represented.

¹⁷See, e.g., the *Waṣīyat Abī Ḥanīfah* (Art. 18): "We confess that the punishment in the tomb shall take place without fail," and the *Fiqh Akbar II* (Art. 23): "The interrogation of the dead in the tomb by Munkar and Nakīr is a reality and the reunion of the body with the spirit in the tomb is a reality. The pressure and the punishment in the tomb are a reality that will take place in the case of all the infidels, and a reality that may take place in the case of some sinners belonging to the Faithful."

so that his or her shrieks can be heard by animals passing through the graveyard.[18] It is fascinating to see how some modern interpreters have dealt with this question of punishment. There is a kind of transition from physical punishment, although the line is obviously not a sharp one, to a semi-psychological torment. This is also closely related, of course, to the question of *what* remains of the human individual after death. When I refer to contemporary interpretations I am not necessarily speaking of a majority perspective, but rather pointing out some of the kinds of thinking that seem to be illustrated by the better-known writers. With the full recognition that the physical body rapidly disintegrates, some have nonetheless felt that despite the death of the brain cells the memory *per se* continues, "remaining alive constantly," as Muṣṭafá Maḥmūd says, "reminding us in our second spiritual life (meaning the life of the grave) of every deed we have done."[19] According to ᶜAbd al-Razzāq Nawfal, another contemporary writer on questions of life after death, "There is no question about the punishment in the grave. In whatever form a person may be buried, the cells start their work to remind him of what he was."[20] The brain cells take a long time to disintegrate, he says, and while they may of course participate in the process of transmutation, appearing in other animals, plants or whatever,[21] they will continue until the day of resurrection to affect and to remind the living soul who is in *barzakh* of his or her good and evil past deeds. Thus the main concern of this *barzakh* life, as with the life on earth, is with activity and human responsibility.

I tried to make the point earlier that the appropriation to oneself of the *tawḥīd* of God, that process through which one lives with integrity, is a way of understanding the possibility of human immortality, as it relates both to life in this world and to the final felicity that comes after God's resurrection of all persons. Now as we move through the time sequence of after-death events, we come to that period dramatically portrayed in the Qurᵓān in

---

[18] A recent study of contemporary Egyptian beliefs about life after death by sociologist Sayyid ᶜUways (*Min Malāmiḥ al-Mujtamaᶜ al-Maṣrī al Muᶜaṣir* [Cairo: al-Markaz al-Qawmī, 1965]) suggests that such beliefs are still held by a large portion of Egyptian society.

[19] *Riḥlat min al-Shakk ᵓilāᵓ l-Īmān* (Cairo: Dār al-Nahḍīyah al-ᶜArabīyah, 1971). Muṣṭafá Maḥmūd is a Cairo journalist, a self-styled theologian whose writings on questions of life after death and other religious subjects are readily accessible and widely read in his part of the Islamic world.

[20] *Yawm al-Qiyāmah* (Cairo: Dār al-Shaᶜb, 1969) 77-80.

[21] Cf. Abuᵓl-ᶜAlá al Maudūdī, *al-Ḥaḍārah al-Islamīyah* (Beirut: Dār al-ᶜArabīyah, 196-?) 247ff.

which the natural order will be disrupted, cataclysmic events signalling that resurrection or *baᶜth*. Keeping in mind the *integratedness* of a life lived in response to God, we can see the force of what is graphically described as a day of *disintegration,* in both cosmic and ethical/moral terms.

According to the understanding of the Qurʾān this is a day when the heavens are split apart (25:27), when the earth will be rent asunder (50:43), when the mountains will be set moving (18:45), when heaven will be rolled up like a scroll (21:104) and many other specific signs given indicating the reversal of the natural order and a disintegration of the structure of the natural universe. It is fascinating to observe that the signal warning of this impending cosmic upheaval in traditional and in many contemporary accounts is actually a disruption of the ethical/moral order, that personal and societal structure through which one in concrete terms lives out the process of integration/integrity consequent of one's affirmation of the being and will of God. Some of these indications, seen in the context of the fabric of Muslim ethics, are that liars and traitors will be trusted and the righteous belied, usury will be acceptable, a man will disobey his parents and obey his wife (thereby upsetting the family structure), men will have open intercourse with women on the streets, wine-drinking will be commonplace, and the like.[22] (It should be noted that there will be a temporary restoration of the ethical order with the coming of the Mahdi.)

The actual arrival of the Hour is made known to all on earth and in the heavens through a series of events which are clearly cosmic in nature. For pure drama and power in description of these events I have found nothing, aside from the Qurʾānic portrayals, as exciting as the passages from Abū Ḥāmid al-Ghazālī's medieval treatise on eschatology, *al-Durrah al-Fākhirah*.[23] Listen to the events to take place at the blowing of the trumpet ushering in the arrival of the Hour:

> Then the mountains will be scattered and will move like the clouds; the seas will gush forth one into the other and the sun will be rolled up and will return to ashes; the oceans will overflow until the atmosphere is filled up with water. The worlds will pass into each other, the stars will fall like a broken string of pearls and the sky will become like rose balm, rotating like a turning millstone. The earth will shake with a tremendous shaking,

---

[22]See, e.g., Muḥammad Ibn Raṣūl al-Ḥusaynī al-Barzinjī, *al-Ishāᶜah li-Ishrāṭ al-Saᶜah* (Cairo, 1384 A.H.) 70–76.

[23]Leipzig: G. Kreysing, 1877 (Arabic text and French translation by Lucien Gautier).

sometimes contracting and sometimes expanding like leather until God orders the stripping off of the spheres. In all of the seven earths and the seven heavens, as well as the vicinity of the Throne, no living being will remain. . . .[24]

No living being will remain. Here, after the final cosmic disintegration, we have a dramatic description of what Islamic tradition has seen as God's absolute oneness in the universe. All else has indeed perished, and there is no living being aside from Him in existence. Here God is not only the sole God, He is all that remains in the universe.[25] Muṣṭafá Maḥmūd calls this the point at which time disintegrates into eternity.[26] It is the moment when all life disappears, when God removes the veil from His face and all the earth is lit by it. God exists at all times, he says, but at that time He will also reveal Himself in His essence. At the day of resurrection, then, will come the manifestation of God's unicity, perfection and sublimity. Again listen to al-Ghazālī's portrayal of this magnificent aloneness:

Then God will manifest Himself in the clouds, seizing the seven heavens in His right hand and the seven earths in His left, saying, "Oh you shameful earth! Where are your masters? Where are your chiefs? You have beguiled them with your splendors and with your beauty you have kept them from concern for things of the hereafter." Then He extols His own praise as He so desires; He glorifies His eternal existence and His lasting power and never-ending dominion and victorious omnipotence and boundless wisdom. Three times He asks, "To Whom belongs the Kingdom this day?" No one answers Him, so He answers Himself, saying, "To God Who is one, victorious!"[27]

As ethical disintegration, a cosmic disintegration, and finally the stunning vision of God's absolute aloneness. Were this the end of the story, we would have to conclude that human claims on immortality are temporary at best, confined to a reflection of divine oneness through the expression of faith and works. But as *tawḥīd* means on the one dimension both the recognition of God's unity and the living of a life in response to that, on the other

[24] Author's unpublished MS, pp. 38-39.
[25] Qurʾān verses such as 55:26-27, "All that is upon (the earth) will perish, but the face of your Lord will abide forever," are being interpreted by many contemporary Muslim exegetes to refer specifically to this eschatological moment of God's aloneness. See, among others, Ṭanṭāwī Jawharī, *al-Jawāhir fī Tafsīr al-Qurʾān al-Karīm* 24:15; ʿAbd al-Karīm Khaṭīb, *al-Tafsīr al-Qurʾānī* 14:675; M. ʿIzza Darwaza, *al-Tafsīr al-Ḥadīth* 7:135; M. Maḥmūd al-Hijāzī, *al-Tafsīr al-Wāḍīh* 27:129-30.
[26] *al-Qurʾān* (Beirut: Dār al-Shurūq, 1970) 96.
[27] Author's unpublished MS, pp. 39-40.

dimension it signifies at once God's absolute oneness *and* the drawing back together of all creation to Him. Thus the very singleness of God's existence is balanced on the day of resurrection by the all-inclusiveness of that time. Of the many names given to this day, the single appellation suggested in 11:84—the *yawm al-muḥīṭ* or all-encompassing day—is the most telling. As the drama of the hour unfolds we see that after the magnificent manifestation of aloneness comes the reversal to a focus on human accountability. God brings all humanity back to life, i.e., back to Himself, in the *baʿth*, the resurrection of bodies, the in-gathering and infusing of new life as the first step in the process of calling human beings to an accounting of their earthly deeds. The *fact* of God's singleness is again balanced by the significance of the *act* through which humans are called to judgment, returning us to the theme of the integral relationship between God's immortal being and human ethical responsibility.

The Qurʾān, along with later eschatological writings, spares us little in describing the day of judgment as one in which even the most pious will be afraid. The resurrection itself is scarcely pictured as a time of great joy or gratitude on the parts of those to whom life is given again. Medieval manuals delight in elaborate portrayals of individuals awaiting in terror the actual judgment, standing in sweat up to their ankles, their waists, their shoulders.[28] It is at this time that souls experience most graphically the results of their deeds and misdeeds on earth. "The things about which they had been niggardly on earth now surround each of them. The one who refused to give a camel carries on his back a braying camel weighing as much as a huge mountain. The one who refused the alms-giving of a cow carries on his back a bellowing bull. . . ."[29]

And then comes the great judgment itself. Those who receive the book in which deeds are recorded in their right hand, says the Qurʾān, will be granted the joys of the Garden, while reception of the book in the left signifies the Fire and the Pit.[30] Tradition, of course, has picked up where the Qurʾān leaves off in describing these edifices of reward and purgation, and contemporary writers are still musing about such questions as their literalness, their inevitability and their eternality. Leaving these questions aside, let us consider briefly what it is that God has promised for those

---

[28] *Ṣaḥīḥ Muslim* 51:60-62; *Musnad* (Aḥmad ibn Ḥanbal) II:70, 105, 112, 125, 418; III:90, 178; IV:157.
[29] *Durrah*, MS pp. 64-65.
[30] Qurʾān 69:18-37; cf. 17:71-72.

who have been of the community of the faithful. The Qur'ānic assurance, apart from descriptions of the Garden, is brief and gentle: "For them there will be a home of peace *(dār al-salām)* in the presence of their Lord. And He will be their friend, because of what they have done" (6:127). This hope of abiding in the presence of God has been drawn more pointedly in some of the orthodox creeds, which specify that God's meeting with the inhabitants of Paradise will be a reality.

With their usual delight in lively detail, some of the traditions carry the story even farther. Ṣoubḥi el-Ṣāleḥ[31] relates the narrative that each Friday on the invitation of God men and women will make a glorious visit to the Lord. They will be taken (the men by the Prophet Muḥammad and the women by his daughter Fāṭimah) before the Throne itself, which is a huge esplanade of musk. There "the veil of light lifts and the eternal appears before His hosts like a full moon." Nor have these matters escaped the attention of contemporary writers. Nawfal talks about the ascent of the spirits in Paradise from one stage to another until they are able to see God face to face.[32] Much of contemporary Islamic thought, however, is remarkably similar to that of the ancient Muʿtazilites, and in response both to a literal interpretation of traditional materials and to writers like Nawfal expresses disdain for the idea that God will be seen plainly on the day of resurrection or any other day.[33]

Common to the various Islamic interpretations of the vision of God, however, literal or symbolic, is the understanding of the final and eternal recognition of the Lordship of the Divine. Even in that timeless stretch of eternity, when the circle has already been drawn from integration to disintegration and back to integration, the proper response to God is *islām*, the total recognition of the unique and abiding Lordship of God alone.

In the Islamic conception, then, God is one, and we are called upon to live lives of integrity. God is just, and we are called upon to deal justly with our fellow creatures. God is immortal, and in carrying out God's commands lies the possibility of human immortality. But as the Qur'ān so emphatically affirms, and it is woven into the fabric of all of the eschatological narratives, God is also merciful and compassionate, *al-raḥmān, al-raḥīm*. Perhaps

---

[31] *La Vie Future Selon le Coran* (Paris: Vrin, 1971) chap. 1, pt. 7.
[32] *Ḥayāt al Ukhrá* (Cairo: Maktabat al-Anglo al-Maṣrīyah) 106-7, 114, 122; *Yawm al-Qiyāmah* 44.
[33] See, e.g., Muṣṭafá al-Kīk, *Rasāʾil ʾIllayhim* (Alexandria: Maktab ʿAlāʾ al-Dīn, 1972) 101-3.

even more than justice, mercy seems a supremely divine quality. With the requirement to live lives of ethical obligation is also the Qur³ānic understanding that as humans we will err, and that mercy is abundant. And so into the stern affirmation of divine retribution comes an injection of hope. The Qur³ān says, *la shafaᶜah*, no intercession on that day, but centuries of Muslims have come to hope for the intercession of the Prophet Muhammad. The *kāfirs* will be in the Fire eternally, says the Qur³ān, yet many contemporary Islamic theologians are interpreting that to mean that as long as the Fire lasts the wrongdoers will be in it—but through God's mercy even that will be brought to an end.[34]

For me no writer, ancient or modern, has more convincingly expressed the essence of the Islamic teaching about divine immortality and human fallibility than Abū Ḥāmid al-Ghazālī. He was keenly aware of the strength of the ethical imperative. In his famous autobiography he writes: "To the road, to the road, little of life is left, and before you is a long journey. . . . If you do not prepare for the future life now, when will you prepare?"[35] And yet his *Ihya ᶜUlūm al-Dīn* and *Durrah* are full of stories of how God will in the last analysis bend and even break the rules, smiling in mercy on the one whose many wrongdoings are balanced by a single act of charity.

The way is clear and the responsibility is ours, says the Qur³ān. But the case is never finally closed until God has had the last word. All the signs are that eternity in the abode of peace must be earned through the ethical response of *tawḥīd*. But we are also assured that waiting beyond our best efforts and our frequent stumbles is the mercy of the Lord from Whom everything—even immortality—must issue, and to Whom, in the end, we all return.

---

[34] Syed Abdul Latif, *The Mind al-Qur³ān Builds* (Hyderabad: Academy of Islamic Studies, 1952) 59-62; Muhammad Zafrulla Khan, *Islam,* 196-97; Maḥmūd Shaltūt, *al-Islam: ᶜAqīdah wa-Sharīᶜa* (Cairo: Dār al-Shurūq, 1975) 43-44. These projections, too, are not without their base in Qur³ānic promise and are meant to explicate such verses as 11:108.

[35] *al-Munqidh min al-Dalāl* (trans. W. M. Watt in *The Faith and Practice of al-Ghazālī*, London: Allen and Unwin, 1967) 57.

THE QUEST FOR THE SPIRITUAL SENSE: THE BIBLICAL HERMENEUTICS OF JONATHAN EDWARDS*

Stephen J. Stein

Indiana University
Bloomington, IN 47401

It is an irony and something of an enigma that the Bible, one of the shaping forces in the theological development of Jonathan Edwards (1703-1758), has largely been ignored in the assessments of this colonial divine. Edwards himself acknowledged its influence, especially during his youthful years. "I had then," he wrote, "and at other times, the greatest delight in the holy Scriptures, of any book whatsoever."[1] From his meditation on its pages he derived great personal pleasure as well as guidance and substance for his preaching. His enthusiasm for scriptural study never failed. Six months before his death he disclosed to the trustees of the College of New Jersey that he had undertaken two major exegetical projects with the hope of publishing "an explanation of a very great part of the holy scripture; which may . . . lead the mind to a view of the true spirit, design, life and soul of the scripture, as well as to their proper use and improvement."[2] Death interrupted his plans, but those nearest him recognized the considerable impact of the Bible upon his work. Samuel Hopkins—student, friend, and first biographer—observed that Edwards had "studied the Bible more than all other books, and more than most other divines do." The "great pains" he had taken in that pursuit, according to Hopkins, laid the foundation for his "religious principles."[3]

---

*The author wishes to thank the National Endowment for the Humanities for a fellowship in 1974-1975 which made possible the research for this essay. An earlier version was read at the annual meeting of the American Society of Church History at Atlanta in December 1975.

[1] Jonathan Edwards's "Personal Narrative" in Samuel Hopkins, *The Life and Character of the Late Reverend Mr. Jonathan Edwards* (Boston: Kneeland, 1765), reprinted in David Levin, ed., *Jonathan Edwards: A Profile* (New York: Hill & Wang, 1969) 32.

[2] Letter of Oct. 19, 1757 (Levin, *Edwards*, 77).

[3] Levin, *Edwards*, 40-41. See also p. 82 for additional comments on Edwards's biblical interests.

Despite such clues, few have taken seriously the place of the Bible in Edwards's thought. Much more attention, by contrast, has been directed to the philosophical side of his endeavors. One nineteenth-century biographer and editor, Sereno E. Dwight, who did investigate some of Edwards's scriptural materials offered a rather unbalanced assessment of his manuscripts, declaring that possibly "no collection of Notes on the Scriptures, so entirely original, can be found"—a judgment that is not substantiated by the notebooks.[4] Dwight's high opinion resulted in the publication of an abridged version of the "Notes on Scripture" in 1830.[5] However, the published exegetical reflections of "America's greatest metaphysical genius"—a tribute rendered by Perry Miller—have not attracted much notice from scholars.[6] The growing body of literature on Edwards reflects little interest in this aspect of his thought.[7]

This essay focuses upon one area in need of investigation, namely, the hermeneutical issue. What leading principles controlled Edwards's interpretation and use of the Bible? And consequently, what were the implications of those principles for his exegetical thought? The answers to these questions provide an occasion to describe his search for the spiritual sense of the Scripture. In this quest Edwards shared certain assumptions with the Reformation tradition, but in other ways he departed from

---

[4] Sereno E. Dwight, ed., *The Works of President Edwards: With a Memoir of His Life* (10 vols.; New York: Converse, 1829-30) 1. 58.

[5] See ibid., 9. 113-563.

[6] Perry Miller, "Jonathan Edwards on the Sense of the Heart," *HTR* 41 (1948) 123.

[7] Much of the literature published in the last twenty-five years has taken its lead from Perry Miller (*Jonathan Edwards* [New York: Sloane, 1949]) who reflects little interest in the biblical influences upon Edwards. Ralph G. Turnbull (*Jonathan Edwards, The Preacher* [Grand Rapids: Eerdmans, 1958]) discusses the subject but lacks critical distance. The same is true of the more recent volume by Harold Simonson, *Jonathan Edwards: Theologian of the Heart* (Grand Rapids: Eerdmans, 1974). The best statement on the Bible in Edwards's thought is Conrad Cherry, "Word and Spirit" (*The Theology of Jonathan Edwards: A Reappraisal* [Garden City, N.Y.: Doubleday, 1966] 44-55). Cherry approaches Edwards as an heir of and spokesman for the Calvinist tradition. William A. Clebsch hints at the significance of the Bible in his recent study on Edwards (*American Religious Thought: A History* [Chicago: University of Chicago, 1973] 11-56). Perry Miller did display an interest in Edwards's use of images; see the introduction to his edition of *Images or Shadows of Divine Things by Jonathan Edwards* (New Haven: Yale University, 1948); see also the essay by Mason I. Lowance, Jr., "'Images or Shadows of Divine Things' in the Thought of Jonathan Edwards," *Typology and Early American Literature* (ed. Sacvan Bercovitch; Amherst: University of Massachusetts, 1972) 209-44.

prevailing patterns of Protestant exegesis. In contrast to the Reformation accent upon the sufficiency of the singular literal sense of the Bible, he underscored the multiplicity of levels of meaning in the text and the primacy of the spiritual. Edwards spoke of the Bible as the source and the norm of his theology, but often it appears that the Scripture was more the occasion than the origin or measure of his reflections. For him the biblical principle was an open and expansive factor.

Edwards derived his basic perspective on the Bible from the Protestant Reformation. He was fully aware of the hermeneutical heritage of the sixteenth century. He too celebrated the power and sufficiency of the Word of God, a term he used interchangeably with Bible and Scripture, submitting to its authority as he conceived it in his thought and life. As a young man of twenty he called the Scripture "the only rule of our faith and practice."[8] From that perspective Edwards never deviated during his lifetime. Through the years he strenuously resisted a number of challenges which he regarded as attempts to displace the Bible from its position as the foundation of Christian theology.

For example, in response to the rising claims on behalf of reason and natural religion articulated by spokesmen for the Enlightenment, Edwards developed an extended argument supporting the necessity of revelation in Christianity. A catena of entries on this topic stretches through the manuscripts of his principal notebook, the "Theological Miscellanies."[9] In that chain of reflections he described the natural restrictions upon human knowledge of God and the insufficiency of other sources of information about him. Even the best efforts of philosophers and the learned cannot transcend these limitations. Edwards found the remedy for this situation in an undeniable inclination on the part of God to communicate with his creatures. "Revelation may be argued," he wrote in 1723, "not only from the necessity we have of it, by reason of the darkness we have contracted by the fall; for seeing man is created for that end [for]

---

[8]"Theological Miscellanies" (Manuscripts, Beinecke Rare Book and Manuscript Library: Yale University, New Haven) no. 160. Hereafter this series is cited as "Miscellanies," and individual entries are identified by number, not page. The texts of the "Miscellanies" quoted in this essay are from typescripts prepared by Thomas A. Schafer of McCormick Theological Seminary, an editor on the Yale edition of *The Works of Jonathan Edwards*. Here and elsewhere in this article, manuscript citations have been edited by the author in accordance with the general editorial principles of the Yale edition.

[9]E.g., see "Miscellanies," 127, 181, 358, 359, 514, 582, 979, 1170, 1126, 1239, 1304, and others including some cited below.

which he certainly is, it is a strange thing, that there should be no mutual communication between him and God."[10] The ultimate goal of God's creation requires communication between the Creator and the creatures. Later Edwards made the same point in a different manner by underscoring the "gross darkness and brutal stupidity" prevailing in areas of the world without revelation. "I am of the mind," he wrote, "that mankind would have been like a parcel of beasts, with respect to their knowledge in all important truths, if there never had been any such thing as revelation in the world, and that they never would have rose out of their brutality."[11] The natives of America, he thought, confirm this judgment.

It is only through the light of biblical revelation, Edwards argued, that humankind attains "certainty, clearness and satisfaction in things that concern their welfare."[12] Without the Bible, "endless disputes" would have persisted concerning the being of God, the nature of the world, and the character of moral responsibility. "The doctrines of the Word of God are the foundation of all useful and excellent knowledge." For Edwards even most of the truth obtainable through philosophy derives, at least indirectly, from "the reliques of revelation." Accordingly, philosophy assumes a secondary position at best. "'Tis therefore unreasonable to suppose," he wrote, "that philosophy might supply the defect of revelation; for without revelation there would be no such thing as any good philosophy: that is, except now and then in some rare instances, and those attended with abundance of darkness and imperfection."[13] From his standpoint, all of Christian theology "depends on divine revelation."[14] The light of nature comes off a poor second to the "gospel scheme" revealed in the Scripture.

Secondly, as a response to a different challenge against the Bible, during the years of the religious awakenings in the American colonies Edwards organized an attack upon the enthusiasts, the radical revivalists, who offered visions and private revelations as authentication of their own religious experiences. He dismissed their efforts and scorned their claims.

[10] "Miscellanies," 129.
[11] Ibid., 350.
[12] Ibid., 1297.
[13] Ibid., 350.
[14] Ibid., 837. Edwards probably intended to publish his reflections on the nature of revelation in his contemplated "Rational Account of Christianity." See his outline of the proposed "Rational Account" (Manuscript, Beinecke Library).

The manifestation of bright lights, the appearance of glorious personages, voices from heaven, even scripture verses miraculously on the tip of the tongue—none of these was for him a convincing sign of true religion. In the treatise on *Religious Affections* Edwards condemned these and other extraordinary impressions as products of the imagination, charging that such delusions detracted from the Word of God and led people to reject the gospel for unbelief and "bastard religion."[15] He lumped the radical evangelicals with other seers and visionaries who deceive the faithful.

Edwards was particularly bothered by the claim of the enthusiasts that the spontaneous recitation of Bible passages was an "undoubted evidence" that their affections were truly from God. Furthermore, those observing the revivalists in this practice were inclined to regard this phenomenon as conclusive proof that the speaker and his message were above reproach. "What deceives many of the less understanding and considerate sort of people, in this matter, seems to be this; that the Scripture is the Word of God, and has nothing in it which is wrong, but is pure and perfect: and therefore, those experiences which come from the Scripture must be right." Not necessarily so, said Edwards. One must distinguish between that which is occasioned by the Bible and that which is properly derived from it. The former is an abuse of the Word of God, whereas the latter is its "genuine fruit," the result of "a right use of it."[16] Satan, Edwards reminded his readers, cited the texts of Scripture when he tempted Christ in the wilderness. Frequently "corrupt and heretical teachers" follow the example of their master and in that are deceivers. The Word of God, noted Edwards, cautions against those who "pervert the Scripture, to their own and others' damnation (2 Pet 3:16)."[17]

Edwards responded to a third perceived attack against biblical revelation rising from Roman Catholic dogma and practice. A lifetime of study on the apocalyptic sections of the Bible combined with his uncritical acceptance of the cultural heritage of New England to feed this polemic.[18] He rejected the sugges-

---

[15] Jonathan Edwards, *Religious Affections*, ed. John E. Smith, *The Works of Jonathan Edwards* (New Haven: Yale University, 1959), 2. 287; see also 266-70.

[16] Ibid., 143.

[17] Ibid., 144-45.

[18] See my essays, "A Notebook on the Apocalypse by Jonathan Edwards," *The William and Mary Quarterly* 3rd ser., 29 (1972) 623-34; and "Cotton Mather and Jonathan Edwards on the Number of the Beast: Eighteenth-Century Speculation about the Antichrist," *Proceedings of the American Antiquarian Society* 84 (1975) 293-315. The text of Edwards's "Notes on the Apocalypse"

tion—whether real or imagined makes no difference—that the Catholic church was a sufficient teacher and guide for Christians, and he condemned the impression created by some that everything the priest says is true. In fact, according to Edwards, the priest feeds on deceit, laying claim to all sorts of miracles to enhance his influence and reputation. Bulls and anathemas, transubstantiation, dispensations and indulgences, holy water —these and other claims to the miraculous including the ability "infallibly to know the truth" are signs of the beast. The clergy, including both the pope and the priests, usurp the prerogatives of God and bear the mark of Antichrist.[19] In the judgment of Edwards, the priesthood has replaced the Bible in the Catholic church, ignoring the fact that the Word of God contains "all things that are necessary" for salvation.[20] He further determined that "too much weight is laid upon the testimony of the fathers" by some within Christianity, again notably the Church of Rome. The voice of tradition pales alongside the Bible. "I think," he wrote, "that God never intended that we should ever have any other sure rule of faith but the holy Scriptures, and has left everything else uncertain, that we might prize and improve them."[21]

Edwards thought that the "sword of the Spirit," the Word of God, would in the end be the efficient cause and instrument for the downfall of the antichristian forces—a kind of poetic justice. On the basis of his apocalyptic speculations he affirmed a continuing belief in God's providential care for the church and the imminent overthrow of the Antichrist as described prophetically in the book of Revelation. Each plague represented in that book brings the antichristian forces one step closer to their final destruction. The seven vials of Revelation 16 deliver the decisive blows as the forces of Antichrist are driven back by the "clear light of the gospel." For example, the great hailstones falling during the execution of the last vial are the "strong reasons and forcible arguments and demonstrations" derived from the Bible which contribute to the gradual weakening of Antichristianism. As the sphere of the Word increases, the Church of Rome will be destroyed.[22]

(Manuscript, Beinecke Library) is available in *Apocalyptic Writings,* ed. Stephen J. Stein, *The Works of Jonathan Edwards* (New Haven: Yale University, 1977), 5. 95-305. Below "Notes on the Apocalypse" is cited as "Apocalypse."
[19] See Edwards's discussion of Revelation 13 in "Apocalypse," 110-13.
[20] "Miscellanies," 61.
[21] Ibid., 72.
[22] See Edwards's discussion of Revelation 16 in "Apocalypse," 115-18.

In all three foregoing cases, against Enlightenment spokesmen, radical revivalists, and Roman Catholics, Edwards reaffirmed the Protestant ideal of the centrality of biblical revelation. For him that scriptural principle was linked to a basic theological assertion. "It seems to me," he declared, "that God would have our whole dependence be upon the Scriptures because the greater our dependence is on the Word of God, the more direct and immediate is our dependence on God himself."[23]

In pursuit of a full understanding of the Bible, Edwards invested himself heavily. As a young man he resolved "To study the Scriptures so steadily, constantly, and frequently, as that I may find, and plainly perceive myself to grow in the knowledge of the same."[24] He remained true to his resolution, spending a lifetime writing commentary on the Bible in his private notebooks. The "Notes on the Scriptures," the "Miscellaneous Observations on the Holy Scriptures" (also known as the "Blank Bible"), and several other manuscripts including the "Notes on the Apocalypse" contain thousands of exegetical entries ranging in length from a few lines to full expository treatises.[25] Edwards wove this network of commentary from his own observations on the Bible and from his reading of other sources. A youthful list of "Books to be Enquired for" was expanded through the years into his "Catalogue" of reading in which is documented his unending search for concordances, lexicons, chronologies, and commentaries to enhance his understanding of the Bible.[26]

The two projects described in 1757 also bear witness to Edwards's continuing commitment to biblical studies. The first he proposed to call a *History of the Work of Redemption,* a work of divinity "in an entire new method."

> This history will be carried on with regard to all three worlds, heaven, earth and hell: considering the connected, successive events and alterations, in each so far as the Scriptures give any light; introducing all parts of divinity in that order which is most scriptural and most natural: which is a method which appears to me the most beautiful and entertaining, wherein every divine doctrine, will appear to greatest

---

[23]"Miscellanies," 535.

[24]Dwight, *Works,* 1. 70.

[25]"Notes on Scripture" (Manuscripts, Beinecke Library) was published as described above; see n. 5. A small number of the entries in the "Blank Bible" (Manuscript, Beinecke Library) were published in the limited edition by Alexander B. Grosart (*Selections from the Unpublished Writings of Jonathan Edwards, of America* [Edinburgh: Ballantyne, 1865]).

[26]See the "Catalogue" (Manuscript, Beinecke Library), compiled throughout Edwards's lifetime, for examples.

advantage in the brightest light, in the most striking manner, showing the admirable contexture and harmony of the whole.[27]

The second project, less well-known, was entitled *The Harmony of the Old and New Testament.* It included a discussion of "the prophecies of the Messiah" considering their relationships and fulfillments, an exposition of "the types of the Old Testament" as they bear on the activities of Christ, and a particular explanation of "the harmony of the Old and New Testament, as to doctrine and precept." These projects occupied a high position on Edwards's agenda of activities. "My heart is so much in these studies," he wrote to the trustees at the College of New Jersey, "that I cannot find it in my heart to be willing to put myself into an incapacity to pursue them any more, in the future part of my life. . . ."[28]

This commitment relates to a second hermeneutical principle embraced by Edwards, one with a very Protestant ring. The Reformation had featured the literal sense of the text as bearer of the essence of the faith. The clarity and perspicuity of Scripture followed naturally, for the words of the Bible convey meaning and truth to all who read and understand. The Christian gospel, according to the Reformers, rests on the *sensus literalis* and is not hidden underneath layers of verbal camouflage. In particular the Protestant Reformation rejected the idea that each passage of the Scripture was subject to a variety of interpretations. The Puritan William Ames (1576-1633) summed up the prevailing judgment: "Hence there is only one meaning for every place in Scripture. Otherwise the meaning of Scripture would not only be unclear and uncertain, but there would be no meaning at all—for anything which does not mean one thing surely means nothing."[29] Edwards too was concerned with the literal sense. Indifference to it would have been tantamount to abdication of the Protestant principle.

---

[27]Letter of Oct. 19, 1757 (Levin, *Edwards,* 76-77). Edwards's project must be distinguished from the series of sermons on the work of redemption delivered in 1739 and published posthumously (*A History of the Work of Redemption* [ed. John Erskine; Edinburgh: Gray, 1774]).

[28]Letter of Oct. 19, 1757 (Levin, *Edwards,* 77).

[29]*The Marrow of Theology* (trans. & ed. John D. Eusden; Boston: Pilgrim, 1968) 188. For a traditional view of the Reformation hermeneutic, see Frederic W. Farrar (*History of Interpretation* [New York: Dutton, 1886] 307-54), and Hans W. Frei for an insightful discussion of "Precritical Interpretation" (*The Eclipse of Biblical Narrative: A Study in Eighteenth and Nineteenth Century Hermeneutics* [New Haven: Yale University, 1974] 17-50).

But the literal meaning Edwards pursued was not singular in appearance. Rather it embraced a variety of aspects, manifesting itself in numerous ways. The *sensus literalis* was a mixed interpretive category for him, united only in its basic communicative function. The various dimensions Edwards ascribed to the literal must be derived from examples of his exegesis. He wrote no systematic treatise on hermeneutics, although he commented at length on hermeneutical issues in his commentaries and notebooks, his sermons and published works.

Edwards commonly associated the literal sense with the meaning of the words themselves. In one case, e.g., he used the category as a near synonym for textual, explaining the phrase "see through a glass darkly" (1 Cor 13:12) by noting that the meaning of "darkly" hinges upon the fact that the term (Greek: *en ainigmati*) "would have been literally translated 'in an enigma or dark saying,'" as in a riddle.[30] The historical was another frame of reference he associated with the literal. It was in this framework that he interpreted the Old Testament prohibition against a woman entering a fight between two men. She who enters the fray on behalf of her husband and grabs the genitals of the opponent shall lose her right hand, according to Deut 25:11-12. In the view of Edwards, this rule "literally forbids" such a low blow. (He also maintained, interestingly, that the "mystical signification" of the statute demands application of the "great rule of equity," that we should do to another only "as we would that he should do to us.")[31] Edwards repeatedly applied the category of the literal to the fulfillment of prophecy. A case in point is his suggestion that the scriptural passages (Isa 34:4; Rev 6:13-14) which tell of the heavens being dissolved at judgment day and rolled together as a scroll and the stars falling from the sky will be accomplished literally.[32] The text, he believed, prophetically describes an actual future event. In all these examples the interpretation rests directly on the words in the text.

Edwards was emphatic about the communicative role of the Bible, a role closely associated with the literal sense. In a sermon preached to his congregation in November 1739 he sounded the theme that every Christian must strive to grow in the knowledge of divinity which, according to him, concerns "God and the great business of religion." Unlike other sciences, divinity is not learned "by the improvement of man's natural reason, but is taught by

[30] "Blank Bible," 826.
[31] Ibid., 162.
[32] "Miscellanies," 863.

God himself in a certain book that he hath given for that end, full of instruction." The Bible is the "guide" supplied by God to the world in the search for knowledge and the "summary" of all that is necessary to be known. Christians should pursue such knowledge, he contended, by diligent and regular study, an objective demanding more than a "cursory reading" of the Bible. "When you read," Edwards directed his congregation, "observe what you read. Observe how things come in. Take notice of the drift of the discourse, and compare one Scripture with another.... And use means to find out the meaning of the Scripture.... Procure, and diligently use other books which may help you to grow in this knowledge."[33] By such means one establishes a command of the literal sense of the Bible. Quite obviously Edwards practiced what he preached.

At this point, however, Edwards began to part company with the prevailing tradition of Protestant hermeneutics. Unlike many, he did not glory in the literal meaning of Scripture. For him investigation of the grammatical and syntactical intricacies of a text, exploration of historical and cultural contexts, and examination of prophetic dimensions produced at best a "speculative knowledge" of divinity. The fullest application of the mind to the biblical text results only in a "rational knowledge of the things of religion."[34] Speculative knowledge of the text has no redemptive value and is obtainable by all. According to him, such knowledge alone merely results in greater condemnation for those who have access to God's Word but reject it. Edwards described the Bible as "a sweet, excellent, life-giving word,"[35] but efficacious use of it requires a second step beyond the mastery of the literal sense of the text.

That something extra Edwards called spiritual understanding or knowledge. A clue to the meaning of this concept is found in the *Religious Affections* where Edwards noted that what is spiritual "in the ordinary use of the word in the New Testament, is entirely different in nature and kind, from all which natural men are, or can be the subjects of."[36] He was drawing upon the New Testament distinction between the flesh (*sarx*) and the spirit (*pneuma*), two separate and opposing forces at work in the

---

[33]"The Importance and Advantage of a Thorough Knowledge of Divine Truth," *The Works of President Edwards* (4 vols.; New York: Leavitt, 1849) 4. 3, 14. Cited below as Worcester reprint.

[34]Ibid., 4.

[35]Edwards's "Personal Narrative," Levin, *Edwards,* 36.

[36]Smith, *Works,* 2. 271.

Christian life. Speculative knowledge of the Bible is accessible to all men including those who are the creatures of the flesh. Spiritual understanding, by contrast, is available only to those who are "Spirit-filled," who have light from God to see and perceive the fullness of the Word. In other words, to possess spiritual understanding "is to have the eyes of the mind opened, to behold the wonderful spiritual excellency of the glorious things contained in the true meaning of it, . . . to behold the amiable and bright manifestations of the divine perfections, and of the excellency and sufficiency of Christ. . . ."[37] Elsewhere Edwards called this sight or insight a "new sense of the heart" produced by the presence of the Holy Spirit and a "spiritual supernatural sense" implanted by God at the time of conversion.[38] This spiritual sense has redemptive value, unlike the speculative knowledge of the Bible.

Edwards's emphasis upon the necessity of spiritual understanding did not eliminate the need for the literal sense. The communicative role carried out by the latter remains indispensable to the effective use of the Bible as a means of grace because a person cannot obtain a spiritual sense of the excellency of Christ without such a notion being conveyed to the mind through speculative knowledge. Although the Scripture is a "dead letter" apart from the Spirit of God,[39] nevertheless it is the interaction of *Word* and Spirit that produces spiritual understanding. In that judgment Edwards remained thoroughly Protestant.

But the hermeneutical position of Edwards is even more complex. He used the concept of "spiritual sense" in a second way, to denote that fuller understanding of the Bible which is one of the results of the sense of the heart implanted by God. That is, Edwards employed the same terms—spiritual sense and spiritual understanding—to refer to both the process and the product of God's grace. The second usage of these terms more properly constitutes a hermeneutical category than the first. This spiritual sense Edwards also distinguished from the literal, contrasting the restricted, confined character of the literal meaning of the text with the sweeping breadth and possibility of the spiritual interpretation. Spiritual understanding in this second sense was the goal and the focus of Edwards's exegetical efforts.

---

[37] Ibid., 280-81.
[38] Worcester reprint, 4. 4; and Smith, *Works,* 2. 275. See "Miscellanies," 782, published by Perry Miller in the essay cited above, n. 6.
[39] "Miscellanies," 204.

It may sound like double talk, but for Edwards the new spiritual sense received at conversion, or the impartation of spiritual understanding, allows the exegete access to the spiritual sense of the text, that is, to a spiritual understanding of Scripture. Often he mixed the two uses of the concept in a single context. At times it is difficult, if not impossible to separate the two, as in the following observation where Edwards says that a person who has not been

> spiritually enlightened beholds spiritual things faintly, like fainting fading shadows that make no lively impression in his mind, like a man that beholds the trees and things abroad in the night. The ideas ben't strong and lively and very faint, and therefore he has but a little notion of the beauty of the face of the earth. But when the light comes to shine upon them, then the ideas appear with strength and distinctness, and he has that sense of the beauty of the trees and fields given him in a moment, which he would not have obtained by going amongst them in the dark in a long time.[40]

Here his mixture of the two ideas seems natural.

The practical effect of Edwards's priority upon the spiritual sense was that he seldom rested content with an explanation of the literal meaning of a passage. Grammar, history, and prophecy were not enough. At best the literal sense provided the materials for reflection and meditation. Edwards described his own method of study in the following words: "Often-times in reading it [i.e., the Bible], every word seemed to touch my heart. I felt an harmony between something in my heart, and those sweet and powerful words. I seem'd often to see so much light, exhibited by every sentence, and such a refreshing ravishing food communicated, that I could not get along in reading. Used often-times to dwell long on one sentence, to see the wonders contained in it; and yet almost every sentence seemed to be full of wonders."[41] The wonders on which he reflected were the deeper insights into the text he ascribed to the spiritual sense.

Edwards relentlessly pursued the fuller interpretation of the spiritual sense in Old and New Testament alike. For example, in an entry on Gen 3:7 describing the nakedness of Adam and Eve, he conjectured that the first sin of the original parents was accompanied by the loss of physical beauty as well as by the first voiding of "excrements," for "they had never done this before." This interpretation appealed to Edwards because the external "vileness" resulting from the first sin described as the "sense of

---
[40] Ibid., 408.
[41] Edwards's "Personal Narrative," Levin, *Edwards*, 32.

spiritual filthiness" contrasted sharply with the holiness obtained through Christ.[42] This spiritual understanding he derived from reflection and meditation. In an exposition of Luke 11 where Christ denounced as hypocritical the Jewish practice of building tombs for the ancient prophets, Edwards distinguished two levels of meaning. The literal sense was the physical rebuilding of the tombs, and the spiritual sense was the continuation of the persecution of the saints in a manner similar to the abuses against the ancient prophets. "This is not the only instance," he commented, "wherein Christ is to be understood in two different senses when speaking of a thing, the one a literal sense and the other mystical."[43] (Often he used "mystical" and "allegorical" as synonyms for spiritual.) On another occasion Edwards's pursuit of the spiritual interpretation led him to state that the term "widow" in Scripture frequently means more than a literal widow, one whose husband is dead. In many places, he wrote, "by the widow seems to be intended one that is so in a spiritual sense, or the soul to whom those things are dead that formerly it was wedded [to]."[44]

The quest for the spiritual carried Edwards from symbol and metaphor to typology and allegory. Like the Puritans he was fascinated by typology, an interest he began cultivating at an early age. He spent a lifetime exploiting traditional typological associations between Old Testament figures and Christ, as in the case of 2 Kgs 13:21 where he noted that "as the man was raised to life by being cast into Elisha's sepulcher and touching his bones, so are souls restored to life by the death of Christ. His bones or his body slain does, as it were, impart life to us."[45] Edwards also extended the range of typology beyond its conventional bounds, making the category all-embracing in scope. In an early observation entitled "Types" he wrote,

> The things of the ceremonial law are not the only things, whereby God designedly shadowed forth spiritual things; but with an eye to such a representation, were all the transactions of the life of Christ ordered. And very much of the wisdom of God in the creation appears, in his so ordering things natural, that they livelily represent things divine and spiritual, [such as] sun, fountain, vine; as also, much of the wisdom of God in his providence, in that the state of mankind is so ordered, that there are innumerable things in human affairs that are lively pictures of the things of the gospel, such as shield, tower, and marriage, family."[46]

[42]"Blank Bible," 95.
[43]Ibid., 721.
[44]Ibid., 459.
[45]Ibid., 296.
[46]"Miscellanies," 119.

The natural order, the human sphere, and the whole realm of Scripture—all these fall into the expanded definition of typology.

Edwards declared that the Exodus was "the most eminent type" of Christ's redemption,[47] but for him almost everything in the Old Testament was typical. God used all kinds of things as "shadows of spiritual [things]." "Persons were typical persons, their actions were typical actions, the cities were typical cities, the nation of the Jews and other nations were typical nations, the land was a typical land, God's providences towards them were typical providences, their worship was typical worship, their houses were typical houses, their magistrates typical magistrates, their clothes typical clothes, and indeed, the world was a typical world," wrote Edwards.[48] Everything invited spiritual reflection, as in the case of Exod 27:20 where Edwards declared that the beating of the oil used in the temple lamps of ancient Israel was a type of the sufferings of Christ because "the Holy Spirit is procured for the enlightening of his church by his [i.e., Christ's] sufferings."[49] These typological associations were formed so readily in his mind that one must be reminded that Edwards himself insisted that some types remain unclear, reasoning that "we cannot now particularly explain what gospel and heavenly things they signified."[50]

For Edwards the gap between typology and allegory was small and the step over easy. His hermeneutical category of the spiritual sense makes it impossible to say when typology ends and allegory begins. He can be deceptively conjectural about both. For example, he wrote of 2 Samuel 20: "It is probably the design of the Holy Ghost to represent something spiritual in this story." That chapter describes the seige of the city of Abel of Beth-maacah by Joab, an officer of king David. Edwards had little to say about the historical situation, but immediately he constructed a full-blown allegory from the story. The city represents the heart of a person. Sheba, the object of Joab's pursuit, who had rebelled against David, symbolizes sin. Joab and his army personify the wrath of God. Joab demands that the head of Sheba be thrown over the wall before he will lift the siege; so God's wrath, wrote Edwards, stands against men until sin is given up. A wise old woman in the city persuades the people to save themselves by getting rid of Sheba. She (i.e., the old woman) is the symbol of the church or "a

[47]Ibid., 691.
[48]Ibid., 362.
[49]"Blank Bible," 71.
[50]"Miscellanies," 1139.

principle of true wisdom and grace in the heart of a particular person." Joab then lifts the siege. "So when once we have given up sin," concluded Edwards, "God proclaims liberty and peace to us."⁵¹ Here the spiritual sense of the chapter, according to him, had little if anything to do with the literal sense of the text.

Nevertheless, on another occasion Edwards explicitly warned against equating the explanation of "the mystical meaning of the Scripture" with the spiritual understanding of the Bible. "'Tis possible that a man might know how to interpret all the types, parables, enigmas, and allegories in the Bible," he warned, "and not have one beam of spiritual light in his mind; because he mayn't have the least degree of that spiritual sense of the holy beauty of divine things which has been spoken of, and may see nothing of this kind of glory in anything contained in any of these mysteries, or any other part of the Scripture."⁵² This judgment makes no sense alongside his exposition of 2 Samuel 20 unless one recognizes his twofold use of the categories of spiritual understanding and spiritual sense.

In his quest for the spiritual sense, Edwards gave himself free rein. His exegetical creativity was constrained only by the length of his attention. His commentaries contain long strings of ideas tied together by diverse miscellaneous associations, forming a vast complex of scriptural materials. Edwards simply assumed that every passage in the Bible held the possibility of multiple interpretations. He judged it appropriate that God "who is infinite in understanding" should "adapt his words to many things" and "speak so as naturally to point forth many things."⁵³ Edwards's interpretation of any given text could and often did randomly result in a statement about Christ, the church, or heaven; or in a statement containing a mixture of Christology, ecclesiology, and eschatology; or in none of these, but something else. Accordingly, the Bible did not function for him as a theological norm or source in any usual Protestant fashion because the literal sense of the text did not restrict him. On the contrary, the freedom and creative possibilities of the spiritual sense beckoned, and he pursued them with abandon.

---

⁵¹"Blank Bible," 256.
⁵²*Religious Affections,* ed. Smith, *Works,* 2. 278.
⁵³"Miscellanies," 851. For an illustration of the multiple meaning found in Scripture by Edwards, see my article "Jonathan Edwards and the Rainbow: Biblical Exegesis and Poetic Imagination," *The New England Quarterly* 47 (1974) 440-56.

A FORM OF ONTOLOGICAL ARGUMENT
Robert R. N. Ross
Skidmore College
Saratoga Springs, NY 12866

Tillich is widely held to be among those Protestant theologians who proclaim considerable scepticism about the arguments for the existence of God. This particular form of scepticism is not an attack on any individual argument or set of arguments, but rather is a wholesale rejection of the possibility of there being any "argument" for the existence of God at all.

The best evidence for attributing this view to Tillich derives from his own testimony. According to Tillich, "there can be little doubt that the arguments are a failure insofar as they claim to be arguments."[1] The primary reason cited for this "failure" is the suggestion that "the method of arguing to a conclusion" (1.204) is "*inadequate* for the idea of God";[2] indeed, it "*contradicts* the idea of God.[3]

More precisely, Tillich seems to hold that God's existence cannot be made a matter of *inference* from any given data about the world because that *method* of argument is inconsistent with a proper understanding of the *concept* of God:

> Every argument derives conclusions from something that is given about something that is sought. In arguments for the existence of God the world is given and God is sought. Some characteristics of the world make the conclusion "God" necessary. God is derived from the world. (1.205)

In contrast, Tillich claims the belief that God can be derived from the world opposes the idea of a transcendent God: "if we derive God from the world, he *cannot* be that which transcends the world infinitely."[4] The concept of a transcendent God and arguments which depend on "characteristics of the world" are, therefore, contradictory.

Since Tillich does not offer any defense of this view, there is little to say about it as it stands. However, it is curious that Tillich

---

[1] Paul Tillich, *Systematic Theology* (3 vols.; Chicago: University of Chicago, 1951-63) 1.204 (hereafter referred to by volume and page number in parentheses in the text).
[2] Ibid., my emphasis.
[3] Ibid., 1.205, my emphasis.
[4] Ibid., my emphasis.

makes these remarks at the beginning of his analysis "rejecting" the ontological argument, since the criticism, of course, is relevant to the *cosmological* argument. In fact, it is precisely the appeal of the ontological argument that God's existence is *not* made a matter of inference from any given data—from some objective feature of the world—but rather is discovered to be the *presupposition* of our ability to conceive of God at all.

It turns out that Tillich displays a rather peculiar attitude toward the ontological argument. First, he does not regard it as really an "argument." Second, his explanation of *why* the ontological argument is "no argument at all" (1.206) is ambiguous:

> The question of God is possible because an awareness of God is present in the question of God. This awareness precedes the question. It is not the result of the argument but its presupposition. (1.206)

Is Tillich offering us a reason to "reject" the ontological argument or is he making some form of it necessary?

I think it is correct to interpret these remarks as suggesting, in part, that it is in some way *intrinsic* to the concept of God that God is identical with that of which it is impossible "not to be aware." That is, in even raising "the question of God" we somehow come to discover that we are *already* aware of God. But from this, according to Tillich, it also follows that we cannot *meaningfully* ask the question of whether God *exists*.

> . . . there is no place to which man can withdraw from the divine thou, because it includes the ego and is nearer to the ego than the ego to itself. Ultimately, it is an insult to the divine holiness to talk about God as we do of objects whose existence or nonexistence can be discussed.[5] (1.271)

Tillich's indictment of the question of the existence of God as "meaningless" is made with considerable frequency:

> . . . the question of the existence of God can neither be asked nor answered. If it is asked . . . the answer—whether negative or affirmative—implicitly denies the nature of God. (1.237)

> . . . the discussions about the existence or nonexistence of God [are] meaningless.[6]

---

[5] Cf. also Paul Tillich, "Escape from God," in *The Shaking of the Foundations* (New York: Scribner's Sons, 1948) 47.

[6] Paul Tillich, *Dynamics of Faith* (Harper Torchbook; New York: Harper & Row, 1957) 46. See also Paul Tillich, "The Philosophy of Religion," in *What Is Religion?* (James Luther Adams, ed.; New York: Harper & Row, 1969) 71: "It is meaningless to ask . . . whether the Unconditioned 'exists'. . . ."

From the above it is clear that what Tillich rather loosely calls "the question of God" needs to be distinguished from a further question he considers: viz., "the question of God's *existence*." The former question is one that it is possible to ask meaningfully; the latter is not.

"The question of God" is a possible question because the concept of "God" is intelligible. In asking it, presumably we are asking about *what* "God" is. "The question of God's existence," however, is not a possible question. But it is not because of a certain feature Tillich attaches to the *former* question: viz., that an *awareness* of God is present in "the question of God" and this awareness is a *presupposition* of our asking it. The former question, then, establishes the basis for the impossibility of the latter.

What seems, in effect, to be happening is that Tillich regards the question of God's existence as "meaningless" only because he begs the question. If it is possible, as Tillich seems to think it is, to speak of an "awareness" of God which always precedes any question of his existence, then the question of whether God exists is "meaningless" precisely because Tillich has assumed there is necessarily only one possible answer to it even before it is asked.

Further, it is important to note that this awareness of God in "the question of God" must have the force of *logical* (not just psychological) necessity[7] in order for Tillich to be able to call "the question of God's existence" *meaningless*. One might, for example, think Tillich is simply saying that God's presence is so powerful in our awareness that to question his existence is psychologically unimaginable. This would be wrong because it would miss just that sense in which Tillich claims the question of God's existence *to be* meaningless: viz., that *any* answer to the question—yes or no—is meaningless. In short, Tillich argues the question is *nonsense*.

Of course, the psychological fact of any awareness of God is contingent upon *my having* it. Nor does this bear on the linguistic fact that one can still *sensibly* ask the general question: But *is* there, after all, a God?[8] To call that question *meaningless* presupposes that to simply *state* the question is to commit some *logical* absurdity. Thus, Tillich is guilty of begging the question just because he says there can *be* no answer either way (the

---

[7] In other words, the awareness must be *logically* prior to the question.

[8] Moreover, I can sensibly ask this question of myself even given "my awareness" of God, because I can question whether my awareness is veridical.

question is nonsense, improper), yet he assumes there *is* one (moreover, *only* one).

Far from rejecting *all* forms of argument for God's existence, then, Tillich himself seems committed to some *version* of one. It runs, roughly, as follows: If one properly understands the concept "God" to mean "that of which it is impossible not to be aware" (God "includes" the ego; an awareness of God is the "presupposition" of the question of God), then it is senseless to raise the question of God's existence. It is senseless to question the existence of that of whose presence one logically *cannot* be unaware.

The reason for thinking Tillich *intends* this is made stronger by his insistence that we are "immediately" aware[9] of God's presence in the question of God. According to Tillich, "man is immediately aware of something unconditional";[10] ". . . the ontological awareness [of the Unconditioned] is immediate, and not mediated by inferential processes. It is present, whenever conscious attention is focussed on it, in terms of an unconditional certainty."[11] Indeed, "the immediate awareness of the Unconditioned has not the character of faith but of self-evidence."[12]

Tillich apparently holds, then, that there is an awareness we *must* have of God which renders his existence both self-evident and indubitable:

> It is meaningless to ask . . . whether the Unconditional "exists," . . . .
> For the question whether the Unconditional exists presupposes already . . . that which exists unconditionally. The certainty of the Unconditional is the grounding certainty from which all doubt can proceed, but it can never itself be the object of doubt. Therefore, the object of religion is not only real, but is also the presupposition of every affirmation of reality.[13]

Thus, Tillich has "built into" his concept of God a sense of necessity that ranges over *our* awareness of God, as a result of which he regards it as senseless to raise the question of his existence.

This form of argument is also displayed in Tillich's

---

[9] Paul Tillich, "The Two Types of Philosophy of Religion," in *Theology of Culture* (Robert C. Kimball, ed.; A Galaxy Book; New York: Oxford University, 1964) 22.
[10] Ibid.
[11] Ibid., 23.
[12] Ibid., 27.
[13] Tillich, "The Philosophy of Religion," 71.

identification of God with "being-itself." Here, instead of saying with the ontological argument that God necessarily exists, Tillich implies that God's reality is a necessity of thought *when* anything is said to exist. Being-itself, according to Tillich, is that "which is always thought implicitly, and sometimes explicitly, if something is said to *be*" (1.163). However, being-itself is not simply an object of thought; it is also something which *itself* exists. That is, being-itself is the Unconditional which *itself* "exists unconditionally . . . [and] can never itself be the object of doubt." Moreover, that which is the presupposition of all thought—"the presupposition of every affirmation of reality"—*must itself exist* because our immediate awareness of it *in* thought has given its existence the character of "self-evidence."

II

Thus far I have intended only to give a rough picture of how Tillich's analysis of the concept of God bears *some* relation to the ontological argument. I think the evidence that there is a connection is sufficiently convincing to warrant further examination of the several remarks Tillich has to make about Anselm and the argument itself.

To begin with, Tillich indicates that he accepts as valid what he calls the "Anselmian statement."

> . . . the Anselmian statement that God is a necessary thought and that therefore this idea must have objective as well as subjective reality is valid in so far as thinking, by its very nature, implies an unconditional element which transcends subjectivity and objectivity. . . . (1.207)

This is not the clearest "statement" nor is it the clearest *re*statement of Anselm. Nevertheless, it is clear enough to see that at least Tillich agrees with some position whose conclusion is this: (1) the concept of God is subjectively intelligible; (2) it has an instance, in some sense, in objective reality.

Let us bracket for the moment the business about precisely *how* "thinking implies an unconditional element," since I will return to that shortly. (It is, in any case, a consideration that does not substantially alter the possibility of seeing Tillich as making the above claims.) What I want to consider first is the rather surprising fact that Tillich seems to want to deny that the ontological "statement" demonstrates the existence of God: "the statement is not valid if this unconditional element is understood as a highest being called God" (1.207). Nor can "the experience of an unconditional element in man's encounter with reality [be] used for the establishment of an unconditional being (a contradiction in terms) within reality" (1.207).

It is hard to know what to make of this. In the first place, Tillich cannot be worrying about the validity of Anselm's deduction, since he doesn't even state it. Consequently his "rejection" of the argument—for whatever reason—cannot be directed at the logical form of the argument itself. What is perplexing is that Tillich accepts the conclusion of the argument as valid on the one hand, yet then appears to deny that the conclusion has anything to do with the existence of God.

The issue forced out seems to be that of equivocation. The equivocation here is not, as it might first appear, between the "objective reality" and the "existence" of God, but between two different senses of the term "God" Tillich inadvertently uses.[14] To bring this out more clearly, consider what it is that Tillich is denying. Tillich denies that the ontological "statement" can establish the existence of "a highest being" or "an unconditional being" *within* reality. The ambiguity of these remarks lies in the fact that a highest being or an unconditional being "within reality" is precisely what Tillich could *not* mean by "God." Why? Roughly, because to be "a" (singular) being is to be *within* reality, where "within" has the force of "exists as a conditioned *part* of." More exactly, to be "within reality," on Tillich's account, is identical with membership in the class of "the totality of beings" (1.205). But God, properly understood as the *ground* of being, "*cannot* be found within the totality of beings."[15] The reason is that membership in this class entails being "subject to the categories of finitude"(1.235).

Now, clearly, something could not be both "subject to the categories of finitude"—i.e., a spatio-temporal object, an object "conditioned by space and time"—and also identical with God who is *un*conditioned.[16] However, it is important to note that the whole matter arises as a result of the rather arbitrary entailment relation Tillich sees between membership in the class of "the totality of beings within reality" and the notion of finitude. Traditionally, of course, it has been regarded as possible to say that God *is* a member of the class of the total number of beings

---

[14] However, sometimes Tillich equivocates on the term "exists" as well, as has often been pointed out.

[15] *Systematic Theology,* 1.205, my emphasis.

[16] Consequently, Tillich calls "an unconditioned being" a "contradiction in terms," because to be "a" being is to be *within* reality and therefore to be conditioned.

within reality, only a *unique* member of that class. For Tillich, however, that is quite impossible: for, by definition, a being "within the totality of beings" is a finite being—even if it is the highest being in that class. And God, of course, cannot be a finite being. On the other hand, Tillich's "rejection" of the ontological argument now seems quite misplaced. For Tillich does not deny that the argument establishes the existence of God as Tillich thinks "God" *must* be understood (viz., as being-itself), but only that it does not establish the existence of an unconditional being "within the totality of beings." Yet since that is precisely what Tillich does *not* mean by "God," who, as Tillich also puts it, is not a being "among others" (1.172), it remains entirely open that he is committed to such an argument insofar as it establishes what *Tillich* thinks must be God.

The question, then, is this. Is Tillich committed, if not to a formal argument, to some ontological "principle" which establishes the existence of God *when* "God" is understood as being-itself? It is my intuition that Tillich *is*. Since Tillich himself has no explicit argument to offer, it is difficult to identify the moves involved. Nevertheless, whatever form of argument it is, it is associated with Tillich's view of the relation between God as being-itself and the nature of "thinking," and what must be presupposed in order for it to be possible for there to be thought at all.

According to Tillich, there is a "principle"[17] that lies within the ontological "statement" which awakens us to the discovery that God *is* being-itself. Furthermore, since being-itself is the presupposition of all thought, it is, consequently, the presupposition of any possible conception of God.

Now Tillich says he wants to accept the "principle" of the ontological argument only, not the conclusion (viz., that God exists). But I see no reason to believe that Tillich is not committed to the conclusion as well. For being-itself, as we have seen, must have not only subjective but also *objective* reality. Thus, since being-itself is identical with God, the objective reality of God must be the presupposition not only for any possible concept of God but for the possibility of any thought at all.

Because being-itself is the presupposition of all thought, it is, according to Tillich, "a *necessary* thought."[18] It is that behind which thought "cannot go," that on which thought is "based" (1.163). It is that which *must* be thought whenever something is

---

[17]Tillich, "The Two Types of Philosophy of Religion," 22.
[18]Ibid., 15, my emphasis.

said to be. Being-itself is the *unconditional* element in our encounter with reality which transcends subjectivity and objectivity.[19] It is something of which we have an immediate awareness, and which transcends the distinction, in any analysis of thought, between the thinking subject and that which thought is about.

While not everything Tillich says here is entirely clear, I think it is clear that, according to Tillich, Anselm's argument views God as a "necessity of thought" in this way. That is, Tillich understands Anselm's "statement" to be the statement "that God is a necessary thought . . . an unconditional element in man's encounter with reality" which is the basis of all thought. Thus, it seems reasonable to assume that Tillich thinks Anselm has in mind what *he* has in mind by being-itself.

Furthermore, Tillich thinks Anselm is right in claiming this idea has *objective reality,* because Tillich believes that thought itself presupposes the reality of being-itself. That is, *when* God is understood as being-itself—a necessity of *thought*—then Anselm is right when he argues "that therefore this idea must have objective as well as subjective reality." Why does Tillich think Anselm is right? Anselm is right because he has recognized that *thinking* itself—the very nature of thought—presupposes the existence of being-itself. Consequently, since Tillich accepts from Anselm that being-itself has objective reality, it would seem that Tillich has accepted this as an argument that being-itself must *be*.

There are, one can say, two steps to Tillich's interpretation of Anselm's argument. For Tillich, it is part of the concept of "thinking" that (1) we necessarily think of being-itself if we are to think of anything at all (being-itself has subjective reality), and (2) being-itself must be (being-itself has objective reality).

III

I suggest we now examine more carefully what Tillich means when he identifies being-itself as the "objective presupposition of all thought." Tillich says that being-itself "remains the content, the mystery, and the eternal *aporia* of thinking" (2.11). It is "the basis of the being of all things whereby 'being' is taken absolutely, transcendentally as the expression of the secret into which

---

[19] Cf. *Systematic Theology,* 1.207.

thinking cannot penetrate, because as something existing it itself is based on it."[20]

Sometimes, however, Tillich tries to make this "secret into which thinking cannot penetrate" explicit. In Tillich's view, thinking requires "a point of identity [between subject and object] which makes the idea of truth possible" (1.207). This point of identity, present in every true judgment, is being-itself. The unconditional element which "transcends" subjectivity and objectivity is "the Absolute in which the difference between knowing and known is not actual."[21] Furthermore, "this Absolute as the principle of Being has absolute certainty. It is a necessary thought because it is the presupposition of all thought."[22]

What, first of all, does Tillich mean by the "point of identity" between subject and object which makes truth possible? What does he mean by the idea that being-itself, as that which subject and object share in common, "transcends" their separation?

Tillich's analysis of thinking entails that the distinction between subject and object be regarded as an *ontological* separation. On Tillich's account, any intelligible experience of an object consists not simply in having a certain relation to some object external to the thought of it, but entails, in some manner, a *uniting* of subject and object.[23] "Knowing" is said to be a "union" in which "the knower *participates* in the known."[24]

Because the separation between the thinking subject and any object is viewed as a *real* separation, to think that some x is F must involve, according to Tillich, a *real* participation in the form (what Tillich also refers to as an object's "true being"; 1.101) which constitutes the essence of that x. When one thinks of some F-ness, what exists in the subject is not just a relation to the F-ness of that object; rather, there is a union such that what exists in the subject, in some sense, *is* that F-ness.

Tillich is *not* saying that when I have a thought of something, say, of a stone, I somehow become identical with the stone or that it is the stone itself which is in my mind. Rather, my thought is an occurrence of an *essential structure* which is in some sense the

---

[20]Paul Tillich, *The Interpretation of History* (trans. N. A. Rasetzki and Elsa L. Talmey; New York: Scribner's Sons, 1936) 83, quoted in James Luther Adams, *Paul Tillich's Philosophy of Culture, Science, and Religion* (New York: Schocken Books, 1970) 45.
[21]Tillich, "The Two Types of Philosophy of Religion," 15.
[22]Ibid.
[23]Cf. *Systematic Theology*, 1.94.
[24]Ibid., 1.177, my emphasis.

same or identical with another individual occurrence in that stone: "The particular object is strange [ontologically separate] as such, but it contains essential structures with which the cognitive subject is essentially united and which it can remember when looking at things" (1.94-95).

Tillich, however, never fully explains in *what* sense my thinking that x is F is the *same* form as occurs in x. To avoid the suggestion that it is the stone which is in my head, Tillich seems to regard the distinction between a thing's "essence" and its "being" as a real distinction. What my thought is "united" with is the essence of the stone, not its "own" being. But the essence of that stone is not "in my head" either, and Tillich's account not only remains largely unclear, but, further, his talk of a union between *myself* and the stone doesn't do much to alleviate the idea that I—in my head—somehow *become* that stone.

Finally, there is a distinct sense in which to know that some x "is a stone" I *must* participate in (i.e., share) its "own" being. For Tillich argues that "the essences of things . . . have being, too."[25] At this point the ontological distinction between essence and being simply dissolves. For if the essence of a stone is not only that which is common to all stones, but also the "being" individuated in each particular stone, then my participation in the essence of that stone is identical with participation in its "own" being.

In any case, insofar as there is a sense of "being" which is common to both me and the stone in each thought of a stone, there is a being we both share. This common sense of "being"—that by which there is a union between the being of the knower and the being of the known—is the "unconditional element which transcends subjectivity and objectivity," the "Absolute" Tillich refers to as being-itself. This is the "point of identity" which makes truth possible. It is "actually present"[26] in both the subject and the object, and what makes it possible to speak of the form in my mind and the form of that stone as the *same* form. Since it is present in both the subject and the object, it "transcends" that ontological separation, and as such becomes that which the thought of anything presupposes.

By laying emphasis on the idea that the reality of being-itself is a necessary presupposition for all thought, Tillich has in effect replaced the concept of a "necessary being" with the notion of that being which is necessary for thinking. Tillich's remark that

---

[25]D. Mackenzie Brown, ed., *Ultimate Concern* (Harper Colophon Books; New York: Harper & Row, 1965) 45. Cf. also *Systematic Theology*, 2.21.
[26]Cf. *Systematic Theology*, 1.192.

thought itself is "something existing," and must, therefore, be *based* on being[27] indicates why Tillich feels he must accept Anselm's statement that being-itself has objective reality. Since thinking, in Tillich's view, is never *simply* a subjective phenomenon, it always involves a real participation of the knower in the being of that which is known. Thinking, therefore, always has objective reality. Thus, if God is being-itself, and if thinking presupposes the objective reality of being-itself, one can see why Tillich's reflection on the presuppositions of thought leads him to the conclusion that in "thinking" we must be immediately aware of the presence of God.

This somewhat involuted argument for the reality of God can be found in Tillich's earliest works. The ontological reality of God is described as a matter of *immediate awareness* to the self—an awareness upon which the possibility of any self-awareness, indeed of any knowledge at all, must be based:

> . . . the self grasps *within itself* the Unconditional as the basis of its own self-certainty . . . the Unconditional is neither object nor subject, but rather the presupposition for every possible antithesis of subject and object . . . the Unconditional is certainly the supporting ground of every theoretical judgment . . . there can be absolutely no certainty in which the certainty of God is not *implicite* present.[28]

Moreover, the certainty of God's reality is self-evident: "the certainty of the Unconditional is *un*conditional."[29]

Despite Tillich's insistence that he can accept only the principle of the ontological argument but not its conclusion, then, he is clearly committed to its conclusion as well. Tillich wants to say the argument is not about the existence of God but about the nature of thought. Nevertheless, Tillich's analysis of the nature of thinking *entails* the objective reality of being-itself. Indeed, its existence cannot be subject to doubt, for it is "affirmed" in every statement which attempts to deny it.[30] But being-itself and God are identical. Hence, Tillich's analysis of thought entails the existence of God. It is not so much that Tillich fails to see this, but that he simply refuses to make the conclusion explicit.

---

[27]Tillich, *The Interpretation of History*, 83, quoted in Adams, *Paul Tillich's Philosophy*, 45.

[28]Paul Tillich, "The Conquest of the Concept of Religion in the Philosophy of Religion," in *What Is Religion?*, 139-40, my emphasis.

[29]Ibid., 124.

[30]Tillich, "The Two Types of Philosophy of Religion," 13.

IV

One must acknowledge that Tillich's interpretation of Anselm's argument is not itself an argument. It is, rather, a claim about an argument—and a claim that is none too clear at that. Why, for example, does Tillich seem to agree that being-itself is "known in such a way that it cannot be thought not to be,"[31] but also hold that the ontological argument is not really an argument for God? By examining one further aspect of Tillich's grounds for "rejecting" the argument, we can see why Tillich holds such a view.

Tillich thinks there is a general line of criticism of the argument which can be made[32] and which is right: namely, that there cannot be "a logical transition from the necessity of Being itself to a highest being, from a principle which is beyond essence and existence to something that exists."[33] While it is not entirely clear just *what* transition Tillich thinks cannot be made, it seems reasonable enough to assume that the remark is meant as a version of a certain line of criticism that runs: one cannot argue from conceptual being to being in reality. That is, from an investigation of certain features intrinsic to a given concept one cannot determine whether that concept has any instances. Now Tillich states that his "ontological way is not a logical conclusion from the idea of the Unconditioned to its existence . . . a procedure that, of course, is impossible."[34] The problem, however, is that Tillich has no objection to talking of "ideas" necessarily *presupposed* in thinking as themselves having being. We have already seen how being-itself must be presupposed to *have* being when Tillich accepts Anselm's argument that this "idea" must have not only subjective but also *objective* reality. However, there are other "less universal,"[35] ontological concepts and categories,[36] constituting the "structure" of being-itself, which also *have* being. In fact, according to Tillich, "everything which can be conceptualized must have being" (1.179).

---

[31] Ibid., 15.

[32] And which has been made "from Gaunilo and Thomas to Kant." Ibid.

[33] Ibid.

[34] Tillich, "The Conquest of the Concept of Religion in the Philosophy of Religion," 129.

[35] That is, less universal than being-itself, but more universal than class concepts "designating a realm of being," (*Systematic Theology,* 1.164).

[36] Namely, the concepts of individuality and participation, dynamics and form, freedom and destiny, and the general categories of space, time, causality, and substance (*Systematic Theology,* 1.164-65).

Tillich's use of "being" is indeed ubiquitous, and appears to commit him to an extreme form of realism similar to that once held by Russell: "*Being* is that which belongs to every conceivable term, to every possible object of thought . . . being is a general attribute of everything, and to mention anything is to show that it is."[37]

What does Tillich have in mind by the thesis according to which everything that can be conceived must have being? I suggest Tillich is attempting to provide some sort of general principle upon which the existence of God as being-itself must be *presupposed*. For if the reality of God is the *presupposition* of any argument for his existence, Tillich apparently feels he can avoid the problems he believes are attached to any method of "arguing through a conclusion" in which a logical move from idea to existence is involved. That is, by getting us to admit to the reality of certain concepts presupposed by thought, Tillich believes we will be led to an awareness of an *ultimate* concept, being-itself, whose existence is the necessary presupposition of our being able to entertain any concept at all.

There are two kinds of concepts whose reality Tillich is interested in having us acknowledge. In ascending order of abstraction, they are: (1) the concepts of essences which distinguish things into "classes,"[38] or what Tillich sometimes calls non-actualized possible beings,[39] and (2) the general ontological concepts that are universally predicable, applicable to the members of every class.[40]

Beyond them lies the concept of that which is most universal—being-itself. It is more universal than even those general ontological concepts applicable to things of every class, because "being" must be applied to every concept itself (1.179). It is in this sense that Tillich calls being "the basic *transcendentale*, beyond the universal and the particular" (2.11). The notion of a concept of being which is *utterly* universal, incidentally, also lies behind Tillich's rejection of nominalism's claim that "universals . . . have no reality of their own" (2.10). For Tillich denies that

---

[37]Bertrand Russell, *The Principles of Mathematics* (2nd ed.; New York: Norton, 1937) 449.

[38]For example, the essence "treehood" (cf. *Systematic Theology*, 2.21).

[39]Cf. ibid., 2.20. See also Brown, ed., *Ultimate Concern,* 45, where Tillich refers to the "potentialities of existence which we usually call the essences of things . . . they have being, too; they are the power of being, which may become beings."

[40]For example, the general ontological concepts of individuality and participation.

"Being as such . . . does not designate anything real" (2.11) in his claim that it *must* have objective reality. But if being-itself designates something real, then *all* concepts—including universals—must designate something real as well, since something is a possible concept only by virtue of its participation in being-itself, the presupposition of all thought. Getting us to admit the reality of these two classes of concepts less universal than being-itself thus "points to" the reality of being-itself. For only by participating in being-itself can they share the "being" Tillich claims must belong to every concept.

If Tillich's use of "being" as a universal predicate is a paradigm of his ontology of thinking, the question is how this usage results in a position from which Tillich thinks he can eliminate the worry of an illegitimate transition from concept to reality in his *own* version of Anselm's "statement." Tillich's doctrine that "being" is a universal predicate has two relevant features. The first is stated in Tillich's claim that "everything which can be conceptualized must have being." This statement urges the general view that whatever we conceive, we must conceive to have being: i.e., we can't conceive of anything without also attributing being to it. Hence, "being" is made the necessary property of every possible object of which we have some concept.[41]

The second feature is implicit in the first, but can be brought out in the following way. From the general form of Tillich's doctrine there follows a further claim: viz., that "all concepts" are themselves included as members of "everything which can be conceptualized" and must, therefore, have being (1.179). Here, in other words, it is the concept itself that becomes the object. Now while a "concept" is clearly not some *thing*—it "cannot be thought of something that is"(1.179)—neither, according to Tillich, "can it be thought of something that is not" (1.179). It must, in some way, have being, since it can itself be *conceptualized,* or thought about. Further, it must itself have form: for "there is no being without form" (1.179). "Being," then, is a necessary property not only of every existing object, but of every conception itself.

The consequence of the doctrine that "being" is a universal predicate is simply to *identify* the being of the conception with the being of what is conceived. With respect to "being," concepts and objects share the same thing: i.e., there is an identity between the formal reality of every concept we entertain and its objective reality, because concepts are said to participate in the *same* being

[41]Cf. *Systematic Theology,* 2.20.

as do existing objects. Thus, there is no *ontological* distinction between the fact that we can *entertain* some concept and the objective reality of that concept.

It is, then, the very ubiquity of Tillich's use of the term "being" that obviates the possibility of any "transition" from concept to reality. Since "being" is that which has *transcendental* application, no question of any transition can even arise. "Being" *must* be involved in every conception simply because it is the necessary predicate of everything conceivable.

Of course, if it is true that "everything which can be conceptualized must have being," then attributing being to anything one conceives becomes tautological. For "being" is already involved in every conception. But the most significant consequence of the notion that "being" is a universal predicate is that it makes *denials* of the reality of anything not readily intelligible. Indeed, in the case of God, Tillich seems quite anxious to make denials of God's being *impossible*. The fact that Tillich believes he can, and does, deny God's "existence" (1.205) is immaterial. For Tillich still gives himself the option of talking about God's "being," and otherwise implying that God nevertheless *is*, even in denials of his existence. This is made perhaps most explicit in Tillich's claim that the being of God is affirmed by the very act of doubting him.[42] In fact, it turns out that God's being is "implied in every statement about the relation between subject and predicate."[43] The problem is that what *we* mean to deny, when we deny there is a God, is what Tillich means by God's *being*—not simply his "existence." Tillich's denial that God "exists," therefore, is gratuitous because he has never given up God's being.

In sum, Tillich's notion of "being" simply *bypasses* the necessity for any transition from concept to reality. The bare thought of anything—including the thought of God in "the question of God"—is already objective. Thus, once Tillich identifies God as the "presupposition" of thought, God is no longer the object of that question but its *objective basis*.[44]

V

It remains to ask how the two general classes of concepts Tillich distinguishes *within* thinking "point to" the reality of being-itself.

---

[42]Tillich, "The Two Types of Philosophy of Religion," 13.
[43]Ibid.
[44]Ibid.

Tillich refers to these concepts, respectively, as "ontic" and "ontological."

An "ontic" concept, it has been suggested, is a "class" concept, since, according to Tillich, it is a concept that designates "a realm of beings" (1.164). An ontic concept, then, is simply the notion of an *essence,* since it has application to the several members of any given class of things. Tillich's example for such a concept is the essence "treehood."

"Ontological" concepts, on the other hand, are concepts which are more universal than ontic or class concepts, for they are universally predicable—that is, they are applicable to the members of *every* class. The reason ontological concepts are universally predicable is that they form part of the very *structure* of thinking itself. In this connection it might be noted that ontological concepts are themselves comprised of two subgroups: the three pairs of "polar" *elements,* including "individuality" and "participation," and the *categories* of space, time, causality, and substance. Now, while ontological concepts are in one sense transcendentals (i.e., universally predicable), they are, all the same, still "less universal" than being-itself (1.164), which, according to Tillich, is *fundamentally* transcendental. That is, being-itself must have application to every *concept* itself as well as to any object, including those structures of thought which are treated, analytically, as objects.

In any case, because both ontic and ontological concepts must possess "being," they are both, in that way, objective. Thus, for Tillich, talking about the concepts which form the various operations of thinking at the same time tells us something about the nature of objective reality.

How do ontic concepts "point to" the reality of God? We have seen that ontic concepts, or essences, are real, since what they designate "is not nothing" but possesses being. But it was also pointed out that a concept must have *form.* Tillich calls the "form" by which an *essence* has its being the form of an "unactualized potential being." Before anything can come into actuality, in other words, it must first have its being as something potential. Moreover, Tillich emphasizes that this state is not one of mere logical possibility; it is a state of *real* being (2.20).

Tillich sometimes characterizes the being of unactualized possibles as "relative non-being" or "not-yet-being" (2.20). This is misleading insofar as it implies that potentiality is a realm of "partial" being, of things "just emerging" into reality. In fact, the opposite is the case.

What Tillich in effect does is to associate a quasi-Platonic understanding of "existence" as the realm of imperfection with the Christian doctrine of creation. Thus, coming into existence is understood to be an "estrangement" from the essential or perfect being in potentiality—a *fall* from essence to existence. Tillich argues that the existence of created things "stands out of their essence as in a 'fall.' On this point, the Platonic and the Christian evaluations of existence coincide" (2.23). Existence, from a religious point of view, is not a "perfection," but is a "falling away from what [something] essentially is . . . a loss of true essentiality" (2.22). It is the realm of opinion and error; it "lacks true reality" (2.22).

Consequently, the state of potentiality could hardly be a world of "half-real" beings. Rather, it is the realm of essences, of "true being," of the "really real." "The potential is the essential, and to exist . . . is the loss of true essentiality" (2.22). Essential being is *true* being, and is present to us in the form of the eternal essences, which are man's "remembrances" of perfect being, "the essential realm from which he fell into existence" (2.22).

Tillich implies that this realm of potentiality is also a divine one, that "essences are ideas in the divine mind . . . the patterns according to which God creates" (1.254). "The essential powers of being belong to the divine life in which they are rooted . . ." (1.254). What is significant about such remarks is that they suggest Tillich sees the "principle" that the potential is what is truly real as a way of "pointing to" the reality of God. This comes about, for Tillich, since claims about potentialities of human thought can also be understood as claims about God. For example, when Tillich talks about "the power of infinite self-transcendence [as] an expression of *man's* belonging to that which is beyond being and nonbeing, namely, to being-itself,"[45] this is *also* meant as an implicit claim for the reality of being-itself. How? Because "the potential presence of the infinite (as unlimited self-transcendence)" (1.191) in us not only "points to" the reality of being-itself. In fact, it is a *manifestation* of being-itself: "Being-itself manifests itself to finite being in the infinite drive of the finite beyond itself" (1.191).

Ontic concepts, then, appear to function as a means for exhibiting the reality of God. There are, of course, some problems Tillich's doctrine of essences generates. For example, while Tillich clearly wants to admit the reality of essences, he is troubled about making them so individualized that they become a mere "duplicate of reality" (1.255). Yet it is just that idea of making

---

[45]*Systematic Theology,* 1.191, my emphasis.

essences into individually existing things that Tillich himself finds it impossible to avoid.

The problem originates in the very way Tillich states his doctrine that "being" is the basic transcendental, the necessary predicate of everything conceivable. According to Tillich, being "is the power in everything that has power, be it a universal or an individual, a thing or an experience."[46] But if it is the *same* being that is predicated of both essences and individuals, then there can be no distinction in reality between essences and individuals. The consequence is that in talking about the ontological reality of essences, Tillich finds it difficult to avoid referring to essences as if they were, themselves, individually existing things.

Tillich falls into this difficulty on at least one occasion when he suggests that if *all* the individuals of a given species should cease to exist, the form which constitutes the essence of that species would still be "there," and, given the right conditions, would come into actuality again:

> . . . the potentialities of existence which we usually call the essences of things . . . have being, too; they are the power of being, which may become beings. For instance, even if suddenly a scourge should cause all trees to disappear, the tree, or the power of becoming a tree, would still be there; and given the right conditions, living trees might come into existence again.[47]

Now, if all the individuals of a certain species of tree should, for some reason, suddenly cease to be (say, a blight), it is not only logically possible,[48] but also, perhaps, a real possibility that individuals of that same species should one day reappear.[49] Nevertheless, it is absurd to think they should reappear *for the reason* that their "essence" is still around. For even if it makes sense to speak of the essence of an individual tree or of all the trees there are, there is not, in addition to those trees, any entity designated by the word "treehood" or "the tree"[50] and which exists after all those individual trees have ceased to be. The essence "treehood" which remains after all trees no longer exist becomes just another possible *individual* tree, eternally waiting in the wings, as it were, to make its appearance.[51]

[46] Tillich, "The Two Types of Philosophy of Religion," 26.

[47] Brown, ed., *Ultimate Concern,* 45.

[48] In other words, in the sense that there is nothing self-contradictory in the concept of a tree that rules it out that there should *be* trees.

[49] For example, from some as yet unexplained process of generation.

[50] Brown, ed., *Ultimate Concern,* 45.

[51] One of the strongest objections to entities which are treated as "possible beings" is that it seems impossible to provide any consistent criteria of identity

Now, what about the group of concepts Tillich refers to as "ontological"? How do they also point to the reality of God? According to Tillich, these concepts constitute the conceptual structure through which any experience is made intelligible, for ontological concepts are concepts of those "general structures that make experience possible"(1.19). These "structures, categories, and concepts which are presupposed in the cognitive encounter with every realm of reality" (1.18) are "the forms in which the mind grasps and shapes reality" (1.192).

In a rough way Tillich's "ontological" concepts bear a certain resemblance to Kant's categories of the understanding.[52] In this sense "ontological" concepts are features of our subjective cognitive constitution; they are "in us," prior to experience. They relate to the general thesis that for experience to be possible at all, we must be able to experience things as falling under very general concepts which govern the operations of thinking.[53] They are "subjective" in the sense that they are those features of our cognition by which we actively order experience.[54]

But when Tillich calls these concepts "ontological," he clearly means to indicate that they are not *merely* subjective. For ontological concepts are *also* said to be "the forms of being" (1.192). "They are ontological . . . ," and, according to Tillich, this means they are actually "present in everything" (1.192).

In effect, Tillich is treating these ontological concepts, which constitute the elements of the conceptual structure through which

---

for them. If something, e.g., "the possible tree," is treated as a subject of which we can make predications, it is necessary for it to be possible to tell in what circumstances two predications are made of that same subject—lest we give up the notion that contradictory predications cannot be made of the same subject. Now while we have criteria by which we decide whether two statements are being made about the same actual tree, by what criteria can we decide whether two statements are being made about the same *possible* tree? How, for example, would we decide whether "the possible male tree" and "the possible spruce tree" are the same possible tree or two? But if we can't decide that, then how can the concept of identity be applied to "possible beings"? Yet what sense can be made of talking of entities which cannot meaningfully be said to be identical with themselves and distinct from others? (Cf. Anthony Kenny, *Descartes* [New York: Random House, 1968] 168. Cf. also W. V. O. Quine, "On What There Is," in *From A Logical Point of View* [2nd ed.; Harper Torchbooks; New York: Harper & Row, 1963] 4.)

[52]Tillich notes (*Systematic Theology*, 1.166, n. 1) that space and time, which Kant had distinguished as the "forms of intuition," are assimilated under his own model of the categories of the understanding.

[53]Cf. P. F. Strawson, *The Bounds of Sense* (London: Methuen, 1966) 72.

[54]What Tillich means by the form by which the mind "shapes" reality.

experience is actively ordered, as if they were properties of *things*. Unlike ontic concepts, essences which determine things into classes, *ontological* concepts are universally predicable of things of every class. Nevertheless, they are, like essences, objective—for they are actually "present in everything." Tillich reinforces this idea most strongly when he identifies the ontological concepts which constitute our cognitive structure as "the structural elements of being-itself"(1.238). What Tillich has done, that is, is to identify the structure of our *cognition* with God, who is the structure of *objective reality*. Tillich makes this quite explicit when he states that God simply "*is* this structure" (1.238, 239) in terms of which our experience of the world is ordered.

Now, if the concepts presupposed by thought are identified as "the structural elements of being-itself," then they are identical with that which must have *objective* as well as subjective reality. What Tillich appears to have accomplished, then, is a way of talking about the nature of thinking and the nature of God at the same time. For in talking about those ontological concepts presupposed by thought, Tillich also takes himself to be informing us about the nature of the *ultimate* structure presupposed by thought: being-itself.

But if theology is thought about God, and God is being-itself, the presupposition of all thought, then the reality of God has simply become the presupposition of any theological inquiry.[55] By some such move, that is, Tillich has established his own form of ontological argument. We are justified in referring to Tillich's procedure as a form of *ontological* argument precisely because the procedure is an a priori one in the required sense. That is, Tillich's analysis of God as being-itself, and the relation of this concept to Tillich's understanding of the nature of thinking, does not proceed from an a posteriori investigation of our actual experience. Rather, it is an a priori analysis of what must be presupposed in order for there to be intelligible experience at all. The reality of God, consequently, becomes the presupposition of any possible epistemic theological inquiry, because, as being-itself, God is simply identified with the presupposition of the *possibility* of all thought. But from this it follows that God cannot sensibly be the "object" of any question about his existence, because God must be its *basis*. And that move, I take it, is identical with Anselm's denial that it is possible to conceive the

---

[55]Cf. Stuart C. Brown, *Do Religious Claims Make Sense?* (New York: Macmillan, 1969) 163.

nonexistence of God. In Tillich's case, it turns out that it is impossible to conceive the non-being of being-itself, since being-itself is both present in, and the presupposition of, any act of conceiving. What Tillich has done, in effect, has been to recast the ontological argument in epistemic terms. Unfortunately, Tillich's epistemology is far too laced with problems of its own to consider his enterprise successful.

BEING AND SOME THEOLOGIANS
O. C. Thomas
Episcopal Divinity School
Cambridge, MA 02138

Introduction

A crucial issue in contemporary theology is the doctrine of God and especially the nature of the divine reality. What kind of reality is God? How is God's reality like, unlike, and related to other kinds of reality? There are many ways to talk about the reality of God. I want to focus on one way, namely, God as being or being-itself, not because I believe that it is the best way to talk about God but because it is one of the oldest ways, because it seems to be undergoing something of a revival, and because I am baffled and intrigued by it.

In this essay I want to explore the various attitudes which some theologians in this century have taken toward the doctrine of God as being-itself. This will include various ways in which the doctrine has been affirmed and denied.

Terminology

What are the possible meanings of the term "being"? Linguistically the term is the present participle of the verb "to be," but we are not concerned with its simple participial use, e.g., "He's being funny." The linguistic form with which we are concerned is "being" as a verbal substantive. The *Oxford English Dictionary* lists four usages:

1. "Existence, the fact of belonging to the universe of things material or immaterial."
2. "Existence in some relation of place or condition."
3. "Existence viewed as a property possessed by anything."
4. "That which exists or is conceived as existing."

These can be summarized as the fact of existence, existence in relation, the property of existence, and the existent itself.

The main philosophical usages of the term "being" include the above and also others; a realm of true reality beyond the sensible world, a genus or class to which everything belongs that is. A number of other less clear philosophical usages will be considered below.

It is sometimes asserted that the doctrine of God as being-itself has been affirmed by the Greek Fathers, Augustine, and Aquinas.[1] However, this kind of generalization obscures a great complexity and even greater diversity of interpretation on this question.

The main source of this complexity is that of the Aristotelian doctrine of being or substance.[2] But this complexity is increased by the other sources of Greek patristic thought in Platonism and Stoicism. It is further increased by the differing contexts in which the terms for being or substance are used, namely, the apophatic theology and the doctrine of the Trinity. The final source of complexity is the variety of possibilities of translating the Greek terms (*einai, ousa, on, ousia*) into the Latin terms (*esse, ens, essentia, entitas*) and all of these into English terms (being, beingness, entity, substance, essence).[3]

This complexity and confusion is brought out by Michael Durrant in his study of *ousia* in Aristotle, the Greek Fathers, and the Latin equivalents in Augustine. He concludes that none of the Aristotelian or Greek patristic usages of *ousia* can be applied legitimately to the Christian God and that Augustine's usage is hopelessly confused.[4]

The diversity of possible interpretations of all this can be seen by comparing Durrant with Gilson's study which treats the issue from Plato to Kierkegaard (but omits the Greek Fathers) and comes to the opposite conclusions.[5] Furthermore, Alasdair MacIntyre has dubbed Gilson's approach as the "Neo-Thomist myth of the history of philosophy," in which a doctrine of being as such is foisted on Aristotle and Aquinas and the history of philosophy is interpreted as a series of answers to the question, What is being?[6]

About all that we can conclude from this is that the doctrine of God as being-itself is obscure in the Greek Fathers, that it is affirmed but unexplored in Augustine,[7] and that it is affirmed and

---

[1] See, e.g., John Macquarrie, *Principles of Christian Theology* (New York: Scribner's, 1966) 107.

[2] See Joseph Owens, *The Doctrine of Being in the Aristotelian 'Metaphysics'* (Toronto: Pontifical Institute of Mediaeval Studies, 1951).

[3] See ibid., 139-43.

[4] *Theology and Intelligibility* (London: Routledge and Kegan Paul, 1973) xvi, 71, 110, 124.

[5] Étienne Gilson, *Being and Some Philosophers* (2d rev. ed.; Toronto: Pontifical Institute of Mediaeval Studies, 1952).

[6] "Being," *The Encyclopedia of Philosophy*, ed. Paul Edwards (8 vols.; New York: Macmillan/Free Press, 1967) 1.275a.

[7] See *De Trinitate* 5.2.

explored by Aquinas and not again until the Neo-Thomists and Tillich. An important sidelight is that there is a recurring theme to the effect that God transcends being, which can be found in Clement of Alexandria, perhaps the Cappadocians, Victorinus, Pseudo-Dionysius, Maximus the Confessor, John of Damascus, Erigena, and Gregory Palamas.[8]

GILSON

Roman Catholic theologians have generally identified God with being-itself since Thomas Aquinas. This is especially true of the Neo-Thomist tradition of Garrigou-Lagrange, Gilson, and Maritain. It is also true of the school of Transcendental Thomism which originated in the work of Maréchal and has been developed by Rahner, Coreth, and Lonergan. We shall look particularly at the thought of Gilson, Rahner, and Lonergan on this question.

For Gilson, the concept of being has a dual meaning. It can mean an existent thing or the act of being by which this existent is a thing. "In a 'that which is' (*id quod est*) or a 'having being' (*esse habens*), we can spontaneously emphasize either the *id quod* and the *habens* or the *esse* and the *est*." Gilson maintains that the latter meaning is primary in Thomistic philosophy. "What characterizes Thomistic ontology thus understood is . . . the primacy of the act-of-being, not over and above being, but within it." Thus, he holds that it is preferable to translate *ens* by "being" and *esse* by "act-of-being."[9] The *esse* or act of being in a thing is its very core, its "secret energy."[10]

However, the act of being cannot be conceived or defined because it has no essence or quiddity of its own.[11] The act of being or existence per se can only be signified by a judgment which always takes the form, It is, or, It is not.

---

[8] See Gilson, *Being*, chap. 1; Vladimir Lossky, *The Mystical Theology of the Eastern Church* (London: Clarke, 1957), chap. 2; A. H. Armstrong, ed., *The Cambridge History of Later Greek and Early Medieval Philosophy* (Cambridge: Cambridge University, 1967); Brooks Otis, "Nicene Orthodoxy and Fourth Century Mysticism," *Actes du XIIe Congrès International des Études Byzantines* (Geograd: 1964) 2.475-84.

[9] Étienne Gilson, *The Unity of Philosophical Experience* (London: Sheed and Ward, 1938) 320; see idem, *The Christian Philosophy of St. Thomas Aquinas* (trans. L. K. Shook; New York: Random House, 1956) 40.

[10] *Elements of Christian Philosophy* (Garden City, NY: Doubleday, 1960) 123; idem, *The Spirit of Thomism* (New York: Harper & Row, 1964) 64, 68-69, 72; idem, *Christian Philosophy of Thomas*, 374.

[11] *Spirit of Thomism*, 76; see 65-66; *Christian Philosophy of Thomas*, 44.

For Gilson, God is "He who is," being-itself, *esse*, the act of being. Furthermore, God as the pure act of existence is all, everything and anything, that it is possible to be, and nothing can be conceived as being which the pure act of being is not.[12]

Sometimes Gilson asserts that God has no essence, because then God would be subject to becoming and would not be a necessary being.[13] Other times he states that God's essence is identical with his existence or act of being.[14] Finally, he concludes that God is "a beyond essence." "God is the being whose essence is to be beyond essence or, in other words, God is the being whose essence it is to be."[15]

The main problem I have with Gilson's doctrine of God as being-itself or the pure act of being is the meaning of the concept of pure act. As Sidney Hook asks, "What acts in the act of Being or existing? Certainly not possibilities, essences, or natures. The meaning of 'death' is not lethal; the notion of 'fire' burns nothing."[16] I suppose that it is possible to conceive of the existence of a being as an action or activity, although this is rather odd. But to abstract from this odd notion to the idea of being in general as activity and thus to the idea of a pure act without any agent is unintelligible to me.

Gilson is very much aware of this difficulty. In his latest extended treatment of this idea, he asks,

> How did Thomas Aquinas achieve the awareness of the very possibility of this notion? It certainly results from a supreme effort of abstraction, since, in order to form it, the intellect must conceive, apart from the condition of being an existent, the act owing to which the existent finds itself in this condition. . . . It is not a notion universally evident to all human minds.[17]

Gilson concludes that Thomas learned of the notion of being as act through divine revelation in Exod 3:14:

> Moses could not learn this sublime truth from our Lord [that God's essence is His very *esse*] without at the same time learning from Him the notion of what it is to be a pure existential act. . . . In order to reach the

---

[12]*God and Philosophy* (New Haven: Yale University, 1941) 51-52.
[13]*Being*, 180; *Christian Philosophy of Thomas*, 91; *Elements*, 114, 119.
[14]*Christian Philosophy of Thomas*, 91, 371; *Elements*, 126; *The Spirit of Mediaeval Philosophy* (trans. A. H. C. Downes; New York: Scribner's, 1940) 51.
[15]*Elements*, 133.
[16]Sidney Hook, *The Quest for Being and other Studies in Naturalism and Humanism* (New York: Dell, 1934) 154.
[17]Gilson, *Elements*, 131.

new metaphysical notion of being, which identifies it with its very act, one has only to accept the words of Scripture at their face value.[18]

Again, what is it that Moses, Thomas, and Gilson learn from the Lord? It is something which is indefinable and inconceivable.[19] What does it mean to learn of a concept that is indefinable and inconceivable? What is Gilson really trying to say here? It seems to me that he is trying in this way to assert the transcendence of God. "When we reach the question, what is God? the time has come for our intellect to cast off its moorings and to set sail on the infinite ocean of pure *esse*, or *act*, whereby that which is actually is. Then, of course, we no longer can say where we are, because there are no landmarks where there is no land."[20]

Thus the concept of the pure act of being seems to join those of ineffability, unknowability, incomprehensibility, absoluteness, etc., in the language of transcendence. This particular concept of act of being is useful in this connection in that it at the same time indicates the mode of the divine immanence. God is "innermost" in all things because "God is present in the totality of all the elements of which the substances consist as well as in all their operations, from the mere fact that he is present in the act of *esse* owing to which they are." As the pure act of being, God is the "ontological energy" that causes everything to be.[21]

Rahner

Karl Rahner's thought on this doctrine is rather confusing. At first he affirms the traditional Thomist doctrine of God as being-itself, but in his more detailed exposition of the doctrine of God, he seems to move away from this position.

Rahner begins by asserting that being can be known but is essentially indefinable. Then he states "the first proposition of a general ontology." "The essence of being is knowing and being known in an original unity, which we call the (conscious) being-present-to-itself of being." Furthermore, "the most general structures of being in general, that is, all that is attributable to being" or "the transcendental definitions of being" are as follows:

---

[18]Ibid., 132. Cp. Tillich's idea below, that the understanding of being requires a conversion.
[19]See above, p. 139.
[20]*Elements*, 134.
[21]*Spirit of Thomism*, 71, 72.

"Being is being-present-to-itself. Being is knowing or luminosity. Being is self-affirmation, the will, and the good."[22]

Rahner clearly identifies being-itself with God, and all that he affirms of being-itself he affirms of God as the Absolute Being. However, a possible qualification of Rahner's identification of God and being-itself is the frequent suggestion in *Hearers of the Word* that God is *a* being possessing absolute "having-being." Rahner begins by asserting that having-being is a matter of degree. This is the basis of his interpretation of being as an analogical concept.[23] Then this distinction is applied to God. "God also in this sense may not be thought of as simply 'being,' but . . . as the existent possessing absolute 'having-being' and thereby as the existent of pure and absolute self-clarification."[24]

To be sure, this statement occurs in a footnote which has been added by J. B. Metz to the second revised edition of the work, but Metz asserts that the concept of "having-being" has the "explicit assent" of Rahner. That this is in fact Rahner's view is indicated by further statements that God is "the thing of which is affirmed absolute 'having existence,'" "an existent thing of absolute 'having being,'" and a "supra-mundane existent thing." He also describes God as "a free autonomous and powerful person."[25]

These statements imply that God is subordinate to being or that being is a property in which all beings, including God, participate. This interpretation is supported in turn by Rahner's assertion that the concept of being-itself is arrived at by abstraction.[26] We shall note that Tillich and Macquarrie are quite concerned to avoid the idea that God is a being, since this would make God subject to the categories and subordinate to being-itself and thus not the ultimate reality.

Perhaps we should interpret Rahner's doctrine of being-itself (mystery, horizon, etc.) as the limit of metaphysical knowledge apart from revelation. Then in the Christian revelation being-itself as mystery and horizon is perceived as the personal God, and the former concepts become no longer necessary.

---

[22] Karl Rahner, *Hearers of the Word* (trans. Michael Richards; New York: Herder, 1969) 39-40, 147; see idem, *Spirit in the World* (trans. William Dych; New York: Herder, 1968) 67-69, 71; idem, *Theological Investigations* (Baltimore: Helicon, 1961) 4.50-52.
[23] *Hearers*, 47; see *Spirit*, 69-72.
[24] *Hearers*, 48 (note); see 50 (note).
[25] Ibid., 63-64, 89, 147-49, 151-53.
[26] *Spirit*, 171, 179, 408, chap. 3 *passim*.

LONERGAN

Lonergan's approach to being is through the analysis of human cognition. As a notion, being is "the objective of the unrestricted desire to know." This includes all that is known and all that remains to be known. Being is what is to be known by the totality of true judgments, the complete set of answers to the complete set of questions. "It refers to all that can be known by intelligent grasp and reasonable affirmation."[27]

Lonergan notes that this is a "second order" definition; i.e., it indicates not what is meant by being but how that meaning is to be determined. At another point he states that being cannot be defined but only characterized.[28]

Lonergan distinguishes proportionate and transcendent being. Proportionate being is defined as "whatever is to be known by human experience, intelligent grasp, and reasonable affirmation." Transcendent being is what may be known beyond human experience. "Being is proportionate or transcendent according as it lies within or without the domain of man's outer and inner experience."[29]

In discussing transcendent knowledge or knowledge of transcendent being, Lonergan distinguishes the idea of being from the notion of being. The idea of being is the content of an unrestricted act of understanding which grasps everything about everything. In the idea of being Lonergan distinguishes a primary component which is identical with the unrestricted act of understanding or with this act's understanding of itself, and a secondary component which consists of the unrestricted act's understanding of everything else because it understands itself.

Then Lonergan proceeds to argue on the basis of contingency and causality for the existence of such an act of unrestricted understanding which is a transcendent being, an ultimate being, an ultimate ground of the universe.[30] He develops the notion of God through further analysis of the concept of an unrestricted act of understanding. He identifies God with the primary component of the idea of being, namely, the unrestricted act of understanding itself or this act's understanding of itself.[31]

---

[27]Bernard J. F. Lonergan, *Insight: A Study of Human Understanding* (New York: Philosophical Library, 1956) 348, 360.
[28]Ibid., 350, 360.
[29]Ibid., 391, 640.
[30]Ibid., 646, 655-56.
[31]Ibid., 658, 674.

Thus Lonergan identifies God with being only in a limited sense. He cannot identify God with the notion of being, because this is defined as the objective of the unrestricted desire to know, which objective includes both transcendent and proportionate being, both God and world. Furthermore, Lonergan cannot identify God with the idea of being as such for the same reason. For the idea of being is the content of an unrestricted act of understanding. "Content" here apparently means the object of such an act, and in the case of the notion of being, this would include proportionate as well as transcendent being.

Can Lonergan consistently identify God with the primary component of the idea of being? Sometimes he defines this primary component as the unrestricted act of understanding itself and sometimes as this act's understanding of itself.[32] It is not clear that these are identical concepts. In any case, since the unrestricted act of understanding is presumably an analogous concept based on the restricted human act of understanding, the question arises as to the agent of the act. If God has or engages in the unrestricted act of understanding, it is not clear how he can be identical with it. (The concept of *actus purus* is not relevant here, since it refers to the absence of potentiality rather than the absence of an agent.) Lonergan confirms this distinction between God and being in his statement, "Unrestricted understanding pertains only to God."[33] I take this to mean that God is the subject of the unrestricted act of understanding and thus is not identical with the idea of being as defined.

This leads to another difficulty in Lonergan's view of the relation of God and being. He often refers to God as *a* being, for example, as "the primary being," "a transcendent being," "the ultimate being," "a rational self-consciousness."[34] Thus Lonergan seems to overlook the "ontological difference" between being and beings. As one commentator puts it,

> It would seem, then, that Fr. Lonergan is in no way interrogating Being as *different* from beings, indeed (as far as the present writer can see) there appears to be no indication that he takes account of such a difference at

---

[32] Ibid., 646, 648.
[33] Philip McShane, ed., *Language, Truth and Meaning: Papers from the International Lonergan Conference 1970* (Dublin: Gill and Macmillan) 311.
[34] *Insight*, 655, 658, 668.

all. A beetle-browed Heideggerean would probably say, then, that Fr. Lonergan is a victim of the "forgetfulness of Being" (*Seinsvergessenheit*), or, more precisely, of a "forgetfulness of the ontological difference."[35]

Finally, Lonergan's approach to the idea of being through the analysis of human cognition and understanding makes these latter concepts prior to that of being. "All other divine attributes follow from the notion of an unrestricted act of understanding. Moreover, since we define being by its relation to intelligence, necessarily our ultimate is not being but intelligence."[36]

TILLICH

Paul Tillich is the main Protestant theologian who has affirmed the doctrine of God as being-itself in this century. His doctrine of being is extraordinarily complex. This is indicated by the fact that Tillich equates the concept of being with the power and ground of being,[37] the structure of being and reality,[38] existence itself,[39] the basis of thought,[40] and the presupposition of knowledge.[41]

It is clear that the exploration of the nature of the relationships among these concepts and the problems arising therefrom would be a task too extended for this essay. A few examples will have to suffice. Being-itself can hardly be identified with the power of being or the ground of being. If the genitives are taken in the subjective sense, it must be objected that being-itself can have no ground or power other than itself. If they are taken in the objective sense, the term "being" must refer to beings and not to being-itself.

Being-itself as the object of existential concern can hardly be identified with the structure of being, understood as the generic

---

[35] William J. Richardson, "Being for Lonergan," in McShane, *Language, Truth and Meaning*, 277, see 283.

[36] *Insight*, 677.

[37] Paul Tillich, *Systematic Theology* (3 vols.; Chicago: University of Chicago, 1951-63) 1.72.

[38] Ibid., 1.18-20; idem, *Love, Power and Justice: Ontological Analysis and Ethical Applications* (New York: Oxford University, 1954) 19; idem, *The Protestant Era* (trans. James Luther Adams; Chicago: University of Chicago, 1948) 85.

[39] *Protestant Era*, 85; *Biblical Religion and the Search for Ultimate Reality* (Chicago: University of Chicago, 1959) 6; *Systematic Theology*, 1.163.

[40] *Systematic Theology*, 1.163, 2.11; *Theology of Culture* (ed. Robert C. Kimball; New York: Oxford University, 1959) 15.

[41] *Systematic Theology*, 1.18.

traits of any and all subject matters as in the Aristotelian metaphysics. The first is similar to the One of Neo-Platonism and the Absolute of Idealism, while the second is simply the proper object of free metaphysical inquiry, as carried out by Tillich in his analysis of the four levels of ontological concepts. Yet, Tillich identifies God as being-itself with the structure of being. "He *is* this structure."[42]

Finally, if being-itself is the presupposition of all thought and knowledge, it could be argued that it cannot be thought or known per se. Indeed, Tillich declares that being-itself is indefinable "since it is the presupposition of every definition." Therefore, concludes Tillich, "every assertion about being-itself is either metaphorical or symbolic."[43] This may be the root of our difficulty and the explanation of why many sympathetic philosophers are hard put to grasp the meaning of Tillich's concept of being-itself.[44]

Tillich grants that the concept of being is a difficult one for us modern people. He argues that the later medieval criticism of the ontological approach has undermined it for the larger part of Western humanity.[45]

> It is hard for the modern mind to understand the Latin *esse-ipsum*, being-itself, or the Greek *on e on*, being-insofar-as-it-is-being. We are all nominalists by birth. And as nominalists we are inclined to dissolve our world into things. But this inclination is an historical accident and not an essential necessity.[46]

In another book Tillich speaks of the necessity of conversion for understanding the ontological approach.

> Ontology presupposes a conversion, an opening of the eyes, a revelatory experience. It is not a matter of detached observation, analysis and hypothesis. Only he who is involved in ultimate reality, only he who has encountered it as a matter of existential concern, can try to speak about it meaningfully.[47]

---

[42] Ibid., 1.238; see W. Kegley and Robert W. Bretall, eds., *The Theology of Paul Tillich* (New York: Macmillan, 1952) 139-40, 160-61, 335.

[43] *Biblical Religion*, 19; *The Courage to Be* (New Haven: Yale University, 1952) 179; see *Love, Power and Justice*, 35.

[44] See, e.g., Charles Hartshorne, "Tillich and the Other Great Tradition," *ATR* 43 (1961) 157; Dorothy Emmet, "The Ground of Being," *JTS* n.s. 15 (1964) 289.

[45] *Theology of Culture*, 16.

[46] *Love, Power and Justice*, 18.

[47] *Biblical Religion*, 65.

In his *Systematic Theology* Tillich asserts that God is being-itself and not *a* being, not even the highest or most perfect being, for if God were *a* being, he would be subordinate to being-itself and subject to the categories of finitude and thus not the answer to the existential question of human finitude. God as being-itself means that God is the ground of being or the power of being. Also, God is the ground of the structure of being. "He *is* the structure."[48] God as being-itself is not the universal essence (pantheism) but rather beyond the contrast of essential and existential being.

Tillich asserts, "The statement that God is being-itself is a non-symbolic statement. It does not point beyond itself. It means what it says directly and properly." This is "the most abstract and completely unsymbolic statement which is possible." "Other assertions about God can be made theologically only on this basis."[49] This would seem to be a serious mistake. I would argue that the concept of being in its original or proper meaning has a finite reference. Thus, when it is applied to God, it is used symbolically.

In the second volume of his system, Tillich tacitly withdraws this statement and asserts that the only non-symbolic statement we can make about God is that "everything we say about God is symbolic."[50] This is indeed a non-symbolic statement, but it is not a statement about God but rather about statements about God. Then Tillich goes on to assert that the equation of God and being-itself is both symbolic and non-symbolic because it designates the boundary line at which the symbolic and the non-symbolic coincide. I have no idea at all what that means.

Tillich's claim that the identification of God and being-itself is a non-symbolic statement also contradicts his assertions in his shorter works that being-itself is indefinable and that statements about it are metaphorical or symbolic. If we can speak of two concepts only symbolically, then any statement about their relation must also be symbolic. (E.g., "The Father begets the Son.") It would seem that consistency requires Tillich to hold that all statements about God, being-itself, and their relations are symbolic or analogous.

Tillich's concept of being is highly ambiguous and diffuse. As we have seen, he identifies being-itself with the power, ground,

---

[48] *Systematic Theology*, 1.238; see 1.235-37.
[49] Ibid., 1.238-39.
[50] Ibid., 2.9.

and structure of being, with existence, the basis of thought, and the presupposition of knowledge. It is very difficult to get one's head around a concept which does all these jobs. The vagueness of Tillich's doctrine of God as being-itself seems to derive from the interplay of two concepts which are equally diffuse in Tillich's writings. In particular, the vagueness of the concept of being seems to be derived from the influence of the traditional doctrine of God rather than vice versa. Thus, being-itself is indefinable, transcendent, can be spoken of only symbolically, and can be understood only through a turning or conversion. If this is the case, then it is not surprising that the concept of being turns out to be very little help in clarifying the doctrine of God.

MACQUARRIE

John Macquarrie is one of the few theologians who has made extensive use of Heidegger's doctrine of being in connection with the doctrine of God.[51] He believes that theology has shared in the "forgetting of being" with which Heidegger charges philosophy. The forgetting of being can take place in two ways. Being can be considered more and more transcendent until it is forgotten, or it can be considered more and more immanent until it is fragmented and absorbed into the beings. Macquarrie is also able to define sin as the forgetting of being, as the turning away from being to the beings. Thus, theology too must be recalled to being and to the fight against the forgetting of being.[52]

Macquarrie begins his doctrine of being by stating what being is not. Being is not *a* being, a property, a class, or genus, a substance or substratum, or the absolute understood as the all-inclusive being or the totality or sum of beings. Being is not "some invisible, intangible realm that is supposed to lie back of the appearances, as a world of 'things-in-themselves.'" Furthermore, being is to be distinguished from nothing, becoming, appearance, and the ideal.[53]

The direct definition of the concept of being is difficult because it does not fall under any of our usual categories. It is

---

[51] For another attempt to make use of Heidegger's doctrine of being in the doctrine of God, see Heinrich Ott, *Denken und Sein: Der Weg Martin Heideggers und der Weg der Theologie* (Zollikon: Evangelischer Verlag, 1959) 139-52. He concludes that if one is to speak of God and being in Heidegger's terms, God must be understood as *a* being.

[52] *Principles*, 106, 150-51, 238, 288.

[53] Ibid., 102; see pp. 98-101.

incomparable. It is a *transcendens* which must remain mysterious. (*Transcendens* is Heidegger's term for the scholastic *transcendentia* or universally applicable characters.) Macquarrie has two main characterizations of the concept of being. One is that being is the prior condition that anything may be or that there may be anything whatsoever. The other is that being is the dynamic letting-be of beings in the sense of enabling to be, empowering to be, bringing into being. Being is present and manifest in every being.[54]

Macquarrie points out that the terms "God" and "being" are not synonymous. Some people experience being as indifferent or alien. "God" is synonymous with "holy being" or being understood as gracious.[55]

There are certain difficulties in Macquarrie's doctrine of God as being. First, if being is not a being, a property, a class, a substratum, the totality of being, or the all-inclusive being, it is not clear what it is. His two key terms are condition and letting-be. By "condition" he apparently means prerequisite, but the prerequisite of beings is the source of beings. This points to the idea of letting-be which he also defines as the source of beings. However, it is not clear why a source of beings must be or can be being-itself and not, e.g., God understood analogously as a being. Macquarrie's only response to this is that "such a being would not be an ultimate because we could still ask about *his* being."[56] This seems to be a begging of the question. Similarly, we could say to Macquarrie, if being is ultimate reality, we can still ask about the reality of being.

However, there is a more serious difficulty in Macquarrie's doctrine of God as being. On the one hand, he asserts that "being is nothing apart from its appearances"; "there is no being apart from beings"; "apart from the beings, Being would become indistinguishable from nothing."[57] On the other hand, he asserts that being is the *transcendens*, the transcendent which is distinct from the beings, beyond every possible being.[58] It is not clear how these statements can be held together. Furthermore, it is also not at all clear how the first set of assertions is coherent with the independence or aseity of God, which Macquarrie also wants to affirm.

[54] John Macquarrie, *Studies in Christian Existentialism* (Philadelphia: Westminster, 1965) 89, 255; *Principles*, 87, 99, 103-6, 132, 183, 186, 194.
[55] *Principles*, 79, 95, 105-06; *Existentialism*, 11.
[56] *Principles*, 106; see 103, 183.
[57] Ibid., 102, 109, 126; see 287.
[58] Ibid., 103, 109, 126, 187.

Neville

Robert C. Neville is the third main protestant thinker who identifies God and being-itself, but he writes on this issue as a philosopher. One of Neville's definitions of being-itself is "that of which the determinations of being are determinations." Being-itself is the being that [things] have considered in abstractions from them."[59]

His second definition is that being-itself is the ontological one for the many, that which unifies the diversity of the world, the ground of the most comprehensive unity. But this requires that the concept of being-itself be used univocally. "For if the concept of being is applied to different things only analogically, then being-itself is not sufficiently unified in its relations to the many determinations of being to unify them."[60]

The main thesis of Neville's book is that in order for being-itself to be the ontological one, it mut be indeterminate. The argument runs as follows: If being-itself is construed as determinate, then it must have a determinate contrast term to be meaningful. However, according to "the principle of the ontological equality of reciprocal contrasts," being-itself cannot have a contrast term because it is the ontological one, and there is nothing on the same ontological level with it or nothing outside of it to contrast with it. Therefore, being-itself must be indeterminate. Put more simply, since being-itself is ubiquitous, it must be present in or apply to the significant contrast to any determinate characterization of being-itself as well as to the determinate characterization itself, which is contradictory. Thus, being-itself is indeterminate.[61]

Next Neville argues that if being-itself is indeterminate, it must transcend the determinations of being in the sense of "being outside of" the determinations. Then using a form of the cosmological argument, he concludes that being-itself is the creator of the determinations of being and that this justifies the identification of being-itself with God.[62]

It is further argued that God as being-itself is one, real, infinite, mysterious, and unintelligible. The latter two terms are attributed to God because as being-itself he is indeterminate.

---

[59] Robert C. Neville, *God the Creator* (Chicago: University of Chicago, 1968) 12, 15; see 40, 91.
[60] Ibid., 12.
[61] Ibid., 28, 40-41, 91.
[62] Ibid., 60-61, 64.

> What the creator is apart from all such connections [with the determinations] is a mystery. Furthermore, it is a mystery in the philosophically acceptable sense of that word. A mystery is *un*acceptable to philosophy when it means that we do not understand something well enough. But a mystery is quite proper when it means that there is nothing to understand. If the creator is indeterminate, then any alleged understanding of it in those indeterminate respects would be in error.[63]

Being-itself is unintelligible because it is not determinate. As creator of the determinations, "God is prior to intelligibility, for only what is determinate can be intelligible in any ordinary sense." Hence, God is "essentially unintelligible."[64]

Neville's claim that God as being-itself is indeterminate leads him into some difficulties because he also wants to assert that God is personal, has intentions, creates, acts providentially, forgives, etc. It would seem impossible to affirm that the God to whom these things can be attributed is indeterminate. Neville attempts to solve this problem by means of a distinction between essential and conditional features in God.

All determinations of being have essential and conditional or non-essential features. The essential feature of a determination is what it is apart from its relations to any other determination. The conditional features derive from the real distinctions that pertain between the determination and that with respect to which it is determinate. Thus, Neville describes the above-mentioned attributes of God as conditional features. God as being-itself has no essential features, and there are no real distinctions between God and the world, because God as being-itself is indeterminate. Therefore, God's conditional features are different from those of determinations of being in that they arise from God himself as creator and not from the created determinations.[65]

The problem becomes acute when Neville asserts that "being-itself gives itself [its conditional] features in creating the determinations of being."[66] But what is it that gives to God as being-itself its conditional features of creator? Neville's only answer can be that God as being-itself creates its conditional feature of God as creator, but this would seem to lead to an infinite regress.

---

[63] Ibid., 76.
[64] Ibid., 99; see 84.
[65] Ibid., 45-46, 97-98.
[66] Ibid., 97; see 75, 100, 104.

Neville claims that an infinite regress is avoided by the indeterminate character of being-itself and thus by the heterogeneity of being-itself with respect to the determinations of being or the created order. "It is in virtue of the heterogeneity that the procession of explanations is halted, for there is nothing in the indeterminate transcendent, such as *de facto* unity, that allows the explanation to move out of the transcendent term."[67]

But then it is not clear how the procession of explanations gets *to* the transcendent term. If God as being-itself *gives himself* his conditional feature of creator, then God as being-itself is determinate. If God as being-itself does not give himself his conditional feature of being creator, then he is not creator. If the fact that God as being-itself gives himself his conditional feature of being creator is a conditional feature of God, then we have an infinite regress of conditional features, and we do not arrive at the transcendent term.

Although God as being-itself is indeterminate and therefore has no essential features, Neville wants to affirm his essential character and reality in some sense.

> That being-itself has conditional features would seem to imply that it has essential features. . . . Although being-itself does not have essential features, there is still a contrast between essential and conditional, for it is the character of the conditional features, in their very determinateness and hence contingency to bespeak their dependence on what is essential. There would be no conditionals without the essential.[68]

Furthermore, although we cannot say that being-itself "is," we can say that it is real. "Part of the meaning of being creator is that God must *also* have reality apart from that determinate connection [with the creation] and that this other reality is prior to his reality as creator."[69] Thus, Neville is forced to claim that while God as being-itself is in some sense real and has something like an essential character and is creator, etc., yet he is also absolutely indeterminate and cannot be said to be.

Neville runs into similar difficulties in regard to the question of the unity of God as being-itself. Although God as being-itself is the ontological one for the many and constitutes itself as the one by creating the many, in no sense can he be called one or unified because he is indeterminate.[70]

[67] Ibid., 135; see 102.
[68] Ibid., 97-98.
[69] Ibid., 99; see 76, 93.
[70] Ibid., 60, 86, 71.

Another difficulty arising from the indeterminate character of God as being-itself is the problem of his relation to the determinations of being. On the one hand, Neville asserts that God as being-itself is present in all the determinations of being, that all the determinations participate in being-itself, that being-itself is the being which all the determinations of being have, and that therefore God as being-itself is closer to the determinations than they are to themselves.[71] On the other hand, because God as being-itself is absolutely indeterminate, he is "unconditioned by any relation to the determinations of being."[72] Presumably this apparent contradiction is overcome by the distinction between essential and conditional features, but this simply moves the difficulty to the next stage. Neville would have to say that there is no relation between the conditional features and that which is essential in God as being-itself. But then it is not clear in what way the conditional features are features of God as being-itself.

Another odd result of the indeterminate character of God as being-itself is that the distinction between creator and creature tends to dissolve. On the one hand, because God as being-itself must be indeterminate, God's "character as creator is an actual part of the created product." On the other hand, "insofar as the created realm is a conditional feature of God . . . it can be called divine." "We have found every determinate thing to be the creative presence of God; there is nothing whose whole being is not the immanence of God."[73] This is the result of identifying God with being-itself, for then God must be defined as that of which the determinations of being are determinations, the being that things have in abstraction from them, and that which all things have in common.[74]

Finally, we must raise the question of the status of indeterminateness in God. Does the alleged indeterminate character of God as being-itself refer to the reality of God in himself or only to our knowledge of God? Is God actually indeterminate in himself, or can we think of him only as indeterminate? Neville seems to mean the latter.

> That the creator is indeterminate . . . is an analytic component of the feature of being creator. Its referent is what the creator must be in order to be creator. It does not refer to any fuzziness or chaos in the creator's essential nature. Rather it points out that the contingent fact that the

---

[71] Ibid., 116, 91, 15, 200.
[72] Ibid., 85.
[73] Ibid., 100, 110, 119.
[74] Ibid., 12, 15, 91.

creator is indeed the creator entails a contradiction in the attribution of a determinate nature to the creator apart from all connection with the determinations. . . . What the creator is apart from all such connections is a mystery.[75]

Here Neville seems to be playing down the significance of his assertion of the indeterminate character of God as being-itself. His description of it as an "analytic component" and a "contingent fact" and as not referring to the creator's essential nature implies that it does not refer to indeterminacy in the creator but rather to an incidental implication of the form of the argument and thus simply to the character of our knowledge of God. "What the creator is in itself we do not know: and we have argued that it cannot be known." "Even the category of being-itself is not a conception of what God essentially is but is only a conception arising from his relation to us that guides our approach to him." Does this mean that God transcends being-itself?[76]

Given the many difficulties cited above which are involved in the conception of God as being-itself and as indeterminate, it can be argued that the alternate view has fewer difficulties. This would consist of the argument that the analogy of being and the determinate character of God involve fewer difficulties than the univocity of being and the indeterminate character of God. Neville states, "To say that the creator is indeterminate is merely to deny of it the character that the determinations have, that is, determinate being."[77] Now Neville is not willing to deny of the creator all of the characteristics which the determinations have, e.g., reality and something essential corresponding to their conditional features. So why not simply deny of the creator the character of *finite* determinate being? We have noted his arguments against such a view. I am only suggesting that it can be argued that it involves fewer difficulties than his own approach.

Dewart

The most influential Roman Catholic theologian who denies the identity of God and being is Leslie Dewart. He attempts a reconstruction of the doctrine of God which can be integrated with contemporary experience. His main thesis is that the Greek-scholastic metaphysical tradition which affirms the identity of

[75] Ibid., 76.
[76] Ibid., 77, 195; see 194.
[77] Ibid., 73.

reality and being must be transcended. This tradition is based on the linguistic structure of Indo-European languages and upon the Parmenidean metaphysical presupposition of the identity of thought and being.[78] This tradition assumes that its way of thinking is the universal human way of thinking. But Dewart argues that this is not the case and offers the example of classical Chinese language and thought.[79]

Therefore, philosophy must transcend its metaphysical stage and initiate what Dewart calls its meta-metaphysical stage. Theology likewise must develop a meta-metaphysical doctrine of God.[80] This means primarily the overcoming of the identification of reality and being or the reduction of reality to being.

Dewart defines being as that which is or that which exists. It is absolutely contingent, and therefore "necessary being" is a contradiction in terms. Being is what is empirically given; it is the sort of reality which is revealed in experience.[81]

Dewart's main concepts for God are "reality" and "presence." Religious experience discloses God not as a transcendent being or as being-itself but as a reality *beyond* being.[82] Dewart describes God as "that which we experience as the open background of consciousness and being." "To be sure, the Christian experience of God *can* be cast in the concept of being. It can also be cast, however, in the concept of reality, as the presence of that which (though not itself being) manifests itself in and through being, that-which-is."[83]

Dewart defines reality as "whatever the self can have real relations towards" and as "*that in relation to which* absolute contingencies can be absolutely contingent upon." Thus God is a reality which transcends being but which is immanent in being and which is manifest in and through being as present to being.[84]

> Among the various ways in which we may conceptualize positively that reality which transcends being, "presence" seems to me particularly apt. . . . I have suggested, therefore, that God is better conceived as a reality which is *present to* being than as a reality which *is* being, that

---

[78] Leslie Dewart, *The Foundations of Belief* (New York: Herder, 1969) 402-13.
[79] *Foundations*, 413-20.
[80] Ibid., 19, 361, 391.
[81] Ibid., 397, 399, 422, 431, 492.
[82] Leslie Dewart, *The Future of Belief: Theism in a World Come of Age* (New York: Herder, 1966) 173, 175.
[83] Ibid., 176, 180.
[84] *Foundations*, 399, 493; see 385, 387, 444, 470; *Future,* 177.

God's reality should be conceived in terms of *real presence* rather than in terms of *real being*.[85]

It now becomes clear that for Dewart being means the totality of being or existence, the world, or the creature. He states, "God creates being."[86] Although Dewart's definition of being is that of the older Neo-Thomism generally ("that which is"), his interpretation of this definition is unique among the theologians we have considered.

DUMÉRY

A position similar to that of Dewart is presented by the French Roman Catholic philosopher, Henry Duméry. Duméry adopts the three-fold reduction of Husserl (eidetic, phenomenological, and transcendental) in order to test the act of faith, but he believes that this is incomplete and must be supplemented by a fourth which he calls the henological reduction.

This leads Duméry to a doctrine of God as the One who is trans-ordinal, trans-categorical, beyond all determinations, and beyond essence and existence.[87] He explicitly follows the apophatic tradition of Plotinus and Pseudo-Dionysius in asserting that God as the One is not being but is beyond being and can be called Super-Being or Nothing.[88]

God as the One is the source of the being which proceeds from him but does not receive a part of him or participate in him. Being appears only at the level of the created. Thus Duméry asserts that there is a clear opposition between a participationist ontology and a processionist ontology which he calls henology. He defines them as follows: "The first holds that the inferior borrows a part of what it is from the superior; the second holds that the inferior receives from the superior the means to be what the superior is not."[89]

Duméry argues that the henology of God as the One more rigorously preserves the transcendence of God than does the ontology of God as being. "The super-being God, that of Plotinus and Pseudo-Dionysius . . . is, so to say, more absolute (the only

---

[85] *Foundations*, 442 and note.
[86] Ibid., 386; see *Future*, 195.
[87] Henry Duméry, *The Problem of God in the Philosophy of Religion: A Critical Examination of the Category of the Absolute and the Scheme of Transcendence* (tr. Charles Courtney, Evanston: Northwestern University, 1964) 49-50, 52 (note), 54, 85-86, 94, 99, 109, 128.
[88] Ibid., 50, 86, 88 (note), 101.
[89] Ibid., 89, see 85-86.

absolute) than the Being-God, who can be placed above the determinations only by means of supplementary correctives."[90]

NEO-ORTHODOXY AND PROCESS THEOLOGY

Protestant neo-orthodox and existentialist theology generally rejects the doctrine of God as being-itself, Tillich being the main exception. Karl Barth resists "the threatened absorption of the doctrine of God into a doctrine of being." The principle to be followed here is *esse sequitur operari* and not the reverse.[91] This is closely connected with Barth's rejection of the *analogia entis* throughout his works.[92]

Emil Brunner sees the identification of God with being as a Neo-Platonist speculative concept which has nothing to do with the Biblical concept of God.[93] From the point of view of an existentialist historicism, Carl Michalson criticizes Heinrich Ott's attempt to use the doctrine of being of the later Heidegger as a basis for systematic theology.

> History is not one among several areas but the horizon of every area of investigation. . . . History is an horizon so inescapable that being itself is a derivative of history. . . . In the eschatological faith of the New Testament, being cannot qualify history because it is history which qualifies being, giving it its end.[94]

Theologians influenced by process philosophy reject the doctrine of God as being-itself because they believe that it implies the changelessness and unrelatedness of God, the immutability and absoluteness of God. This in turn makes incomprehensible either God's knowledge of and presence in the world or the reality of change in the world. Schubert M. Ogden argues that the starting point for a genuinely new theistic conception is what Whitehead calls "the reformed subjectivist principle." This requires that we take as the experiential basis of all our most fundamental concepts the primal phenomenon of our own

---

[90] Ibid., 88 (note); see 128.

[91] Karl Barth, *Church Dogmatics*, vol. 2: *The Doctrine of God* (ed. G. W. Bromiley and T. F. Torrance; Edinburgh: Clark, 1957) 1.260; see 83, 261.

[92] See my article, "Barth on Non-Christian Knowledge of God," *ATR* 46 (1964) 268-71.

[93] Emil Brunner, *The Christian Doctrine of God* (Philadelphia: Westminster, 1950) 248-49.

[94] Carl Michalson, *Worldly Theology: The Hermeneutical Focus of an Historical Faith* (New York: Scribner's, 1976) 104-05. For a summary of these and similar views, see Ronald Gregor Smith, *The Doctrine of God*, ed. K. Gregor Smith and A. D. Galloway (Philadelphia: Westminster, 1970), chap. 3.

existence as experiencing subjects or selves. The result is a complete revolution of classical metaphysics. "In consequence the chief category for finally interpreting anything real can no longer be 'substance' or 'being' (as traditionally understood) but must be 'process' or 'creative becoming,' construed as that which is in principle social and temporal. . . . God, too, must be conceived as a genuinely temporal and social reality."[95]

Arguing along similar lines, Charles Hartshorne affirms the priority of becoming to being.

> In general, all attempts to explain becoming as a special case of being, novelty as a special case of permanence, have failed. . . . We shall see that, by contrast, being can very well be explicated as an aspect of novelty.[96]

CONCLUSION

The theologians who affirm the doctrine of God as being-itself fall into two main groups, neither of which is successful in maintaining this identification. The first group defines God as the one who has being in the highest degree in the sense of self-knowledge. For example, Rahner defines being as knowing and being known or being present to oneself, and he asserts that God possesses absolute having-being in this sense. Lonergan defines the idea of being as the unrestricted act of understanding of itself and asserts that this pertains only to God. Neither achieves the identification of God and being-itself, for in both cases God is the subject of a predicate which is distinct from the subject.

The second group asserts that God as being-itself is the act or power of being in everything (Gilson, Tillich), or the dynamic empowering of the being of beings (Macquarrie). This involves either the use of the term "being" in two different senses or the definition of being in terms of itself, neither of which is very clear or satisfactory.

Neville's approach does not fall into either group. His preliminary definition of being-itself is clear enough, namely, the being that things have considered in abstraction from them. However, the identification of God and being-itself in this sense would make God simply an abstraction or universal property in

---

[95]Schubert M. Ogden, *The Reality of God and Other Essays* (New York: Harper & Row, 1963) 58; see also Delwyn Brown, Ralph E. James, Jr., and Gene Reeves, eds., *Process Philosophy and Christian Thought* (Indianapolis: Bobbs-Merrill, 1974) 179-81.

[96]Charles Hartshorne, "Introduction: The Development of Process Philosophy," in *Philosophers of Process*, Douglas Browning, ed. (New York: Random House, 1965) xiv.

spite of Neville's denial. The insurmountable problems involved in his further assertion that God as being-itself is indeterminate have been noted.

This situation leads one to ask why anyone would want to use the concept of being in his theology. What are the possible motives for the assertion of the doctrine of God as being-itself?

1. Because it is a central element in a canonized tradition which needs reinterpretation (Gilson, Rahner, Lonergan).

2. Because it is the fundamental and unavoidable concept in any philosophy or theology (Tillich, Neville).

3. Because it is the fundamental concept of the most important contemporary philosophy (Macquarrie).

4. Because it is useful or helpful in elaborating the doctrine of God.

No. 1 is not decisive for me because this doctrine is not canonized in the tradition in which I stand. I am not persuaded that no. 2 is the case. In regard to no. 3, I would agree that Heidegger's philosophy is one of the most influential in this century and therefore that the interpretation of the doctrine of God in its terms will be an important means of elaborating and communicating the meaning of Christian faith. However, this is qualified by the fact that Heidegger's doctrine of being seems to be more obscure than the received doctrine of God which is being interpreted. Thus the interpretation of the latter in terms of the former may shed light on the doctrine of being but not on the doctrine of God. No. 4 would be decisive if it were the case, but in all the examples we have investigated it seems to me that the doctrine of being is too obscure or problematic to be useful in elaborating the doctrine of God.

This is not surprising in light of the fact that all the theologians who affirm that God is being-itself also state that being-itself is indefinable, inconceivable, and unintelligible. A concept which can be characterized in this way is not going to be very helpful in clarifying the doctrine of God. If it is argued that the appreciation of the concept of being requires revelation or conversion (Tillich, Gilson), I would respond that while concepts may require revelation or conversion for their affirmation, they should not require it for their intelligibility. It is asserted by some of these theologians that the very inconceivability of the concept of being points to the transcendence of God, but this is to confuse unintelligibility with transcendence.

As a matter of fact, one of the main problems in the identification of God with being-itself is the tendency to pantheism. For Gilson, God is the act of being in all things; God is everything that it is possible to be. For Tillich God is the power and structure of all being. For Macquarrie God as being is nothing apart from the beings. For Neville there is nothing whose whole being is not the immanence of God. Duméry notes that God as being-itself can be placed above the determinations of being only by means of "supplementary correctives."

Furthermore, the reasons given for the indefinability, inconceivability, and unintelligibility of being-itself are logical rather than theological. Being-itself cannot be conceived or defined because it has no essence or quiddity of its own (Gilson). It is indefinable because it is the antecedent of knowing and being known (Rahner) or because it underpins and transcends the content of every definition (Tillich, Lonergan) or because it does not fall under our usual categories of thought (Macquarrie). It is unintelligible because it is indeterminate and prior to intelligibility (Neville).

However, it can be argued that the transcendence of God is not a logical matter but rather a theological one. The transcendence of God is manifest in the character of his presence in the contingencies of history, in his free activity. Early Christian theology should "have been able to understand the otherness of God more radically than philosophy as not only the incomprehensibility of the world-ground but as the otherness of the freedom of God precisely in his acts which cut across and surpass all expectations and planning."[97] It can also be argued that the incomprehensibility of God is not a logical matter but rather the mysteriousness of God which emerges through his self-disclosure on the analogy of human personal self-disclosure.[98]

Thus I conclude that if the doctrine of being is to be used at all in Christian theology, it should be used in the doctrine of the world or the creation (Dewart, Duméry). Then being would be defined as that which is, or as the totality of existence. Being or some aspect of being could be attributed to God analogically, and the ways in which the being of God is like and unlike the being of the creature could be specified. Thus I would associate myself with the tradition which asserts that God transcends being and is the creator of being.[99] To be sure, this involves many other problems. But that should be the subject of another essay.

---

[97] Wolfhart Pannenberg, *Basic Questions in Theology* (Collected Essays, tr. George H. Kehm; Philadelphia: Fortress, 1971) 2.181.

[98] See Karl Rahner, "The Concept of Mystery in Catholic Theology," *Investigations*, 4.36, 73.

[99] See above, p. 155.

THE TWO I-THOU RELATIONS IN MARTIN BUBER'S PHILOSOPHY

Stuart Charmé

University of Chicago Divinity School
Chicago, Illinois 60637

Maurice Friedman, the leading scholar of Martin Buber's work, notes that "the question must even arise whether the philosophy of dialogue, the I-Thou relation between man and man, cannot stand by itself as an autonomous ethic, grounded in Buber's anthropology, but not necessarily tied with the relation between man and God."[1] Friedman then suggests that Buber's philosophy of religion and interpretation of the Bible do provide an important source of his ethics. An examination of Buber's thought reveals, however, that the tie between his philosophy of dialogue as an ethics and his view of the relation between man and God is indeed not necessary in some ways and perhaps not even possible.

In the Postscript to *I and Thou,* Buber cites the central concern which he has sought to express throughout his work—"namely, the close connection of the relation to God with the relation to one's fellowman."[2] Elsewhere in *I and Thou* and his other writings, Buber emphasizes the need to develop authentic human relations in order to counteract "a progressive augmentation of the world of *It.*"[3] Buber thus sets a dual purpose for himself. He wishes to point the way to a renewed sense of personal relation with God *and* to truly human interpersonal relations. For Buber these two concerns are interconnected because he believes that a personal relation with God is of the same fundamental nature as an authentic relation to one's fellow humans.

Unfortunately, the interconnection Buber suggests is problematic; it falters because Buber's two primary concerns occur on two different levels. Buber's concern with human relation to God is essentially an *epistemological* issue dealing with

---

[1] Maurice Friedman, "The Bases of Buber's Ethics," *The Philosophy of Martin Buber* (ed. Paul Arthur Schilpp; La Salle, Ill.: Open Court, 1967) 171.
[2] Martin Buber, *I and Thou* (New York: Scribner's, 1958) 123-24.
[3] Ibid., 38.

the peculiar ways in which God is known. His concern with developing authentic relations among humans is mainly an *ethical* question regarding the proper way to act toward other human beings. Consequently, Buber's central distinction between I-Thou and I-It is made at both the epistemological and the ethical level. As an epistemological distinction I-Thou and I-It are used to establish a parallel between relations with other people and relations with God. As an ethical distinction, these types of relation reflect Buber's judgment on the moral way to treat other people in the world.

Buber, however, never distinguishes these two different levels of his philosophy of I-Thou and I-It relations. Accordingly, he never considers the possible tension or incompatibility between them. Buber wants to show that human relationship to God is personal, since one can know God only as one knows another person. Because knowledge of God can be neither objectified in particular contents nor validated, our knowledge of other persons or objects in the world must be of an analogous kind if Buber is to be able to show a parallel between relations to God and relations to persons. When Buber describes the I-Thou relation as a way of knowing persons, trees, or God, he is, therefore, concerned with a special kind of knowledge which he regards as intuitive, self-validating, ineffable, momentary, and contentless. It is a virtually mystical knowledge in which all normal knowing *about* a person, an object, or God is eliminated. This fleeting, contentless kind of I-Thou relation in itself, like mystical ecstasy, involves no obvious ethical implications for action in the world, since any type of responsible action rests on some knowledge about the world and takes place in time and space. Buber contrasts I-Thou knowledge with the I-It way of knowing. Here I-It refers to our normal way of organizing the world of perception and sensation. It includes all our ordinary knowledge about the world of space and time.

It is the ethical side of Buber's formulation, however, which has received the most attention and which most of Buber's readers find familiar and valuable. Here Buber is primarily concerned about the increasing tendency in the modern world to treat other persons as objects to be used, manipulated, and exploited. In this context, I-Thou relation refers to an intimate, caring relation which accepts another person for what he is. In contrast, I-It relation refers mainly to the inevitable use of objects and persons for private, selfish purposes. As it will become clear, an I-Thou relation on the ethical level does not preclude all knowledge *about* another person.

The tension in Buber's philosophy is apparent. If the I-Thou relation is simply a contentless, timeless knowledge of the other person, one can perhaps compare knowledge of God with knowledge of other persons; but it is difficult to base ethical relations with other people on this type of knowledge. Conversely, if I-Thou relation, as a model for ethical relations with other people, requires a certain knowledge about these others and action within a spatio-temporal context, then the parallel between relation to God and relation to humans breaks down, precisely because analogous knowledge *about* God is lacking. Rather than struggling to harmonize Buber's contradictory characterizations of I-Thou relations, it is probably more valuable simply to recognize Buber's two different kinds of I-Thou relations. Buber's error is to assume that the one kind of I-Thou relation implies the other, or that they are in fact the same.

The Epistemological Meaning of I-Thou

It is not without justification that one may interpret I-Thou knowledge as a "mystical" way of knowing. In so doing we must be careful to distinguish mysticism as a specific metaphysical doctrine from the more general characteristics of mystical knowing. As a metaphysical doctrine, mysticism commonly asserts such things as the illusory nature of ordinary reality, the underlying unity of the world, and human oneness with God. Indeed, mysticism as Buber first encounters it and understands it throughout his life is a fundamentally monistic doctrine.[4] In his introduction to an anthology of mystic texts, Buber describes the essence of mystical ecstasy as a perfect unity in which the world and the I are one and all multiplicity has disappeared.[5] Many years later Buber states succinctly, "As far as I understand mysticism, its essential trait is the belief in a (momentous) 'union' with the Divine or the absolute, a union occurring not after death but in the course of mortal life, i.e. as interruption."[6]

When Buber insists that I-Thou is not a mystical relation, he is criticizing this doctrine of monism, since it eliminates relation.

---

[4] For an account of Buber's relation to mysticism, see Maurice Friedman, "Martin Buber's Encounter with Mysticism," *Human Inquiries: Review of Existential Psychology and Psychiatry*, 10 (1970) 43-81.

[5] Martin Buber, *Ekstatische Konfessionen* (Jena: Diederichs, 1909) xi-xxvi.

[6] From a letter from Martin Buber to Maurice Friedman superscribed "Tübingen 23.8.54" quoted by Friedman, "Buber's Encounter with Mysticism," 62-63.

His criticism, moreover, is largely of the ethical consequences of mysticism. Buber is concerned that mysticism may inhibit committed action in the world and genuine ethical relations with other people. He notes, "mysticism is wanting in the element of activity in the state of unconditionality, the tendency to realized undivided life in the world of man, in the world of being with one another."[7] The mystic's experience of unity can become a substitute for life with other people. The mystic begins "to regard everyday life as an obscuring of the true life."[8] The mystic constantly leaves it for the mystical experience of unity above life in the world and thereby forsakes authentic relations. By ignoring relation in the human world, mysticism leads to passivity and inauthentic existence. As Buber develops his dialogical philosophy, he emphasizes the ethical dimension of I-Thou in order to remedy this danger.

In addition to the specific monistic doctrine of most mystics, the mystic also makes claim to a special type of knowledge which is contrasted with ordinary sense experience and reason. He believes in a special kind of wisdom which is immediate and infallible. This knowledge presents itself more as mystery and revelation than particular beliefs. The mystic doubts common knowledge because it is slow, partial, fallible, and concerned only with the appearances revealed to the senses. Mystical knowledge grasps an object in its wholeness; it is absolute.

Buber's early interest in various mystical traditions is well known.[9] Although his dialogical philosophy made him increasingly critical of mysticism as the basis of authentic living, Buber's rejection of a mystical way of knowing is far less clear. Indeed, as Maurice Friedman points out,

> Buber's "conversion" did not mean, as some have thought, a rejection of mysticism *in toto*. On the contrary, much remained with him and informed his lifetime of work on Hasidism and his own philosophy. Presence, presentness, immediacy, ineffability, a meaning which can be lived and confirmed but cannot be defined, the action which appears like non-action because it is whole and does not interfere—all these accompanied Buber on his long way forward.[10]

---

[7] Martin Buber, "The Holy Way," *On Judaism* (ed. Nahum Glatzer; New York: Schocken, 1967) 126.
[8] Martin Buber, *Pointing the Way* (New York: Schocken, 1957) ix-x.
[9] See Maurice Friedman, *Martin Buber: The Life of Dialogue* (New York: Harper, 1960) chap. 4.
[10] "Buber's Encounter with Mysticism," 81.

Buber's descriptions of I-Thou knowledge frequently resemble those of traditionally mystical ways of knowing. The I-Thou encounter is immediate and timeless. The person treated as Thou is "not . . . a specific point in space and time within the net of the world."[11] I-Thou exists in the "spaceless, timeless present on the shore of existence."[12] A Thou has no dimensions. "When *Thou* is spoken, the speaker has no thing for his object. . . . *Thou* has no bounds."[13] I-Thou relation is beyond all experience of the world. A Thou is not "a nature able to be experienced and described, a loose bundle of named qualities."[14] All experience of the world occurs only by leaving the relation. "I do not experience the man to whom I say *Thou*. . . . Only when I step out of it do I experience him once more. In the act of experience *Thou* is far away."[15] In addition, the relation is indescribable and ineffable. "You cannot make yourself understood with others concerning it, you are alone with it."[16] It is a "mystery" which "every word would falsify."[17]

In I-Thou relation one encounters the indivisible unity and uniqueness of the Thou. One meets the object *in itself* and one is relieved of all specific knowledge *about* it and all sense perception of it. One grants an object like a tree its full independence only

> by freeing it from the sense world, from its sensible representation. What then remains as it-self, emptied of all properties that it has acquired in the meeting with me, in the sense-world, may here be designated by a small x. It exists but not as imageable. . . . Of x we know what Kant points out to us of the thing-in-itself, namely, that it is. Kant would say: "And nothing more," but we who live today must add: "And that the existent meets us."[18]

This thing-in-itself which one encounters is "propertyless and uncanny."[19] It is an "unfathomable darkness."[20] Only later is there a stimulation of my senses out of which arise "clearly outlined forms that people my sense world in color and sound."[21]

---

[11] *I and Thou*, 8.
[12] Ibid., 14.
[13] Ibid., 4.
[14] Ibid., 8.
[15] Ibid., 9.
[16] Ibid., 33.
[17] Ibid., 15.
[18] Martin Buber, *The Knowledge of Man* (New York: Harper, 1965) 157.
[19] Ibid.
[20] Ibid., 158.
[21] Ibid.

There are no cognitive contents which one takes from I-Thou relations. All the cognitive categories by which one orders the world are eliminated. One is simply confronted with the brute existence of the world. Buber says,

> With all deference to the world continuum of space and time, I know as a living truth only concrete world reality which is constantly, in every moment, reached out to me. I can separate it into its component parts, I can compare them and distribute them into groups of similar phenomena; and when I have done all this I have not touched my concrete world reality. Inseparable, incomparable, irreducible, now, happening once only, it gazes upon me with a horrifying look.[22]

Despite the lack of all experience, sense data, and content regarding the Thou, one still achieves an absolute kind of knowledge which cannot be doubted even if it is not fully understood. "We have 'known' it, but we acquire no knowledge from it which might lessen its mysteriousness."[23] Even without factual knowledge about it, the Thou is "clearer than all the clearness of the world which is experienced."[24] Error is not possible since there is no knowledge of objective facts which might be compared and corrected.[25]

I-Thou relation is thus a momentary glimpse of the naked existence of an object, the apperception of the Kantian thing-in-itself. I-It relation, in turn, is our ordinary way of thinking about the nature and characteristics of the world as we represent it to ourselves by means of our senses and our conceptual categories. I-It includes all our normal mental processes. It is the realm of "transitive verbs," i.e., all activities which have some thing for their object. Buber notes, "I perceive something. I am sensible of something. I imagine something. I will something. I feel something. I think something. . . . This and the like together establish the realm of *It*."[26] In short, all normal contact with the world, reactions to the world, and activities in the world are part of the realm of It.

---

[22]Martin Buber, *Between Man and Man* (London: Collins, 1964) 30. This type of relation to reality is not very different from the somewhat mystical encounter with a chestnut tree which Jean-Paul Sartre describes (*Nausea* [New York: New Directions, 1964] 170-80) when he recognizes the inability to capture existence in descriptions or language.

[23]*I and Thou*, 111.

[24]Ibid., 10.

[25]Sidney and Beatrice Rome, eds., *Philosophical Interrogations* (New York: Holt, Rinehart, & Winston, 1964) 54-55.

[26]*I and Thou*, 4.

Buber identifies all "experience" with the world of It. Experience for Buber is the way the world is mediated for man through his senses and intellect. Experience is that which "continually reconstitutes the world."[27] It is very much the phenomenal world of Kant, the spatio-temporal world of objects which appears to consciousness.[28] Buber finds experience superficial, since it deals only with appearances and misses the real being of people and things. "Man," says Buber, "travels over the surface of things and experiences them. He extracts knowledge about their constitution from them: he wins an experience from them."[29] Experience, however, is just an accumulation of information. It does not truly involve the world, since it arises "in" a person rather than between the person and the world.[30] Buber claims, "The world has no part in experience. It permits itself to be experienced but has no concern in the matter."[31]

Buber has conceived his epistemology in terms of an opposition between all ordinary experience or knowledge and a special knowing of reality beyond ordinary knowledge. Buber's rejection of sense data in the realm of I-Thou is intended to circumvent criticism regarding the fallibility of our senses and the possibility of error in the interpretation of signs used in ordinary communication. This is crucial if Buber is to establish the plausibility of a personal, infallible, direct relation with God. God, the "eternal Thou," can by its nature never become an object, be measured, or be understood in terms of qualities. God lacks space, time, sense aspects, and can be neither experienced nor thought.[32] Nevertheless, Buber insists that a personal relation with God is possible. He bases this belief on the claim that persons and objects can be known with a similar type of awareness which transcends ordinary experience. If we can have personal relations with other people outside of time, space, and all sense-data and experience, then to have a personal relation with God in this fashion is not inconceivable.

This position, however, results in a peculiar kind of relation. I-Thou relation takes place without any attention to sound,

---

[27]Ibid., 38.
[28]Buber says he read Kant when he was 15 and learned that space and time have nothing to do with the inner nature of the world but are only an appearance to the senses (*Between Man and Man,* 169).
[29]*I and Thou,* 5.
[30]Ibid.
[31]Ibid.
[32]Ibid., 112.

gestures, or words. It is not even the silence between lovers, for they, too, rely on each other's gestures and predetermined attitudes toward each other.[33] Rather, Buber refers to the sudden silent communication which occurs between two persons who do not speak to each other, look at each other, or know anything about each other.[34] This sort of contentless, mediumless communication may be immune to sensible or interpretive error, but it is not clear in what sense we can still speak of communication as having occurred, or of anything having occurred for that matter. Buber finds epistemological infallibility only by emptying communication of all normal meaning.

The entire idea of grasping a person as a thing in itself in a Kantian sense has given Buber a very radical epistemology bordering on the mystical. This type of encounter which is beyond "experience" presents serious questions. If all conceptual categories and all sense information are withdrawn, it may become difficult to maintain the individuality of I and Thou, the distinction between self and other. Without a view of spatial and temporal dimensions, the boundaries between things begin to dissolve. As a result, the very notion of relation is threatened, since relation requires some way of distinguishing the individual sides of the relation. This is problematic since Buber is very concerned with preserving the bipolarity of relation and he strongly opposes a mystical union of I and Thou. For Buber, human relation to God is a personal one because it is like relation to other persons. However, Buber's necessarily radical epistemology has not made knowledge of God personal as much as it has made knowledge of other people mystical and unlike any common way of personally knowing something.

The Ethical Meaning of I-Thou

When I-Thou is proposed as the proper way to treat other human beings, Buber is not concerned with a mystical cognition of another person about whom one has no phenomenal knowledge. Rather, Buber presents I-Thou in this context as an ethical relation based on respect for the uniqueness and integrity of every individual. According to Buber, the chief presupposition for a genuine dialogical situation is regarding the other as what he is. Buber says, "I become aware of him, aware that he is different, essentially different from myself, in the definite, unique way which is peculiar to him, and I accept who I thus see, so that in full

[33] *Between Man and Man,* 19.
[34] Ibid., 19-20.

earnestness I can direct what I say to him as the person he is."[35] Genuine relation, therefore, is mainly based on "acceptance of otherness."[36]

Above all, in an I-Thou relation one does not "use" the other person in any way. Buber insists, "No aim, no lust, and no anticipation intervene between *I* and *Thou*. . . . Every means is an obstacle. Only when every means has collapsed does meeting come about."[37] Buber admits that he is near Kant's belief that one's fellow human being must never be thought of and treated merely as a means, but always at the same time as an independent end.[38] Unlike Kant, however, Buber bases this belief on the dialogical nature of human existence rather than a rationally derived categorical imperative. Buber links the notion of speech and response between two people with the moral notion of responsibility. He wishes to remove the concept of responsibility from the realm of specialized ethics where it lacks real foundation and to place it in the context of a person's lived life. He points out, "Genuine responsibility exists only where there is real responding."[39] When one is addressed by another person one is responsible not simply in the literal sense of being able to respond but in the ethical sense of being obligated to answer in a trustworthy manner. One is accountable to the other person. Buber says, "Responsibility presupposes one who addressed me primarily, that is, from a realm independent of myself, and to whom I am answerable. . . . He addresses me from his trust and I respond in my loyalty. . . ."[40]

When Buber develops his vision of what genuine and authentic relations between people must be, he is mainly concerned with the danger of treating other people as objects of use. This does not mean that one must regard another person as a virtual thing-in-itself. Clearly, even in I-Thou relations of an ethical sort, one experiences and has conscious knowledge about the Thou. What I-Thou adds to one's knowledge about other people is a kind of intuition or inner understanding of the other's point of view. Buber calls the process "imagining the real," which means the capacity to imagine what another person is wishing, feeling, perceiving, and thinking, not as an abstraction but as the other

---

[35] *The Knowledge of Man*, 79.
[36] Ibid., 69.
[37] *I and Thou*, 11.
[38] *The Knowledge of Man*, 84.
[39] *Between Man and Man*, 33-34.
[40] Ibid., 65.

person lives it.⁴¹ This process, however, is not a substitute for experienced knowledge about the other, but a completion of it. Buber explains, "The experiencing senses and the imagining of the real which completes the findings of the senses work together to make the other present as a whole and as a unique being, as the person that he is."⁴²

In the ethical context, the I-It relation does not concern the way reason and the senses represent the world to man. It deals primarily with how one *makes use* of the world. One relates to people and objects in the world in particular, limited ways according to one's specific needs and interests. I-It addresses that part of another person which fulfills a particular need. Buber condemns "the lust to make use of men" and to treat them as things robbed of their distance and independence.⁴³

Similarly, when Buber refers to "the tyranny of the exuberantly growing It,"⁴⁴ he is not referring to the simple epistemological fact that one perceives and senses the world as an object of experience, nor to any obvious consequence of that fact. Rather, he is pointing to how people today have become victims of their own desire to master the world. Buber addresses himself to the specifically modern problems raised by the dominance of a scientific and technological world-view. In this sense he is like many other humanistically oriented thinkers who condemn the objectification of humans into things which can be completely explained and manipulated according to scientific laws. Buber is concerned with the ways in which a technological ideology has extended to more and more aspects of human life and destroyed the human capacity to enter into genuine relation.

Buber's ethical critique of the world of It has very specific targets. In the communal life of modern man, for example, the major compartments of the world of It are economics and politics. Buber claims that the success of the economist and the statesman requires that each of them treat other persons not as

---

⁴¹ *The Knowledge of Man,* 70. To a certain extent Buber, a student of Dilthey, must be seen in the philosophical tradition of "life philosophy" with its concern for lived experience. Dilthey's famous distinction between "explanation" and "understanding" (*verstehen*) obviously influenced Buber. In some ways I-Thou is quite similar to the method of *verstehen,* and I-It may be associated with the explanatory method of the natural sciences.
⁴²Ibid., 85.
⁴³Ibid., 69.
⁴⁴*I and Thou,* 48.

unique individuals but as "centres of work and effort, whose particular capabilities it is his concern to estimate and utilize."[45]

Buber is likewise critical of the overapplication of the notions of causality and determinism which the scientific viewpoint fosters. The "sickness of our age"[46] is largely the pervasiveness of our belief in causality. Buber associates the world of It with "the unlimited reign of causality."[47] The person who lives only in the world of It is enslaved to his sense of biological and historical causality. He thereby eliminates the essential element of human freedom. The world of I and Thou lacks all causality and assures people of their freedom and their capacity for decision.[48]

Buber does not attack the I-It mode without qualification, for he recognizes that the analytical method of the human sciences can provide indispensable knowledge about a phenomenon. He insists only that the I-It relation is limited and is not a fully ethical response to the uniqueness of another person. Buber wants to emphasize that a person treated as a whole, as a unity, and as unique is more than the sum of all that can be scientifically determined about him or her. The specifically modern point of view which treats a person as an object which can be put together and taken apart, reduced to recurrent structures, and derived by general genetic formulas ignores people's basic humanity.

The I-Thou relation avoids the dangers of use, exploitation, and scientific reductionism in its approach to other people. It is an ethical ideal for authentic life with others in the world. I-Thou is an alternative to the utilitarian, technological, and reductionist ethos prevalent in modern times. At this level Buber is not centrally concerned with the similarities he posits between the way God is known and the way human beings are known. Consequently, the "mystical" aspects of I-Thou relation in the latter context are not evident in the ethical I-Thou relation. There is no reason to believe that in an ethical I-Thou relation the Thou is beyond space, time, experience, or sense awareness in any radical way.

Conclusion

One reason Buber develops the notion of the I-Thou relation is to establish a personalistic relation with God. Relating to God as a person encounters difficulties, however, when we admit our lack

[45] Ibid., 47.
[46] Ibid., 55.
[47] Ibid., 51.
[48] Ibid.

of any factual knowledge about God analogous to our factual knowledge of other people. Buber tries to remedy this problem by offering an alternative epistemology in which "knowing" a Thou requires no factual knowledge and entails no possibility of error. Buber claims that when one addresses someone as a person there is no experience or consciousness of that person. This relation goes beyond all phenomenal or conceptual experience and provides only a direct, ineffable glimpse at the "suchness" of the other.

We can understand Buber's dismissal of all experience, sense awareness, and knowledge of the Thou if we keep in mind Buber's desire to make a parallel case for I-Thou encounter with God. It is unlikely, however, that Buber regards this pure, mystical kind of relation with another person as a major goal of authentic living. This spontaneous flash of the existence of the other has a certain passive quality to it. It seems to require the cessation of all action rather than the ethical purification of action. Indeed, one does not "do" anything in the momentary, contentless I-Thou encounters which Buber describes. Even the relationship of love, says Buber, cannot exist in the immediacy of I-Thou relation.[49] It is difficult to imagine any ethical dimension to this kind of relation or any concrete way of life based on it.

But Buber does conceive of an I-Thou relation which is deeply immersed in concrete action in the world. It does not require constant involvement in the intensity of a "mystical" I-Thou relation. The ethical I-Thou relation recognizes other people as unique individuals and treats them as ends in themselves. On this level, a love which wholly accepts and respects another person is paradigmatic of I-Thou. "Love is responsibility of an *I* for a *Thou*."[50] Here one "knows" the other in the Biblical sense of embracing him lovingly. This responsibility for the other entails a continuing relationship and a growing understanding of the other's particular needs. As an ethical relation, moreover, I-Thou need not represent a lack of objective knowledge about the Thou. One is aware of the expression of his eyes and voice, his gestures, and so on. Some knowledge of other people is necessary in order to avoid error and deception. Behavioral checks are essential for judging another person's feelings and needs.

Furthermore, Buber's ethical concern over the increase of the realm of It in the modern world and the attendant dangers of objectification must not be confused with his epistemological

[49] Ibid., 99.
[50] Ibid., 15.

treatment of the realm of It as ordinary phenomenal world of human experience. When we refuse to treat persons as objects we do not mean that they are no longer data of our consciousness, but rather that we consider their freedom and individuality, and we do not see them as machines or servants with purely functional values. Buber may believe that the simple fact that we have experience and knowledge of people inevitably leads us to use and manipulate them as objects. Yet Buber never demonstrates any necessary connection between the two different ways a person may be an "object" for another person. To say that we should not experience another person as an object of use does not mean that we do not experience him at all. Buber holds that when a person is conscious of something, he possesses that object, and the object is dependent on him for its existence. This is an unnecessary assumption if we avoid an idealist view of consciousness and recognize the phenomenological insight that intentional objects are objects *for* consciousness, not *in* it. Indeed, the notion of consciousness without an object is incomprehensible. Relationship makes no sense if I am not conscious of Thou, if I do not experience Thou, albeit in a special way.[51]

In short, Buber's parallel between relation with human beings and relation with God is based on a superior mystical way of knowing which has no contents and cannot be verified. Whether this type of I-Thou relation is convincing in itself, however, does not depend on Buber's ethical vision of I-Thou where knowledge of a non-reductive type *is* present. The understanding of Buber's I-Thou philosophy would be best served by evaluating each of these two modes of I-Thou in its own right.

---

[51] It is somewhat ironic that Buber criticizes the monistic absorption of the mystic precisely for eliminating the object of consciousness. He says, ". . . in lived reality there is not something thinking without something thought, rather is the thinking no less dependent on the thing thought than the latter on the former. A subject deprived of its object is deprived of its reality" (*I and Thou*, 87).

Rewarding reading experiences

THE CHRISTIAN DOCTRINE OF THE CHURCH, FAITH, AND THE CONSUMMATION Now with this new edition of Volume III, EMIL BRUNNER'S complete *Dogmatics* is again available.
Soft cover $7.95

THEOLOGY IN A NEW KEY *Responding to Liberation Themes* by ROBERT McAFEE BROWN. Explores the challenges to North Americans issued by South American liberation theologians.
Soft cover $6.95

THE HUMILITY OF GOD by JOHN MACQUARRIE. Thought-provoking theological discussions which emphasize God's involvement in the life of His creatures.
Paper $4.65

THE REMAKING OF CHRISTIAN DOCTRINE by MAURICE WILES. A distinguished contributor to *The Myth of God Incarnate* develops some of the provocative points he raised in that book.
Soft cover $5.95

BAPTISM IN THE NEW TESTAMENT by OSCAR CULLMANN. Available for the first time in a trade edition, "an indispensable work...on the subject of baptism." —*Reformed Theological Review*.
Paper $3.95

EARLY CHRISTIAN WORSHIP by OSCAR CULLMANN. Another classic work by one of the great Biblical thinkers of our age, available for the first time in a trade edition.
Paper $4.65

SACRIFICE AND THE DEATH OF CHRIST by FRANCES M. YOUNG. "A perceptive treatment of the different theories of atonement. The continuing moral force of the idea of sacrifice is illustrated and defended." —*Journal of Theological Studies*.
Soft cover $4.95

THE RELIGIOUS CARE OF THE PSYCHIATRIC PATIENT by WAYNE E. OATES. An important and innovative book for ministers, psychiatrists, psychologists, nurses, and social workers.
$12.50

THE METHOD AND MESSAGE OF JESUS' TEACHING by ROBERT H. STEIN. A valuable introductory text for colleges and seminaries.
Soft cover $7.95

THE GOSPEL ACCORDING TO ST. JOHN *Second Edition* by C. K. BARRETT. An outstanding commentary on St. John, completely revised and reset.
$25

UNDERSTANDING THE OLD TESTAMENT by A. H. J. GUNNEWEG. How the Old Testament has been understood from the beginnings of the church until today. *Old Testament Library*.
$12

Delayed, but now available
CATHOLICISM BETWEEN LUTHER AND VOLTAIRE *A New View of the Counter-Reformation* by JEAN DELUMEAU.
$19.50

Now in soft cover: four more volumes from The Library of Christian Classics

EARLY LATIN THEOLOGY
edited by S. L. GREENSLADE.
Soft cover $7.95

AQUINAS ON NATURE AND GRACE
edited by A. M. FAIRWEATHER.
Soft cover $7.95

CALVIN: THEOLOGICAL TREATISES
edited by J. K. S. REID.
Soft cover $7.95

LUTHER AND ERASMUS: FREE WILL AND SALVATION
edited by E. GORDON RUPP and PHILIP S. WATSON.
Soft cover $7.95

Ichthus  Edition

Available at your bookstore or direct from the publisher
THE WESTMINSTER PRESS
905 Witherspoon Bldg., Phila., Pa. 19107

NOTES AND OBSERVATIONS

GEORGE BERKELEY'S ATTITUDE TO JOHN WESLEY: THE EVIDENCE OF A LOST LETTER

John Wesley made his third tour of Ireland in 1749. He spent about fourteen weeks there traveling and preaching, and he encountered much opposition. It came in part from clergymen who spoke and wrote their disapproval of his work, in part from angry, rioting crowds. But he also found sympathizers, including the Rev. Richard Lloyd, rector and vicar of Rathcormack. Twice, when Wesley stopped to preach at Rathcormack, Lloyd received him with warm interest and gave him the use of the pulpit in the parish church; and after he had finished his tour and gone home to England, Lloyd wrote to him, thanking him for the good he had done in the town.[1]

During the spring of 1750 Wesley returned to Ireland, and, as in the previous year, stopped in Rathcormack and preached at Lloyd's invitation from the pulpit of the parish church. This time, however, the clergymen of the neighboring parishes decided to complain of Lloyd to the bishop of the diocese. At the episcopal visitation in June they said that Lloyd ought to be kept from letting a troublemaker like Wesley use his pulpit.

The bishop was George Berkeley, the philosopher, and he agreed with the complaining clergymen. He told his archdeacon to write to Lloyd and order that the Rathcormack pulpit be closed to strangers. When Lloyd got the archdeacon's letter, he took offense. Fifty-one years old, and holding a living worth about £250,[2] he disliked getting orders through an intermediary. He made no answer to the archdeacon but, on July 4, 1750, sent Berkeley instead a hot, diffuse letter, displaying his irritation and also justifying his hospitality to Wesley. He said that Wesley was after all a fellow of an Oxford college; that to exclude him from the pulpit would serve only to promote field-preaching and lay-preaching; that lay-preaching had anyway proved beneficial in reforming many sinners; that if those so reformed were continually ridiculed and persecuted, the rich among them would emigrate to England and leave behind only the "refuse"; that Wesley's sermons were "edifying"; and that he himself, for the

---

[1] Nehemiah Curnock, ed., *The Journal of John Wesley* (8 vols.; London: Kelley, 1909-16) 3. 395-417, 426-27.

[2] William Maziere Brady, *Clerical and Parochial Records of Cork, Cloyne and Ross* (3 vols.; Dublin: Thom, 1863) 2. 371-72.

future, begged to get the bishop's orders direct. The same day Berkeley replied with a letter doubtless meant to be mollifying but firm:

> Rev. Sir,
>
> I have that opinion of your prudence, that I doubt not you will be cautious whom you admit into your pulpit; and that you will avoid doing or countenancing any thing that may offend your brethren of the clergy, or give occasion to mobs and riots. I am, Rev. Sir,
>
> > Your faithful Brother
> > and humble Servant,
>
> > G. Cloyne
>
> Cloyne,
> July 4, 1750.[3]

Lloyd never again opened his pulpit to Wesley.[4]

HENRY ABELOVE

DEPT. OF HISTORY, WESLEYAN UNIVERSITY
MIDDLETOWN, CONNECTICUT 06457

---

[3] This letter is missing from every edition of Berkeley's correspondence, including the most recent (*The Works of George Berkeley, Bishop of Cloyne,* ed. A. A. Luce and T. E. Jessop, [9 vols.; London: Nelson, 1948-57] vols. 8, 9); it is not listed in the standard guide to his writings (T. E. Jessop, *A Bibliography of George Berkeley* [2nd ed., rev.; The Hague: Nijhoff, 1973]); nor is it mentioned in any biography of him. It may be found along with the letters of the archdeacon and Lloyd, but without any notation that "G. Cloyne" was George Berkeley, in *The Arminian Magazine* 2 (1779) 252-56. Luke Tyerman (*The Life and Times of the Rev. John Wesley, M.A.* [3 vols.; London: Hodder and Stoughton, 1870] 2. 79-80) reprinted it, but apparently without realizing to whom the episcopal signature belonged, for he also did not name Berkeley. C. H. Crookshank (*History of Methodism in Ireland* [2 vols.; Belfast: Allen, 1885] 1. 69) reprinted it again and did name Berkeley; but because his book is obscure, the letter has persistently eluded notice.

[4] Tyerman, 2. 80.

BOOKS RECEIVED

Biblical Studies

BEAUCHAMP, Paul. L'un et l'autre testament: essai de lecture. Parole de Dieu, 14. Paris: Le Seuil, 1976. 319p.

HAZLITT, Frances Kanes. The concise Bible: a condensation. Indianapolis: Liberty, 1976. 257p.

NINEHAM, Dennis. The use and abuse of the Bible: a study of the Bible in an age of rapid cultural change. Library of Philosophy and Religion. New York: Barnes & Noble / Harper & Row, 1976. xi, 295p.

RUSSELL, Letty M., ed. The liberating word: a guide to nonsexist interpretation of the Bible. Philadelphia: Westminster, 1976. 121p.

SOULEN, Richard N. Handbook of biblical criticism. Atlanta: John Knox, 1976. 191p.

Old Testament and Ancient Near East

ABERBACH, Moses and GROSSFELD, Bernard. Targum Onqelos on Genesis 49. Translation and analytical commentary. Aramaic Studies, 1. Missoula, Mont.: Scholars Press / Society of Biblical Literature, 1976. xiv, 84p.

ANDERSEN, Francis I. Job: an introduction and commentary. Tyndale Old Testament Commentaries. Downers Grove, Ill.: InterVarsity, 1976. 294p.

DE GEUS, C. H. J. The tribes of Israel: an investigation into some of the presuppositions of Martin Noth's amphictyony hypothesis. Studia Semitica Neerlandica, 18. Assen: Van Gorcum, 1976. xii, 258p.

GOWAN, Donald E. The triumph of faith in Habakkuk. Atlanta: John Knox, 1976. 94p.

LEVINE, Étan. The aramaic version of Lamentations. New York: Hermon, 1976. 203p.

METTINGER, Tryggve N. D. King and messiah: the civil and sacral legitimation of the Israelite kings. Coniectanea Biblica, Old Testament series 8. Lund: Gleerup, 1976. 342p.

NOTH, Martin. Storia d'Israele. Biblioteca di cultura religiosa, 25. Brescia: Paideia, 1975. 578p.

VIGANO, Lorenzo. Nomi e titoli di YHWH alla luce del semitico del Nord-ovest. Biblica et Orientalia, 31. Rome: Biblical Institute, 1976. xix, 247p.

WINWARD, Stephen F. A guide to the prophets. Atlanta: John Knox, 1976. 255p.

New Testament and Christian Origins

ANNEN, Franz. Heil für die Heiden: zur Bedeutung und Geschichte der Tradition vom besessenen Gerasener (Mk 5:1-20). Frankfurter Theologische Studien, 20. Frankfurt am Main: Knecht, 1976. vii, 253p.

BARTH, Karl. Erklärungen des Johannes-Evangeliums (Kapitel 1-8); hrsg. von Walther Fürst. Gesamtausgabe, II. Akademische Werke, 1925-26. Zürich: Theologischer Verlag, 1976. xii, 422p.

BIANCHI, Ugo. Prometeo, Orfeo, Adamo: tematiche religiose sul destino, il male, la salvezza. Roma: Ateneo & Bizzarri, 1976. viii, 300p.
CHRISTIAN, Paul. Jesus und seine geringsten Brüder: Mt 25:31-46 redaktionsgeschichtlich untersucht. Erfurter Theologische Schriften, 12. Leipzig: St. Benno, 1975. xxix, 108p.
DAHL, Nils Alstrup. Jesus in the memory of the early church. Minneapolis: Augsburg, 1976. 175p.
FARMER, William R. The synoptic problem: a critical analysis. Dillsboro, N.C.: Western North Carolina, 1976. xi, 308p.
FUNK, Wolf-Peter. Die zweite Apokalypse des Jakobus aus Nag-Hammadi-Codex V. Texte und Untersuchungen, 119. Berlin: Akademie, 1976. xvi, 246p.
KILGALLEN, John. The Stephen speech: a literary and redactional study of Acts 7:2-53. Analecta Biblica, 67. Rome: Biblical Institute, 1976. xiii, 187p.
KYSAR, Robert. John, the maverick gospel. Atlanta: John Knox, 1976. vi, 118p.
MARSHALL, I. Howard. The origins of New Testament christology. Downers Grove, Ill.: InterVarsity, 1976. 132p.
METZGER, Wolfgang. Die letzte Reise des Apostels Paulus: Beobachtungen und Erwägungen zu seinem Itinerar nach den Pastoralbriefen. Arbeiten zur Theologie, H. 59. Stuttgart: Calwer, 1976. 62p.
MIGUENS, Manuel. Church ministries in New Testament times. Arlington, Virginia: Christian Culture, 1976. xvii, 221p.
ORCHARD, Bernard. Matthew, Luke & Mark. The Griesbach solution to the synoptic question, vol. 1. Manchester: Koinonia, 1976. viii, 168p.
SCHWEIZER, Eduard. The good news according to Matthew. Trans. David E. Green. Atlanta: John Knox, 1975. 572p.
STENDAHL, Krister. Paul among Jews and Gentiles and other essays. Philadelphia: Fortress, 1976. ix, 133p.
TOVAR, Severino Talavero. Pasión y resurrección en el IV evangelio: interpretación de un cristiano de primera hora. Bibliotheca Salmanticensis XVII, Estudios 15. Salamanca: Universidad Pontificia, 1976. 277p.

Jewish Studies

THE DEAD SEA scriptures in English translation. With intro. and notes by Theodor H. Gaster. Third ed., revised and enlarged. Garden City, N.Y.: Anchor/Doubleday, 1976. xvi, 580p.
LAPERROUSAZ, E.-M. Qoumrân: l'établissement essénien des bords de la Mer Morte. Histoire et archéologie du site. Paris: Picard, 1976. xii, 257p.
MOTYLEWSKI, Leo F. The Essene plan. New York: Philosophical Library, 1976. 164p.
PANKO, Stephen M. Martin Buber. Makers of the Modern Theological Mind. Waco, Texas: Word, 1976. 135p.
RHOADS, David M. Israel in revolution: 6-74 C.E.: a political history based on the writings of Josephus. Philadelphia: Fortress, 1976. viii, 199p.
ROST, Leonhard. Judaism outside the Hebrew Canon: an introduction to the documents. Trans. David E. Green; Nashville: Abingdon, 1976. 205p.
SAFRAI, S. and STERN, M., eds. The Jewish people in the first century: historical geography, political history, social, cultural and religious life and institutions. Compendia rerum Iudaicarum ad Novum Testamentum, sect. I, vol. 2. Philadelphia: Fortress, 1976. x, 561-1283p.
TWERSKY, Isadore. The Mishneh Torah of Maimonides. Proceedings of the Israel Academy of Sciences and Humanities, vol. 5, no. 10. Jerusalem: Israel Academy of Sciences and Humanities, 1976. 32p.

BOOKS RECEIVED

World Religions

PARRINDER, Geoffrey. Mysticism in the world's religions. New York: Oxford Univ., 1976. viii, 210p.

SINGH, Kirpal. Prayer, its nature and technique. Delhi: Ruhani Satsang, 1973. xii, 153p.

THE TRANSPORT of love: the *Meghadūta* of Kālidāsa. Trans. and intro. Leonard Nathan. Berkeley: Univ. of California, 1976. viii, 116p.

Church History and Historical Theology

BERCIANO, Modesto. Καιρός: tiempo humano e historico-salvifico en Clemente de Alejandria. Publicaciones de la Facultad Teologica del Norte España, 34. Burgos: Ediciones Aldecoa, 1976. 330p.

BOYD, W. J. P. Alred's marginalia: explanatory comments in the Lindisfarne gospels. English Medieval Texts and Studies, 4. Exeter: Univ. of Exeter, 1975. x, 62p.

BUSCH, Eberhard. Karl Barth: his life from letters and autobiographical texts. Trans. John Bowden. Philadelphia: Fortress, 1976. xvii, 569p.

ELMEN, Paul. Wheat flour Messiah: Eric Jansson of Bishop Hill. Carbondale and Edwardsville, Ill.: Southern Illinois for the Swedish Pioneer Historical Society, 1976. xv, 222p.

FEDALTO, Giorgio. La chiesa latina in oriente. Vol. 2: Hierarchia latina orientis. Studi Religiosi, 3. Verona: Casa Editrice Mazziana, 1976. 282p.

FERM, Robert L. Jonathan Edwards the younger: 1745-1801. Grand Rapids: Eerdmans, 1976. 214p.

GENÈVE, Charles de. Les trophées sacrés ou missions des Capucins en Savoie, dans l'Ain, la Suisse romande et la vallée d'Aoste, à la fin du XVI*e* et au XVII*e* siècle. Publiés par Félix Tisserand. Mémoires et documents, 3*e* série, tomes 12-14. Lausanne: Société d'histoire de la Suisse romande, 1976. 3 vols.

GOSSELIN, Edward A. The king's progress to Jerusalem: some interpretations of David during the Reformation period and their patristic and medieval background. Humana Civilitas, 2. Malibu, Cal.: Undena Publications, 1976. 131p.

GRITSCH, Eric W. and JENSON, Robert W. Lutheranism: the theological movement and its confessional writings. Philadelphia: Fortress, 1976. x, 214p.

HAINSWORTH, Cuthbert D. Staretz Paisy Velichkovsky (1722-1794). Doctrine of spiritual guidance. Excerpta e dissertatione ad lauream. Rome: Pontificium Institutum Orientalium Studiorum, 1976. 88p.

IRWIN, Frank. Letters of Thomas Jefferson. Selected and edited, intro. Frank Irwin. Tilton, N.H.: Sanbornton Bridge, 1975. 260p.

LEDIT, Joseph. Marie dans la liturgie de Byzance. Théologie Historique, 39. Paris: Beauchesne, 1976. 363p.

LOZANO SEBASTIAN, Francisco-Javier. San Isidoro de Sevilla: teología del pecado y la conversión. Publicaciones de la Facultad Teológica del Norte de España, 36. Burgos: Ediciones Aldecoa, 1976. 234p.

MEIJER, Albericus de, ed. Gregorii de Arimino O.S.A. Registrum generalatus 1357-1358. Fontes historiae ordinis sancti Augustini: Prima series: Registra priorum generalium, vol. 1. Romae: Institutum Historicum Augustinianum, 1976. xvi, 419p.

MOREAU, Joseph. De la connaissance selon S. Thomas D'Aquin. Bibliothèque des Archives de Philosophie, n.s. 23. Paris: Beauchesne, 1976. 132p.

MÜNCH, Marc-Mathieu. La "Symbolique" de Friedrich Creuzer. Association des Publications près les Universités de Strasbourg, Fasc. 155. Paris: Editions Ophrys, 1976. 165p.

PETERSON, William S. Victorian Heretic: Mrs. Humphry Ward's *Robert Elsmere.* Atlantic Highlands, N.J.: Humanities, 1976. x, 259p.

PROBLÈMES d'histoire du Christianisme. Édités par Jean Préaux. 6, 1975-1976. Bruxelles: Université de Bruxelles, 1976. 93p.

RUSSELL, C. Allyn. Voices of American fundamentalism: seven biographical studies. Philadelphia: Westminster, 1976. 304p.

SCHLEIERMACHER, Friedrich. The Christian faith. English trans. of the second German ed.; H. R. Mackintosh and J. S. Stewart, eds. Philadelphia: Fortress, 1976. xii, 760p.

SMITH, John Holland. The death of classical paganism. New York: Scribner's, 1976. vii, 280p.

SOMMERFELDT, John R., ed. Studies in medieval cistercian history II. Cistercian Studies series, 24. Kalamazoo: Cistercian Publications, 1976. xiii, 207p.

STEINBACH, Wendelinus. Opera exegetica quae supersunt omnia; vol. 1: Commentarius in epistolam S. Pauli ad Galatas. Edidit Helmut Feld. Veröffentlichungen des Instituts für Europäische Geschichte Mainz, 81; Abteilung für Abendländische Religionsgeschichte. Wiesbaden: Steiner, 1976. lxiii, 342p.

STELL, Christopher. Architects of dissent, some nonconformist patrons and their architects. Friends of Dr. Williams's Library, 30th lecture, 1976. London: Dr. Williams's Trust, 1976. 33p.

THEY preached liberty: an anthology of timely quotations from New England ministers of the American Revolution on the subject of liberty. Introductory essay and biographical sketches by Franklin P. Cole. Indianapolis: Liberty, 1976. 176p.

THE UKRANIAN Catholic Church 1945-1975: a symposium, held at La Salle College in Philadelphia, Pennsylvania, April 19, 1975; Miroslav Labunka and Leonid Rudnytzky, eds. Philadelphia: St. Sophia Religious Assoc. of Ukranian Catholics, Inc., 1976. 162p.

WENDEL, François. Calvin et l'Humanisme. Cahiers de la Revue d'Histoire et de Philosophie Religieuses, 45. Paris: Presses Universitaires de France, 1976. 103p.

Theology

BADHAM, Paul. Christian beliefs about life after death. Library of Philosophy and Religion. New York: Barnes & Noble, 1976. 174p.

BARTH, Karl. Das christliche Leben: Die kirchliche Dogmatik IV, 4. Fragmente aus dem Nachlass, Vorlesungen 1959-1961. Hrsg. von Hans-Anton Drewes and Eberhard Jüngel. Karl Barth-Gesamtausgabe, II. Akademische Werke 1959-1961. Zürich: Theologischer Verlag, 1976. xx, 536p.

BENKTSON, Benkt-Erik. Dogma als Drama: der holländische Katechismus von einem schwedischen Theologen gelesen. Arbeiten zur Theologie, 60. Stuttgart: Calwer, 1976. 197p.

BERKOUWER, G. C. The church. Studies in dogmatics. Grand Rapids: Eerdmans, 1976. 438p.

BLOESCH, Donald G. Jesus is victor! Karl Barth's doctrine os salvation. Nashville: Abingdon, 1976. 176p.

DORONZO, Emmanuel. The church. The science of sacred theology for teachers; book 4. Middleburg, Va.: Notre Dame Institute, 1976. vii, 296p.

EVANS, Robert A. and PARKER, Thomas D., eds. Christian theology: a case method approach. New York: Harper & Row, 1976. xv, 269p.

GILKEY, Langdon. Reaping the whirlwind: a Christian interpretation of history. New York: Seabury, 1976. ix, 446p.

GRATSCH, Edward J. The credentials of Catholicism. Washington: University Press of America, 1976. viii, 82p.

HENRY, Carl F. H. God, revelation and authority, vols. 1 & 2. Waco, Texas: Word, 1976.

HISTORY, criticism and faith: four explanatory studies. Gordon J. Wenham, F. F. Bruce, R. T. France, Colin Brown. Downers Grove, Ill.: InterVarsity, 1976. 224p.

KASPER, Walter. Jesus the Christ. New York: Paulist, 1976. 289p.

KEHL, Medard. Kirche als Institution: zur theologischen Begründung des institutionellen Charakters der Kirche in der neueren deutschsprachigen katholischen Ekklesiologie. Frankfurter Theologische Studien, 22. Frankfurt am Main: Knecht, 1976. xi, 338p.

LUCAS, J. R. Freedom and grace. Grand Rapids: Eerdmans, 1976. xiv, 138p.

MARTELET, Gustave. The risen Christ and the eucharistic world. New York: Seabury, 1976. 252p.

RAHNER, Karl. Theological investigations, vol. XIV: Ecclesiology, questions in the church, the church in the world. Trans. David Bourke. New York: Seabury, 1976. 342p.

SALGUERO, José. Biblical revelation: the history of salvation. Trans. Judith Suprys. Arlington, Virginia: Christian Culture, 1976. vii, 202p.

SELBY, Peter. Look for the living: the corporate nature of resurrection faith. Philadelphia: Fortress, 1976. viii, 212p.

SWANSTON, Hamish F. G. A language for madness: the abuse and the use of Christian creeds. Assen: Van Gorcum, 1976. 154p.

THEISEN, Jerome P. The ultimate church and the promise of salvation. Collegeville, Minn.: St. John's Univ., 1976. xx, 198p.

VANDERVELDE, G. Original sin: two major trends in contemporary Roman Catholic reinterpretation. Amsterdam: Rodopi; Atlantic Highlands, N.J.: Humanities, 1975. 350p.

Philosophical Theology and Philosophy

FREE choice: a self-referential argument. Joseph M. Boyle, Germain Grisez, Olaf Tollefsen. Notre Dame, Ind.: Univ. of Notre Dame, 1976. xi, 207p.

HOERES, Walter. La Volontà come Perfezione Pura in Duns Scoto. Teoretica. Padova: Liviana, 1976. xii, 405p.

KENYON, Roger A. Existential structures: an analytic enquiry. New York: Philosophical Library, 1976. 63p.

MELAND, Bernard E. Fallible forms and symbols: discourses on method in a theology of culture. Philadelphia: Fortress, 1976. xvi, 206p.

PROUDFOOT, Wayne. God and the self: three types of philosophy of religion. Lewisburg, Penn.: Bucknell Univ., 1976. 241p.

SARRI, Francesco. Socrate e la genesi storica dell' idea occidentale di anima. Collana di Filosofia Antica, 3. Roma: Abete, 1975. 2 vols.

SCIENCE et métaphysique: Colloque de l'Académie Internationale de Philosophie des Sciences. S. Dockx, T. Settle, et al. Bibliothèque des Archives de Philosophie, n.s. 22. Paris: Beauchesne, 1976. 254p.

VAN DER HOEVEN, Johan. Karl Marx: the roots of his thought. Toronto: Wedge, 1976. 109p.

Ethics

ADAMS, James Luther. On being human religiously: selected essays in religion and society. Ed. and intro. Max L. Stackhouse. Boston: Beacon, 1976. xxx, 257p.
GUINDON, André. The sexual language: an essay in moral theology. Ottawa: Univ. of Ottawa, 1976. x, 476p.
SARDI, Paolo. L'aborto ieri e oggi. Biblioteca di cultura religiosa, 26. Brescia: Paideia, 1975. 389p.
SMITH, Adam. The theory of moral sentiments. Intro. E. G. West. Indianapolis: Liberty Classics, 1976. 546p.

Applied Theology

ALTENÄHR, Albert. Dietrich Bonhoeffer-Lehrer des Gebets: Grundlagen für eine Theologie des Gebets bei Dietrich Bonhoeffer. Studien zur Theologie des geistlichen Lebens, 7. Würzburg: Echter, 1976. 284p.
BLACKWOOD, Andrew Watterson. The fine art of preaching. Grand Rapids: Baker Book House, 1976. ix, 168p.
BROWNING, Don S. The moral context of pastoral care. Philadelphia: Westminster, 1976. 144p.
DUPRÉ, Louis. Transcendental selfhood: the loss and rediscovery of the inner life. New York: Seabury, 1976. x, 118p.
EXPERIENCE of the spirit; Peter Huizing and William Bassett, eds. Healing and the spirit; Georges Combet and Laureat Fabre, eds. Concilium, 99. New York: Seabury, 1974/76. 140p.
HICKMAN, Martha Whitmore. Love speaks its voice: the sights and sounds of life. Waco, Texas: Word, 1976. 123p.
JEEVES, Malcolm A. Psychology and Christianity: the view both ways. Downers Grove, Ill.: InterVarsity, 1976. 177p.
KIRKEMO, Ronald. Between the eagle and the dove: Christian and American foreign policy. Downers Grove, Ill.: InterVarsity, 1976. 218p.
LYON, David. Christians and sociology. Downers Grove, Ill.: InterVarsity, 1976. 89p.
MARTY, Martin E. The pro and con book of religious America. Waco, Texas: Word, 1975. 149p.
PADILLA, C. René, ed. The new face of evangelicalism: an international symposium on the Lausanne Covenant. Downers Grove, Ill.: InterVarsity, 1976. 282p.
RAHNER, Karl. The religious life today. New York: Seabury, 1976. 88p.
SMITH, M. A. The church under siege. Downers Grove, Ill.: InterVarsity, 1976. 277p.
VISSER 'T HOOFT, Willem Adolph. Has the ecumenical movement a future? Atlanta: John Knox, 1974. 97p.